One Day MBA

RICHARD A. D. JONES

icsa.
Publishing

Published by
ICSA Information & Training Ltd
16 Park Crescent
London W1B 1AH

Designed and typeset by Paul Barrett Book Production, Cambridge
Printed in Great Britain by Hobbs the Printers Ltd, Totton, Hampshire

British Library Cataloguing in Publication Data
A catalogue record for this book is available from the British Library

ISBN 978-1-86072-494-7

Contents

Acknowledgements   vi
Introduction   vii
How to use this book   viii
List of figures   x
List of tables   xiii

Part A – Understanding the situation   1

Chapter 1
Strategy – understanding the external environment   2
1.1 Introduction   2
1.2 What is strategy and why does it matter?   2
1.3 Mission and vision   4
1.4 The need for strategy to evolve   6
1.5 PEST analysis   8
Summary   15
Notes   16

Chapter 2
Assessing an organisation   17
2.1 Introduction   17
2.2 Keys to effective organisational assessments   18
2.3 A structured approach to organisational assessments   19
2.4 Running an assessment programme   22
2.5 Identifying the real strengths and weaknesses   26
Summary   31
Notes   32

Part B – Setting the direction   33

Chapter 3
Developing strategy   34
3.1 The context of strategy   34
3.2 The strategic planning cycle   34
3.3 Strategic analysis – tools for formulation   39
3.4 Understanding where to invest   48
3.5 Where should the focus be?   60
3.6 Markets will change   60
3.7 Strategy to action   61
Summary   64
Notes   65

Chapter 4
Marketing   67
4.1 What is marketing?   67
4.2 The marketing concept   68
4.3 Assessing strategic alternatives   69
4.4 Generic marketing strategies   69
4.5 Marketing at a more tactical level   75
4.6 Segmentation   81
4.7 Benefits of segmenting markets   81
4.8 Simple approaches to segmentation   82
4.9 Market estimation   85
4.10 Product and service positioning   86
4.11 Product lifecycle   88
4.12 The BCG Matrix (or Boston Box)   95
4.13 The product diffusion curve   100
4.14 The marketing mix – the 4Ps   104
4.15 Advertising   110
4.16 The value proposition   111

4.17 Pricing and sales volumes 113

4.18 Planning pricing 115

4.19 Identifying opportunities for products/ services 117

4.20 Customer retention and loyalty 120

Summary 130

Notes 131

Chapter 5

Finance 133

5.1 Introduction 133

5.2 Understanding company accounts 134

5.3 Income statement or profit and loss (P&L) 135

5.4 Balance sheet or statement of financial position (SoFP) 142

5.5 The anatomy of a balance sheet 144

5.6 Gearing 150

5.7 Key measures and ratios 151

5.8 Cash flow 158

5.9 Key investment assessment 161

5.10 The importance of timing 169

Summary 170

Notes 171

Chapter 6

Product development, portfolio management and launch 172

6.1 Product development 172

6.2 Why products fail 174

6.3 Portfolio management 179

6.4 The complexity of launching products 187

Summary 189

Notes 189

Chapter 7

Organisational design 190

7.1 Organisational structure 190

7.2 Functional hierarchies 190

7.3 Matrix organisations 193

7.4 The process vector 195

Summary 196

Part C – Staying on track 197

Chapter 8

Understanding and managing people 198

8.1 Being a good manager 198

8.2 Motivation 201

8.3 Motivating 206

8.4 Management and groups 208

8.5 Understanding people and situations 209

Summary 214

Notes 215

Chapter 9

Leadership 216

9.1 The characteristics of leadership 216

9.2 Power 220

9.3 Leadership strength 225

Summary 226

Notes 227

Chapter 10

Change management 228

10.1 Introduction 228

10.2 Types of change 229

10.3 High level fundamentals of change management (unfreeze – change – refreeze) 231

10.4 The context for change – are you ready? 233

10.5 Are you ready – credibility and respect 234

10.6 The story has to be right 234

10.7 The enemies of change 235

10.8 Classic mistakes and problems within change programmes 236

10.9 Models of change 238

10.10 Rewards and metrics 240

10.11 Psychodynamics 240

10.12 Hubbers, saboteurs and fence sitters 241

10.13 What you should do 243

10.14 Structuring a change process   244
Summary   245
Notes   245

Chapter 11
Managing projects   246
11.1 Introduction   246
11.2 What is a project?   246
11.3 Why is it vital to manage projects well?   247
11.4 Diagnosing the state of an existing project   247
11.5 Digging into the plan   250
11.6 Starting a new project   252
11.7 Project initiation   253
11.8 The project charter   254
11.9 Creating the project charter   255
11.10 The project lifecycle   256
11.11 Defining objectives   257
11.12 Milestones   260
11.13 Creating the work breakdown structure   261
11.14 Risk management   262
11.15 Issue management   265
11.16 Scope change management   266
Summary   267
Notes   267

Chapter 12
Problem-solving techniques   268
12.1 Ishikawa diagrams   268
12.2 The five whys   270
12.3 Force field analysis   271
12.4 Drill-down   273
12.5 Swim lane diagrams   274
12.6 Interaction diagram   275
Summary   276
Notes   276

Concluding thoughts   277
Recommended reading   282
Bibliography   284
Index   294

Acknowledgements

I would like to thank Fiona Tucker and Jo Glover at ICSA for the opportunity to convert thinking from the One, Two and Five Day MBA series and my unusual career into a book. Publishing is never an easy thing to do but it's been a pleasure to work with their professional, enthusiastic and driven approach.

Thanks also to John Jeffcock, the founder of Winmark Europe, for getting me involved with the world-class training they provide to CEOs, directors and partners across the FTSE350. He is a man to learn from and one I admire more the longer I know him. His detailed review of this book and support have been more than helpful. It's also been huge fun creating new courses with his team and delivering training and interventions that people seem to consistently value and enjoy. Thank you to Janet Baker, Harry Cummins and Peter Jaques – for keeping it all going.

I also want to thank Stefan Stanislawski and Mikael Sandberg, my partners within Ventura Team (www.venturateam.com). We're into our eighth year and have delivered strategy, business modelling, change management and implementation projects from Curacao to Saudi Arabia and from the US to the UK. I think it's rare to find people you really like and respect to work with, but I'm lucky as they are two of the best.

Thanks to my sisters Sue and Maura for supporting me always, and my late parents for everything.

Finally, but most importantly, I'd like to thank my lovely wife Julie and wonderful sons Harry and Will for the support, love and laughter, as well as allowing me the time to write this book.

Introduction

This book is designed to provide an overview of the key skills required to understand today's businesses. It covers a number of the areas studied during an MBA, combined with pragmatic management tools, models and approaches that help make this learning applicable.

The aim is to help you to understand the interrelationships between different aspects of management and to provide you with an appreciation of the key approaches that can be used to build, monitor and improve organisations.

The book combines:

- theoretical approaches from leading academics;
- real-world experience from seasoned management professionals;
- learning gathered from over 1,000 CEO/Director/Partner-level members across Winmark's professional networks and advisory panels; and
- learning and feedback from One, Two and Five Day MBA training courses and master classes on topics such as finance, change management and project management.

The book takes the reader on a structured journey through the different aspects of business in a readable, pragmatic and actionable way.

This learning shared in this book is now being used by companies to:

- develop new strategies;
- assess the organisation's own situation, or understand potential clients' businesses before approaching them;
- help them understand the real problems they face;
- position themselves better to sell to clients; and
- develop new products and services.

Additional content

You can download many of the templates used throughout this book and other content including additional case studies from www.innovation2execution.com.

How to use this book

The structure of this book is designed to lead you through the tools and techniques needed to understand an organisation from the outside in. The ordering of the chapters means new topics are introduced, and can be understood, on the foundations laid in the previous chapters. This structured approach can help you to understand and improve your own organisation or get inside the thinking and decision making of competitors and clients.

- **Exercises** are included throughout the book to support your own learning and development, or to run as group activities to tackle specific problems.
- **Stop and think** boxes are included to get you to reflect on aspects of your own or your organisation's situation. They are there to help challenge your own thinking and cement learning from the book.
- **Case studies** are used to illustrate points and show how companies tackled particular issues.
- **Snapshots** are brief descriptions of a particular organisation's experience or approach to an issue.
- **Summary** sections are included at the end of each chapter to highlight the key learning points of the chapter.

The book is divided into three parts and you can read the book from front to back or dip into chapters as you wish. The parts are as follows.

Part A: Understanding the situation

This first part describes the role and importance of strategy and looks at how to understand the external environment in which an organisation exists. Then we look inside the organisation to consider resources, skills, systems and structures. This will help you to identify the current strengths and weaknesses of the organisation. This knowledge provides the context for further assessment and strategic decision making.

Part B: Setting the direction

The second part examines the tools and techniques needed to develop strategy and then moves on to marketing, considering the models and approaches a company can use to create sustainable advantage. The finance chapter focuses on the basics of understanding financial information and looking for meaning in the numbers that reflect progress in the organisation. Part B also looks at product and portfolio management in more detail before finally considering the impact of how different organisational designs deliver in different circumstances.

Part C: Staying on track

Once an organisation has been given the right direction, it is important to monitor and maintain progress. This final part covers skills including leadership, managing projects, motivation and change management in the organisation.

Finally, there are a number of useful resources listed to help you deepen your understanding of some of these topics. These include a recommended reading list, useful websites and the location of the online learning tools that support this book.

List of figures

Figure 3.1:   The strategic planning process   35
Figure 3.2:   Porter's Five Forces Model   40
Figure 3.3:   Five Forces – prompt questions for exercise   47
Figure 3.4:   Porter's Five Forces applied to a traditional book publisher   48
Figure 3.5:   Ansoff's Product Development Matrix   49
Figure 3.6:   Potential product and market evolution strategies and risk   51
Figure 3.7:   Bowling pin strategy – example   52
Figure 3.8:   The GE Matrix   53
Figure 3.9:   GE Matrix example   55
Figure 3.10:   Product/market evolution – Example A   56
Figure 3.11:   Product/market evolution – Example B   57
Figure 3.12:   Relative product strength compared to competition   58
Figure 3.13:   A PORTS chart   62
Figure 4.1:   Market and Customer Group Matrix   84
Figure 4.2:   Detailed segment plans   85
Figure 4.3:   Market leakage   85
Figure 4.4:   Perceptual map for the car industry   86
Figure 4.5:   Clusters on a perceptual map   87
Figure 4.6:   Perceptual map with target segments   88
Figure 4.7:   The product lifecycle   89
Figure 4.8:   Scallop pattern lifecycle   92
Figure 4.9:   Cycle–recycle lifecycle   92
Figure 4.10:   The product lifecycle – costs and profit   93
Figure 4.11:   Cash flow in product lifecycle   95
Figure 4.12:   The Boston Box   96
Figure 4.13:   Boston Box – high growth – low market share   97
Figure 4.14:   Boston Box – high growth – high market share   97
Figure 4.15:   Boston Box – low growth – low market share   98
Figure 4.16:   Boston Box – low growth – high market share   99
Figure 4.17:   BCG classifications in the product lifecycle   99
Figure 4.18:   The product diffusion curve   101
Figure 4.19:   The 'chasm' between early adopters and the early majority   104

Figure 4.20:   Example of a 'willingness to pay' curve – monthly subscription product   114
Figure 4.21:   Example value curve for mountain bikes   119
Figure 4.22:   Example value curve with new product   120
Figure 4.23:   Value curve for Smart car vs. average family car   120
Figure 4.24:   The customer cycle   122
Figure 4.25:   Lifetime value against likelihood of remaining a customer (source: Satyam)   125
Figure 4.26:   Prioritising customers to retain   126
Figure 4.27:   The impact of product/service complexity   129
Figure 5.1:   Income statement from revenue to profit   135
Figure 5.2:   Example income statement   140
Figure 5.3:   Example profit and loss statement (percentage change shown year on year)   141
Figure 5.4:   Example balance sheet information   145
Figure 5.5:   Current assets – two examples   148
Figure 5.6:   Example balance sheet   152
Figure 5.7:   Example of abridged balance sheets   153
Figure 5.8:   Example balance sheet 2   156
Figure 5.9:   Annual cash flow and cumulative cash flow total   162
Figure 5.10:   Example of free cash flow over time   167
Figure 5.11:   NPV calculation example   168
Figure 5.12:   Cash inflows and outflows profile – late cost case   169
Figure 5.13:   Cost and income profile – early cost case   169
Figure 5.14:   Net cash profile (income – cost) for early and late cost cases   170
Figure 6.1:   Project lifecycle – typical and 'improved' curve   171
Figure 6.2:   Product risk during the development cycle   173
Figure 6.3:   Relative cost of product change during the development cycle   174
Figure 6.4:   Ideas screening   179
Figure 6.5:   Ranking project attractiveness   181
Figure 6.6:   Example Portfolio A   182
Figure 6.7:   Example Portfolio B   183
Figure 6.8:   Portfolio C – technologies against markets   183
Figure 6.9:   Adventurous and conservative portfolios   184
Figure 6.10:   Various portfolio assessment approaches   185
Figure 6.11:   A Stage-Gate process   186
Figure 6.12:   Milestones and Stage-Gate processes   187
Figure 7.1:   A 'command and control' functional hierarchy   191
Figure 7.2:   A project-focused organisation   194
Figure 8.1:   Competence development model   210
Figure 8.2:   Ladder of Inference   212
Figure 10.1:   Four-stage change curve (derived from Kübler-Ross' Five Stages of Grief)   240
Figure 10.2:   Transition curve during change process   241
Figure 11.1:   Project diagnostic approach   248
Figure 11.2:   Sample resource usage chart   252
Figure 11.3:   Project lifecycle   257

Figure 11.4:   Example work breakdown structure for building a skyscraper   261

Figure 11.5:   Work breakdown structure with numbering   261

Figure 11.6:   Categorising risks   262

Figure 11.7:   Risks – probability vs. severity   264

Figure 11.8:   Probability vs. severity – risk prioritisation   264

Figure 11.9:   Example risk register   265

Figure 12.1:   Ishikawa diagram – high level   268

Figure 12.2:   Ishikawa diagram – more detail   269

Figure 12.3:   Ishikawa diagram – full detail   269

Figure 12.4:   The five whys   270

Figure 12.5:   Force field analysis   271

Figure 12.6:   Forces for and opposing change   272

Figure 12.7:   Strengthening/weakening forces for and opposing change   273

Figure 12.8:   Example of a drill-down   274

Figure 12.9:   Example swim lane diagram   275

Figure 12.10:   Example interaction diagram for a customer complaint   275

List of tables

Table 1.1:   Examples of mission statements   5
Table 1.2:   Comparing mission statements   5
Table 1.3:   Factors that can impact on an organisation   9
Table 2.1:   The 7S Framework   19
Table 2.2:   Areas of investigation   21
Table 2.3:   Different types of processes   24
Table 2.4:   McKinsey's 7S Framework   31
Table 3.1:   GOST theory   38
Table 3.2:   The Ansoff Matrix   50
Table 3.3:   RACI Matrix   63
Table 4.1:   Elements of the marketing concept   68
Table 4.2:   Porter's generic strategies   70
Table 4.3:   Risks of Porter's generic strategies   71
Table 4.4:   Ways to differentiate products   74
Table 4.5:   Market leaders' options   76
Table 4.6:   Defensive strategies   77
Table 4.7:   Attacking strategies   78
Table 4.8:   Following the market leaders   80
Table 4.9:   Scale of socio-economic status   82
Table 4.10:   Stages of the lifecycle   89
Table 4.11:   Sales volume and operating profit   94
Table 4.12:   Rising sales volumes   94
Table 4.13:   The value proposition approach   111
Table 4.14:   Pricing strategies   115
Table 4.15:   Business models   117
Table 4.16:   Categories of change   119
Table 5.1:   The income statement in figures   139
Table 5.2:   Example of low gearing   150
Table 5.3:   Example of high gearing   151
Table 5.4:   Depreciation expenses   159
Table 5.5:   Example of a statement of cash flows   159
Table 5.6:   Payback example   161
Table 5.7:   Working out the cumulative cash flow   161

Table 5.8: Applying the formula to the net cash flow in each year   164

Table 5.9: Net present value   165

Table 5.10: Three different cash flows and their respective IRRs   166

Table 5.11: Cash flows with IRRs of 4 per cent and 19 per cent   166

Table 5.12: Impact on the net present value   170

Table 6.1: Reasons why products fail   174

Table 6.2: Valuing technologies   182

Table 6.3: Challenges at each stage for a product   188

Table 8.1: The continuum of management styles   199

Table 8.2: Vroom and Yetton's categorisation of management styles   200

Table 8.3: Matching the styles to situations   201

Table 8.4: What motivates individuals   201

Table 8.5: Theory X and Theory Y   204

Table 8.6: Hygiene factors and motivators   204

Table 8.7: The three-factor theory of motivation   205

Table 8.8: Rungs on the Ladder of Inference   212

Table 9.1: Types of positional power   221

Table 9.2: Types of personal power   222

Table 9.3: Generic management styles   223

Table 9.4: Descriptions of leadership   224

Table 10.1: Comparing Theory E, Theory O and combined projects   230

Table 10.2: Reasons for complacency   235

Table 10.3: Satir's change model   239

Table 10.4: Tuckman's stages of group development   239

Table 10.5: Managing change (Kotter, 1995)   244

Table 11.1: Elements of a project charter document   256

Table 11.2: Breaking down an objective   258

Table 11.3: The milestone is complete when…   260

Table 11.4: Categories of risk   263

Table 11.5: Prioritising issues   266

Part A

Understanding the situation

1
Strategy – understanding the external environment

Of the companies in the US Fortune 100 in 1970, only 57 remained by 1990. Those on the list in 1990 fared worse with only 26 still there in 2010. Overall, only 16 companies remained on the list from 1970 to 2010 and they were corporate giants like Exxon-Mobil, Coca-Cola and Boeing.[1] It is getting tougher and tougher for businesses to survive and one thing is true: Defining and implementing the right strategy is more important now than ever.

1.1 Introduction

This chapter on strategy will focus on the external environment and looks at the different forces that influence an organisation from the outside. However, before we start on this, it is useful to understand what strategy actually is and why it's important in defining how a company prepares itself to face its customers, competitors and market conditions.

1.2 What is strategy and why does it matter?

Strategy is the long-term plan that defines and shapes the objectives of an organisation – matching resources to the expectations and needs of customers, the market environment and the stakeholders.

This definition of strategy includes a number of important points. Let's break the statement down into smaller chunks and look at each piece to understand why they are so important.

1.2.1 Strategy should be about the long term

Defining a strategy should give an organisation a clear understanding of the direction it has chosen to follow. This strategy should be appropriate and actionable within the organisation over a reasonable period of time. There are several good reasons why you wouldn't want to define a new strategy every few weeks:

- Developing a new strategy typically takes months rather than weeks to complete.
- The actual effort required to produce a strategy is significant and doing this work too often would distract senior management and key resources from their operational responsibilities.

- The external situation doesn't normally change quickly enough to justify recreating a strategy that often.

However, the reasons above don't mean the same strategy should last forever. It also doesn't imply that the strategy should remain in place when the environment or circumstances of the organisation change significantly.

With this in mind, a strategy should typically address at least one year into the future. However, it must be re-evaluated immediately if the situation demands. So, even if you are only one day into implementing a new strategy, a radical change in the environment around the organisation would require an immediate re-evaluation of that strategy.

1.2.2 Strategy defines and shapes the actions of an organisation

The strategy acts as the blueprint that the organisation uses to decide how it operates and what it does. This ranges from setting major objectives down to defining individual tasks that are appropriate, effective and consistent with the desired direction. The strategy therefore needs to be sufficiently detailed, clear and unambiguous to allow this translation from words into action.

1.2.3 Strategy is about using resources effectively

Both market leaders and those challenging them need to marshal their forces very carefully.

Market leaders typically have the luxury of superior resources to their competition. Their higher volumes provide the opportunity to benefit from economies of scale which should in turn give them better profit margins. Leaders may also have wider product ranges, superior channels to market and other attributes that lead to advantages in their market. However, even longstanding market leaders can fade over time if their superior resources are used badly.

Market challengers are normally at a disadvantage in terms of strength. This is like playing chess where you begin with fewer pieces than your opponent. Your pieces will have their particular strengths and weaknesses, and so the way you play needs to be carefully thought out and reflect the capabilities of the pieces at your disposal.

Taking the chess analogy one step further, you don't typically start sacrificing pieces or even exchanging pieces (taking one of your opponent's pieces but immediately losing an equivalent of your own) when you are in a weaker position. The same logic applies in business. Price wars and other attritional activities are normally bad news for market challengers.

1.2.4 Strategy should support the mission of the organisation

The mission statement of an organisation is normally a relatively concise description of what the management team wants the organisation to achieve. It describes the aims of the organisation and may vary in length from one or two sentences through to a few short paragraphs. The short content of a mission statement is very much focused on the 'what' of the situation. The complete strategy document should develop the mission statement with far more detail of *what* will be done; it will also provide a clear description of *how*.

Aligning the mission and strategy is vital, so let's look at mission statements (and the closely related vision statements) in more detail.

1.3   Mission and vision

1.3.1   Defining mission and vision

Henry Mintzberg defined the idea of a mission for an organisation as follows:

> A mission describes the organisation's basic function in society, in terms of the products and services it produces for its customers.[2]

Mission and vision statements can be defined and compared as follows:

- **Mission statements** tend to be internally focused and developed by senior management and shareholders, and then disseminated to the entire organisation. They are also more about the here and now for the organisation, and may change when markets or the focus of the company need to shift.
- **Vision statements** are normally more outwardly focused with the inclusion of the values held by the business and an aspirational vision of the future. They exist to encourage customers and employees to work with the organisation and the vision will normally outlive mission statements – being more about what the organisation stands for than what it does at present.

Example mission and vision statements
The leading toy retailer, Toys 'R' Us, is one of the companies that has explicit versions of each type of statement.

   Toys 'R' Us Mission Statement: 'Our Goal is to be the Worldwide Authority on Kids, Families and Fun.'

   Toys 'R' Us Vision Statement: 'Our Vision is to put joy in kids' hearts and a smile on parents' faces.'[3]

   The differences between those two statements are slight but it can be argued that the mission statement is slightly more 'actionable' than the vision statement.

   In the real world, mission and vision statements are rarely as clearly differentiated as in the definition above and sometimes there is a single statement that is a hybrid of both.

   For the purpose of helping create the right strategy for an organisation, we will concentrate on mission statements as these represent what the organisation is aiming to do in the short and medium term. Below are examples of mission statements for a number of well-known companies.

   The Hershey mission statement is very market friendly and perhaps a little 'fluffy', whereas Proctor and Gamble's mission is more specific, linking the quality and value of products to the achievement of corporate objectives.

Table 1.1: Examples of mission statements

Company	Mission statement
Proctor and Gamble	We will provide branded products and services of superior quality and value that improve the lives of the world's consumers. As a result, consumers will reward us with leadership sales, profit, and value creation, allowing our people, our shareholders, and the communities in which we live and work to prosper.[4]
Google	To organize the world's information and make it universally accessible and useful.[5]
Nike	To bring inspiration and innovation to every athlete in the world.[6]
Skype	To be the fabric of real-time communication on the web.[7]
Hershey	Bringing sweet moments of Hershey happiness to the world every day.[8]

Let's look at a particular industry to compare and contrast mission statements from companies that are actively competing with one other.

Table 1.2: Comparing mission statements

Company	Statement
Ford	We are a global family with a proud heritage passionately committed to providing personal mobility for people around the world. We anticipate consumer need and deliver outstanding products and services that improve people's lives.[9]
VW	It is the goal of the Group to offer attractive, safe and environmentally sound vehicles which are competitive in an increasingly tough market and which set world standards in their respective classes.[10]
Toyota	Toyota will lead the way to the future of mobility, enriching lives around the world with the safest and most responsible ways of moving people. Through our commitment to quality, constant innovation and respect for the planet, we aim to exceed expectations and be rewarded with a smile. We will meet challenging goals by engaging the talent and passion of people, who believe there is always a better way.[11]

Ford's statement is clearly more in the vision category. It doesn't include much of the internally referenced, results-focused wording one would typically expect to see in a mission statement. However, it has evolved from earlier versions and changed the limiting word 'automobiles' to the more flexible and open phrase 'personal mobility'.

In contrast, VW's statement is pretty clear about the type of vehicles it wants to make, and the standards it wishes to set – even against the backdrop of a difficult external market.

Toyota's vision statement is carefully constructed from a number of key phrases that all have more detailed definitions and meaning for the company. The statement combines both the internally and externally focused messages, and fits neatly into the corporate goals and standards that Toyota promotes as a company.

The implication of comparing these three mission statements is that they provide a useful first view of a company's intentions but significant differences will only appear at the strategy level.

STOP AND THINK

For your own organisation, take a moment to consider the following questions:

- Is there a long-term vision for the organisation?
- Is this agreed across the senior management team, founders, shareholders?
- Is there an actionable strategy that has been shared across the organisation?

If the answer to any of the above is no, then where have things broken down? Is the problem defining the direction, gaining agreement or communicating it?

Here's a final thought: If there is a problem, then what are you going to do to fix it or at least make people aware of the issue?

1.4 The need for strategy to evolve

Before you start the process of developing a new strategy, you have to understand where the organisation is now and what's happening around it. These external factors will influence the choice of targets for the organisation, how it will achieve these, the resources required and also how long it will take to succeed.

It's very tempting to skip this step and dive into the excitement of creating new products and services or transforming the business, but it's vital to understand the current situation first and identify if the organisation's position is drifting or even becoming untenable. Matthew Olson and Derek van Bever's book *Stall Points* describes how, once growth in a company stalls, it has less than a 10 per cent chance of ever fully recovering.[12]

1.4.1 Companies do not own a market forever

Being the greatest manufacturer of steam trains was a fantastic market position at one time, but the introduction of diesel engines changed the market completely.

Let's look in depth at two more recent examples where markets have been disrupted. First we will consider how a new entrant completely changed a market.

CASE STUDY

Skype becomes the dominant player for international calls

Telecoms operators used to make huge revenues from international phone calls. The call would need to be routed across the originator's network to an international gateway from where it might cross oceans in dedicated undersea cables or span the globe using satellites. Eventually it would be routed across the copper wire network in the destination country and the call

CASE STUDY continued

established. Each leg of this call's journey and every country crossed would increase the costs. Twenty years ago, many telecoms companies were monopolies and they could charge what they wished in the absence of any real competition – enabling them to make good profits on these calls.

The spread of internet access has now changed the market forever. Companies such as BT were looking at transferring calls across the internet in the early 2000s but looked at this approach as an opportunity to reduce their own internal costs. They did not see it as something that could be used by a completely new entrant to disrupt their core business in the way it eventually would.

Skype was introduced in 2003 as a way to make free calls between PCs, but the opportunity to make a call from a PC and transfer the call around the world on the internet was quickly identified. Rather than paying the significant transit costs for a call over satellite or passing through copper wires in the ground, these calls would only incur a small charge in the destination country where they leave the internet and essentially become a local call.

The result was extraordinary growth in the use of Skype with 24.7 per cent of global international call minutes being carried over Skype in 2011 (up from 12 per cent in 2009).[13] In parallel, Skype-to-Skype calls grew 48 per cent in 2011 and reached a total of 145 billion minutes, with 40 per cent of those calls including video.[14]

The number of users and the potential to dominate the market led to the high valuations of Skype in its purchase by eBay for £1.4 billion in 2005[15] and subsequently by Microsoft for £5.2 billion in 2011.[16]

Skype's entry into the market has both taken away significant market share from the traditional telecoms players and also driven down prices so far that customers are now paying just 1–2 per cent of the price they used to pay for international calls.[17]

Let's look at a second case to see how even the strongest companies can lose their way.

CASE STUDY

New skill requirements mean new entrants in the digital camera market

Sometimes changes in technology allow new players to enter and others to fail.

The camera market in the 1980s and into the 1990s was dominated by big players such as Canon, Nikon, Pentax and Olympus. They made cameras where the optics and internal mechanisms were the key factors governing performance and hence influencing buyer choice. In parallel, companies such as Kodak, Agfa and Fuji provided photographers with the film to go in the cameras.

A Kodak engineer developed the first CCD image sensor in 1975 and this technology started to appear in a significant number of cameras for the consumer market in the early 1990s. The cost of digital cameras reduced as economies of scale and more aggressive competition

CASE STUDY continued

appeared in these markets and the market shifted inexorably towards digital. This change to digital from film technology has helped some companies to reposition themselves while others have fared badly in the transition.

At the start of 2011, the analyst company IDC published a report showing the market share in the global digital camera market (including interchangeable lenses):

Manufacturer	%
Canon	19.0
Sony	17.9
Nikon	12.6
Samsung	11.1
Panasonic	7.6
Kodak	7.4
Olympus	6.1
Fujifilm	4.9
Casio	4.0
Pentax	1.5

Canon continues to thrive in the digital era, having combined their expertise in manufacturing lenses with new electronics capabilities to create a strong range across both the consumer and professional markets. Nikon is the same.

Fuji has established itself as a serious provider of low- to medium-range digital cameras in spite of not being a major player in the 1990s camera market. Sony has entered the market in a very strong position, based on their experience in electronics and video camera technology. Panasonic has partnered with the legendary optics company Leica to complement its strength in electronics and create a powerful presence in the non-professional digital camera market.

These examples illustrate how technology can change a market forever and even powerhouses like Kodak can crumble in the face of such radical change – moving from domination of the film and paper era to a minor position in digital and eventual withdrawal from the market in early 2012[18] while under bankruptcy protection.[19] We will examine some of the reasons why this happened later in the book.

Technology is only one of a number of external forces affecting an organisation. We will now consider the wider set of these forces by introducing PEST analysis.

1.5 PEST analysis

The acronym PEST originally referred to the current (and future) Political, Economic, Social and Technological (PEST) factors that can impact on an organisation. However, it became clear over time that some important external influences were missing.

A fuller and more up-to-date list is shown in Table 1.3.

Table 1.3: Factors that can impact on an organisation

Factor	Questions for the organisation
Political	What impact will changes in the political landscape have? What will happen after local, national or international elections? What new policies may appear and what may change?
Economic	What is happening in the economy? What is the likely impact of that?
Social	How is society changing? How are attitudes evolving over time?
Technology	What new technologies or usage trends are appearing and how will they change the situation?
Legal	What new laws may appear? Which laws may be subject to change and in what ways?
Education	What are the changes in what we are learning and the way we learn it?
Environmental	What changes in the environment are predicted? Which changes have already occurred and what is the impact? What will the results be?
Demographic	How is the population changing in terms of the breakdown by, for example, age and spending power?
Industry	What is happening in the industry around the organisation? What new trends are occurring? What is happening to pricing? Are there any new entrants?

The addition of some or all of these new factors to the original PEST model mean it is now sometimes referred to as PESTLE, PESTLED or even STEEPLED. The Industry category is important but not included as often at this point. This may be because models like Five Forces (discussed in Chapter 3) do such a good job of capturing all the elements relating to this category.

You use the different factors as prompts to consider the potential changes that each may have on the organisation in the future. Some changes may be threats or challenges for the business while others may provide opportunities. At any point in time, one or more of these factors may be completely inconsequential for the organisation while others may be critical. There is also a high degree of interaction between the different factors with causes in one category creating notable effects in another.

Let's examine each category in more detail. The examples given in each section are designed to help understanding rather than describing the detail of every current trend. There is no 'one size fits all' analysis, as every organisation is unique and so will be affected by the external environment differently.

1.5.1 Political factors

Political changes may be driven by external factors. For example, the sudden change in the global economy in the last few years has resulted in many new policies that would not have been considered (or accepted by the public) before. Extreme austerity measures across Europe led to major protests in countries like Greece and to the resignation of the Spanish Prime Minister in

2011. The economic turmoil has also led to calls for greater banking regulation amid the collapse of some banks and the International Monetary Fund (IMF) and European Central Bank having to step in to support some countries' financial systems. These measures were a political response to economic forces, i.e. they were reactive.

However, political measures are normally more proactive and can be more predictable at certain points.

Manifestos set out the changes a particular party will put in place if elected and signpost the policies that might impact an organisation during the next parliamentary term. The biggest potential change will come during an election where very different sets of policies will be put in place after the date of the election. An organisation needs to understand the impact of each of the alternative political parties on them. For example, a reduction in public spending may be bad news for companies involved in capital projects (e.g. road building) or may lead to a reduction in welfare benefits and therefore consumer spending power.

Political changes may even extend to embargoes and trade sanctions that could cripple certain businesses.

1.5.2 Economic factors

This category relates to the general financial outlook in a region or country including output, inflation, trends in output, employment in different sectors and credit. The underlying economic health of a country will be indicated by the Gross Domestic Product (GDP) which measures the production of finished goods and services in financial terms.

The GDP per capita figure is perhaps a more useful measure that divides the total GDP into the country's population. This provides some indication of the spending power of individuals. For example, the UK's GDP per capita figure of £22,360 appears strong against the figure for the Congo that is only £250 according to the CIA World Factbook.[20] However, gas-rich Qatar has nearly five times the UK's figure at £107,150.

A reduction in the total GDP figure in a country for two consecutive quarters is taken as an indicator of recession. The UK has obviously been swept up in the global economic crisis, sliding into recession and suffering consequences that rival the double-dip recession of the 1970s.

In order to function as a country, governments need to borrow money and the ability to generate and hopefully grow tax revenues will underpin the ability of a country to repay these debts. The net government debt in the UK hit £1 trillion in early 2012.[21] Since the crisis started in 2007, governments have been trying to tread a careful path between spending more to stimulate and grow the economy while recognising this so-called 'quantitative easing' increases the debt.

Policies such as these have a direct impact on business, as the level of public spending will have a knock-on effect on the rest of the economy; for example, spending cuts lead to higher unemployment and therefore lowered consumer spending. Similarly, pay freezes reduce the real spending power of individuals as the pound in their pocket buys less year on year as inflation pushes prices up. Inflation itself will have an impact on interest rates which are used by some governments to damp down consumer spending that is driving inflation up to unacceptable levels.

The impact of changes in the economy clearly cast a shadow across every organisation in the countries they serve.

1.5.3 Social factors

Social trends look at changes ranging from life expectancy, birth rates, levels of house ownership and average family size through to how we live and the attitudes we hold.

For example, the emergence of widespread access to the internet has triggered significant social change. Children are now are on the internet for as long each day as they spend watching television (three hours).[13] One in five couples now meets on the internet according to Erik Qualman, an expert in social media trends.[22] Even how we communicate has changed with the rise of e-mail, text messaging and social networks such as Facebook and Twitter.

The nature of work also evolves. For example, more of us are now able to work from home, and access to the internet and e-mail on multiple devices has shifted many of us from a nine-to-five working pattern to an 'always available' lifestyle.

1.5.4 Technology factors

Changes in technology impact the way that we live and how organisations work and interact with their clients and customers. For example:

- 3G-enabled phones provide people with mobile access to e-mail and the internet.
- Smartphones have built-in 3G technology combining multiple functionality that was previously only available in separate devices (e.g. camera, GPS location, maps, video player, music player, guitar tuners).
- Some US universities have stopped providing e-mail accounts to students: free e-mail accounts are easily available, and text messages, Facebook and Twitter have become more 'immediate' means of communication.[22]
- Price-aggregating sites enable consumers to 'comparison shop' financial services (bank accounts, credit cards, insurance, etc.) in a few minutes and select and buy an offer that is the best compromise between requirements and price.

To underline the impact of technology change in the business context, let's look deeper at the recent challenges for Kodak.

CASE STUDY

How the mighty fall – the challenge for Kodak

Kodak popularised photography at the start of the twentieth century with the relatively cheap box Brownie. By the 1980s and into the early 1990s they were one of the dominant providers of photographic film and paper; in early 2012 they filed for bankruptcy protection.

Though a Kodak employee invented the technology used in digital cameras, the company was concerned that following this new technology would have a negative impact on their traditional film and paper businesses. Former VP Don Strickland claims he left the company in 1993 because the company refused to launch a digital camera.[23]

CASE STUDY continued

The company invested in digital technology but did not easily let go of its reliance on the film market even as this all but disappeared under the development of digital technology. It also focused on the low end of the market. The high profitability of the company during the glory days of the traditional film era may also have contributed to the fall from grace as the burning need to improve efficiency was perhaps absent.

Ironically, the digital camera market that displaced traditional film is itself under threat from the increasing availability and performance of cameras in smartphones.[24]

1.5.5 Legal factors

This category looks at the legal environment and the way that existing (and proposed) laws and regulations will impact on an organisation and the markets it serves.

The banking sector faces greater regulation after taking significant blame for the global economic crisis.

CASE STUDY

Aston Martin Cygnet

In the automotive sector, increasingly tough emission laws have prompted Aston Martin to launch the Toyota IQ-based 'Cygnet' to reduce the average CO_2 emissions across their range. In 2007 the EU announced laws to come into force in 2012 which fine manufacturers with a higher average CO_2 emission figure than 130g/km, with plans for a further 10g reduction.[25] High-performance cars typically emit very high CO_2 levels and the V12-engined Aston Martin DB9 emits 389g/km.[26] The Cygnet has emissions of 110g/km[26] and achieving the target sales of 3,000 units will bring the overall level far closer to the target. Manufacturers such as Ferrari and Porsche are in a more fortunate position as they are part of larger automotive groups who produce millions of low-emission cars (Fiat and VW respectively). These sports car companies therefore do not have to comply with these rules on their own range alone.

1.5.6 Education factors

The rise in access to the internet and increasing numbers of devices that can access the web are supporting new ways of learning. Traditional distance learning courses can benefit from greater interactivity through the use of video-based lessons and tutorials, while children in remote locations can be taught by a teacher who is providing lessons to multiple schools via the internet.

At the opposite end of the education spectrum, the shrinking of the manufacturing sector in the UK means there are fewer apprenticeships on offer. In parallel, the extent of the impact of universities charging fees of up to £9,000 a year is yet to be seen – but this change will certainly discourage some students from continuing their education.

1.5.7 Environmental factors

Thinking about environmental factors may immediately suggest global warming to many people, but 'environment' is a very broad topic. It covers everything from the way that consumers use and recycle everyday items, through to government action for controlling pollution to prediction, avoidance and recovery from natural disasters.

Let's consider the oil industry as it clearly illustrates the complexity of this topic. We see actions by governments to secure the continuity of oil supplies for their countries in the future. Within an oil-producing country, there will be legislation covering production methods and the environmental impact. (BP's Deepwater Horizon leak in the Gulf of Mexico in 2010 resulted in US$20 billion being earmarked by the company for compensation for the damage to shorelines, wildlife and livelihoods.)[27]

From an accounting perspective, there will be regulations to ensure the estimation of oil reserves by an oil company is reasonable. (Shell were fined £17 million by the Financial Services Authority (FSA) in 2004 and the share price fell 7.5 per cent after they admitted to overstating their reserves and failing to correct the error promptly.)[28]

Oil products are also affected by environmental concerns, with plastics being recycled to conserve the supply while diesel and petrol are taxed heavily in countries like the UK to reduce consumption and conserve stocks.

1.5.8 Demographic factors

These are really a subset of the social category but specifically deal with the way that society is divided by, for example, age, income and education. We have a population in the Western World with increasing life expectancy, and so pensions need to provide income over a longer period.

CASE STUDY

PEST analysis for telecoms operator

This is part of the PEST analysis carried out for a UK telecoms company that provides voice calls and internet access to subscribers.

Factor	Description
Political	A report from the Human Rights Council of the UN General Assembly has announced that access to broadband is a basic human right.[29] Governments are responding to this and so more basic 'social' tariffs may be necessary to fit in with this drive to make broadband services more accessible to those on lower incomes. This will affect the operator's revenues negatively as these tariffs mean low prices for entry level services.

CASE STUDY continued

Economic	Although the economy means an individual's spending power may be down, telecoms is shown in surveys around the world to be the last item of discretionary spending that people will give up. A BCG survey suggested 77 per cent of Americans would give up chocolate to keep their internet access and 21 per cent would forego sex for a year![30] A TeleNav survey showed 40 per cent of iPhone users would rather give up their toothbrush for a week than their phone.[31] Fifty-seven per cent of Gen Y surveyed in Australia would rather give up food for the day than their phone.[32] This is unlikely to be any different in the UK. This prioritisation of devices and internet access should help to maintain revenues but precautions against bad debt should be increased – for example, change contracts to increase up-front payments and reduce the company's exposure to the risk of non-payment.
Social	The government is concerned that failure to provide good enough internet access in smaller towns and rural communities will cause young people to move to the large towns and cities.
Technology	The iPhone has changed the market with 50-fold increases in data usage compared to previous generation 3G handsets.[17] This puts a huge strain on some parts of the network, requiring accelerated investment and causing operators to look for alternative networks to offload data traffic onto (e.g. Wi-Fi). Fifty per cent of mobile internet traffic in the UK is now for Facebook.[22] YouTube is uploading an hour of video every second – highlighting the impact of content sharing and the huge increases in the use of social media.[24]
Legal	The European Union has ordered a reduction in prices for receiving data when roaming aboard.
Education	Students remain heavy internet users and are keen to have the fastest broadband access in their rooms. They also are significant downloaders of content and so will be 'greedy' users of resources. Planning the network accordingly will be important to avoid any damage to reputation caused by slow connectivity.
Environmental	Eight per cent of power consumption in the EU is by ICT companies and they are responsible for 4 per cent of CO_2 emissions according to the EU.[33] There is pressure to reduce the amount of energy being used across telecom networks and so more efficient base stations will reduce power requirements as well as saving money on battery back-up (to keep the service going in the event of a power outage).
Demographic	Population growth will increase the number of 'new' users coming to the age when they will use mobile phones.

EXERCISE

Carry out a PEST analysis within your own organisation as a way to understand not only your own organisation, but also the organisations with which you want to work. This can also help you to better understand competitors' thinking.

Many advertising agencies and law firms are now using this approach to try to put themselves in the mind of, and therefore get closer to, their existing and potential future clients.

What you do...

1. Assemble a group that provides visibility across the different areas that may impact on the organisation in question. That means people with an understanding of the different PEST factors as well as creative thinkers.
2. Run a brainstorm session to define PEST factors relative to the organisation both now and in the future.
3. Capture the points in each category on a flipchart during the session.
4. If you have time, you can score the different points under each category in terms of their impact on the organisation (for example, 0 is negligible impact and 10 is extremely significant). You can then consider with the group if there are ways to reduce the strength of negative factors and increase the strength of positive factors.
5. During the meeting, ask the group to consider the 'so what' about each factor you have identified. Which ones are serious now? Which will become serious in the future? What should or could be done about each?
6. Finally, agree on next steps across the team. These may be to help the organisation better understand a coming threat or look more closely at something that is facing a client of theirs.

Summary

Strategy is the long-term plan that defines and shapes the objectives of an organisation – matching resources to the expectations and needs of customers, the market environment and the stakeholders.

Any strategy should be consistent with the long-term vision as well as with the mission defined for the organisation. The mission should reflect the more immediate aims of the company in support of the longer-term vision.

Understanding the external environment helps provide a context to the ongoing decision making and PEST analysis provides a useful framework for thinking about what the organisation is facing.

What's next?

After examining the external influences on your organisation, the next step is to focus internally – to look inside the organisation and understand how it can respond to the changes going on around it. This will help to develop strategies that relate to the current (and future) state of the organisation.

Notes

1. CNN Money. Database of 50 years of Fortune Magazine's list of America's largest corporations.
2. *The Fall and Rise of Strategic Planning: Reconceiving the Roles for Planning, Plans, Planners*, Henry Mintzberg, *Harvard Business Review*, 1994.
3. Toys 'R' Us company website and statements 2009.
4. Proctor and Gamble corporate website information on purpose, value and principles – www.pg.com.
5. Mohamad Mourad, Regional Manager Gulf, Google. Speech at Broadband World Forum 2012, Dubai.
6. Nike corporate website – nikeinc.com.
7. *Daily Telegraph*, Josh Silverman, CEO, Skype, 10 May 2010.
8. The Hershey Company, corporate factbook, July 2011.
9. Ford corporate website.
10. Volkswagen AG corporate website.
11. Toyota Global Vision Statement 2011.
12. *Stall Points: Most Companies Stop Growing – Yours Doesn't Have To*, Matthew S Olson, Derek Van Bever, Yale University Press, 2008.
13. Samer Abu Latif, General Manager, Gulf, Microsoft. Speech at Broadband World Forum 2012, Dubai.
14. Telegeography.com, January 2012.
15. BBC news report, 12 September 2005.
16. BBC news report, 10 May 2011.
17. Ventura Team LLP, Presentation at Fibre to the Home Council Conference.
18. Kodak press release, February 2012.
19. *Financial Times*, 19 January 2012.
20. CIA World Factbook 2011.
21. UK Office for National Statistics.
22. *Socialnomics: How Social Media Transforms the Way We Live and Do Business*, Erik Qualman, John Wiley & Sons, New Jersey, 2009.
23. James Cowling for BBC News website, 20 January 2012.
24. *Marketing Week*.
25. European Union Law – Communication from the Commission to the Council and the European Parliament 6 Results of the review of the Community Strategy to reduce CO_2 emissions from passenger cars and light-commercial vehicles.
26. Manufacturer's figures.
27. *Compensating the people and communities affected*, BP corporate website.
28. Financial Services Authority announcement, 24 August 2004.
29. *Report of the Special Rapporteur on the promotion and protection of the right to freedom of opinion and expression*, Frank La Rue, UN Human Rights Council, 17th Session.
30. Boston Consulting Group (BCG) survey of 1,000 respondents, 22 March 2012.
31. TeleNav survey of 514 mobile phone users in the US, 3 August 2011.
32. *Australians would rather go without food than be without their smartphone, survey shows*, INQ Mobile survey reported at news.com.au.
33. EU Digital Agenda: *Major ICT companies join European Commission initiative to reduce electricity consumption*, press release, 28 September 2010.

2
Assessing an organisation

2.1 Introduction

As discussed in the first chapter, the development of a new strategy begins with a clear understanding of the external environment. We will now move on to describe the next two stages.

The first is to look inside an organisation to assess its current capabilities. This is done by considering different elements ranging from individual skills through to business processes.

Once these capabilities are understood, the second stage is to review them within the context of the changing environment and any specific opportunities or threats that face the organisation. It is only at this point, and not before, that a view can be taken about what are really the strengths and weaknesses of the organisation.

SNAPSHOT

In March 2012, Thorsten Heins, the CEO of BlackBerry manufacturer Research In Motion (RIM), reported to the financial markets after his first 10 weeks in post. The company had failed to respond adequately to the arrival of the iPhone and Android-based phones, and had lost £625 million in revenue quarter on quarter, moving from profit to a loss of £78 million in the same period.

The result of Heins's review of the company's fit to the market led him to the stunning announcement that BlackBerry would move away from the consumer market and focus more on business customers. Heins added:

> We can't do everything ourselves, but we can do what we're good at. We believe that BlackBerry cannot succeed if we try to be everybody's darling and all things to all people.[1]

In the face of fierce competition, the announcement suggests the company believes it cannot continue to do everything in house anymore and will be open to developing partnerships with outside suppliers in a bid to survive.

RIM's change of direction illustrates how important it is to recognise what your real strengths and weaknesses are in the markets you serve.

Let's move on to some approaches for that first stage of understanding the capabilities within an organisation.

2.2 Keys to effective organisational assessments

2.2.1 Why strategic assessments fail

A strategic assessment needs to investigate across the breadth of the organisation at an appropriate level of detail. It seems obvious but this doesn't always happen. There are a number of reasons why a full strategic assessment ends up with the wrong focus.

Assessment teams focus on what they understand or relate to best
An individual or team may focus more on the parts of the organisation they are familiar with. This may be because of their experience, their expertise or where they work within the overall structure of the organisation. If there are plenty of issues in their own departments or business units, they may not have the time or inclination to look more widely across the complete organisation.

Alternatively, the focus of the investigation may also simply be skewed by an issue that is 'flavour of the month' within the senior management.

If you are only paying full attention to one part of the picture, any findings may be misleading or even wrong. This type of focused approach may work well when tackling specific issues, but developing strategy involves (and is shaped by) every part of the organisation.

More broad-based assessments may have the wrong emphasis
Even supposedly rigorous assessment processes can be skewed towards answering certain questions within an organisation.

For example, a due diligence study of a company is normally carried out by potential investors before lending money, investing in or buying a company outright. The primary aim of the due diligence process is to verify that the company is capable of delivering what it has promised and so is worth the investment or is safe to lend money to. This investigation ranges from checking over commercial contracts and verifying that any patents claimed during negotiations exist, through to considering the technical and delivery capability of the company to meet future revenue forecasts.

Although due diligence looks across the capability of an organisation, the team is entirely external (to ensure independence and objectivity) and is normally made up of lawyers, investment bankers, analysts and perhaps some technical experts. Their aim is different from a strategic assessment in that they are simply answering the question: Can the business achieve what it says it can (and so should it get the money)?

This is not the same as looking in detail inside the company to help shape future direction. In contrast, strategic assessment answers this question: Given our current capabilities, and the situation around us, what should we do next and how can we do this?

Let's look at how you ensure that strategic assessments are effective.

2.3 A structured approach to organisational assessments

2.3.1 A few simple guidelines for strategic assessments

The issues described previously suggest that any assessment should be carried out by a team with experience and access across the whole scope of the organisation. External guidance and assistance may help at this point, as consultants or other experts can bring a perspective that is lacking within the organisation.

The assessment should obviously take into account any serious challenges for the organisation but this should not prevent a rigorous approach being taken. To ensure the work is not skewed towards any particular aspect, it is helpful to use frameworks that have been developed to address the full scope of capabilities across an organisation.

We will start by looking at the 'what' of strategic assessments, then move on to look at the 'how'.

2.3.2 The McKinsey 7S Framework[2]

Consulting firm McKinsey developed an extensive framework to ensure that all parts of the organisation are considered. It is known as the 7S Framework.

This doesn't just consider the more tangible elements of a business (e.g. the structuring of an organisation or the configuration of business units). It also emphasises the importance of cultural variables related to the people in the organisation.

Whatever the particular focus of a consulting project for a client, McKinsey insists that all parts of the framework are considered. Table 2.1 lists the 7S factors and shows which variables McKinsey considers as hard and soft variables within an organisation. Shared values sit at the heart of the organisation influencing everything else that occurs and so are considered to sit between the hard and soft elements.

Table 2.1: The 7S Framework

	Factor	Description
Hard	Style	The management style used within the organisation.
	Skills	Specific skills and experience of the staff.
	Staff	The people working in the organisation and their high-level capabilities.
Soft	Structure	The way the different parts of the organisation are structured for management purposes – reporting lines and responsibilities.
	Systems	Processes and systems supporting day-to-day operations.
	Strategy	The direction and scope of activities in the company.
	Shared values	The underlying common set of values that drive the culture within the organisation.

STOP AND THINK

Which of the 7Ss do you think is weakest in your own organisation?

When you've decided, spend some time thinking about how this weakness has knock-on effects on the other variables in the list.

Finally, think about problems in other areas that may be making this weakness worse that it otherwise would be.

McKinsey uses detailed checklists for each variable in the framework to ensure that a complete view is taken of the organisation. However, after the exercise we will introduce an alternative approach where the areas of investigation are defined in ways that are more obviously areas for assessment.

EXERCISE

The type of structured thinking defined by the 7Ss can also be applied in a shorter form than a full assessment of the organisation. The outcome of this abbreviated version might be new insight into problems in the organisation or identification of areas to investigate further.

You can select a group that understands the organisation well enough to recognise issues within, or you can employ this type of exercise with those attending a management away-day type of event.

The duration of this work can vary from three hours to a couple of days, but the general outline for the work should be something like the following:

- Create a flipchart for every 'S' and attach them to the walls.
- Identify a 'long list' of issues within the organisation by brainstorming.
- Write down issues on Post-its and place a copy on every category to which each issue relates.
- Identify any of the 7Ss that have few or no issues noted against them. Consider issues within the organisation again but specifically relating to these potentially underrepresented 7S categories.
- Define any knock-on effects of issues (i.e. where a problem in one area creates issues in another). This will help complete the list of issues.
- Prioritise the list in terms of severity to the organisation (or identify just the high-priority issues if the session is a short one).
- Identify the ability to fix the issues within three periods – immediate, next three months (or six months if that fits the way the organisation operates better), longer.
- Define the sources of resistance to resolving the issues (e.g. investment, cultural change, unions).
- Capture the big, easy wins. These will be issues that are serious in terms of impact on the organisation but relatively simple and easy to resolve.
- If time allows, continue this categorisation, but group the other high-severity issues logically (e.g. high severity but high resistance to resolution).
- Decide on next steps.
- Collate the information and deliver a report for review and as a basis for any next steps.

Let's move on to a more capability-focused framework that we will examine in more detail.

2.3.3 A capability-focused approach to assessing organisations

Although similar in concept to the 7S, this framework has evolved over time and been honed in projects from the US to Baghdad. The specific areas of investigation in this approach are shown in Table 2.2.

Table 2.2: Areas of investigation

Area	Questions
Processes (using process benchmarking and mapping to identify how things are done at present)	• What processes exist for key areas and operations within the organisation? • What are the actual processes that are followed (the 'As Is')? • What are the processes that are supposed to be followed (the 'As Intended')?
Performance measures	• What measures are applied to individuals, groups and the organisation overall? • How do these measures relate to the overall strategy?
Roles and responsibilities	• What are individuals and groups supposed to be doing (job definitions)?
Systems, facilities and technical capabilities	• What technical facilities are available to support the operations of the organisation? (E.g. intranets, CRM systems, databases.)
Personal attributes	• What are the skills, capabilities and experience of people relative to the roles they are trying to fulfil? • What gaps exist and what further resources will be needed for the organisation to be successful in achieving its current strategy? • What technical skills are available in the organisation? • How do the skill levels compare to competitors?

2.3.4 Assessing how well strategy is embedded in the organisation

As well as thinking about capabilities, it is also important to understand how well the organisation understands and is implementing the current strategy. If there are failings now, these are likely to carry over as issues when the new strategy is defined. Let's look at the critical factors regarding how strategy is embedded into an organisation.

Strategy must be shared at the appropriate level of detail throughout the organisation
You expect an organisation to work from top to bottom in a way that is in line with the mission and, in particular, the current strategy. Logically, this can only happen if the strategy has been shared throughout the organisation. You cannot expect people to act in line with a strategy if they are unaware of its existence.

Strategy must be clear enough to enable individuals to act on it

The CEO and management team should understand the current strategy as they will have played a big part in defining it. However, if nobody else in the organisation 'gets it', implementing the strategy will be nigh on impossible. Simplicity, clarity and a communication plan are needed to spread the message in an effective way.

Behaviour will follow how performance is measured and rewarded

Assuming there is complete understanding of the strategy throughout the organisation will still not automatically guarantee that parts of the business operate in line with it.

The problem stems from the way that group and individual performance is measured and how this makes them respond. Most of the time, if staff bonuses, job security and/or chances of promotion are at stake, employees will look at what they are supposed to achieve and the associated performance measures. Reaching or exceeding those performance measures is a clear way to either safeguard their position or show they are excelling. It's human nature.

SNAPSHOT

A car company may have a reputation for quality, but if a plant manager is only measured against a challenging target for numbers of cars produced each day, the risk is that the manager may begin to let sub-standard cars leave the factory just to keep up. It's not in line with the 'quality' strategy for the company, but is perfectly understandable as the manager's own performance measure is not aligned with what the business needs.

Now let's imagine someone asked you to generate £10 million and offered you £1 million if you could do it within a month. They might be hoping for sensible turnaround measures and improvements. However, influenced by the huge bonus on offer, you might sell a factory, the company's offices or the patent portfolio. Admittedly the company might not be able to operate properly, but at least you'd have your bonus! The metric on your performance drives you possibly to do the wrong thing for the company and this is the same case in most organisations.

If the metrics are not aligned with the strategy of the business, results will not be as expected.

STOP AND THINK

Consider how your own performance (and any groups you are part of) is measured. Is achieving those targets strongly aligned with the strategy of the company or is there only a tenuous link?

2.4   Running an assessment programme

A strategic assessment is carried out using a combination of workshops, interviews, reviews of documentations and other forms of information gathering during an intensive period.

The team carrying it out should be familiar with all parts of the organisation and have the skills to gather and interpret data accurately. The team should ideally include at least one member of senior management to provide positional authority if and when needed, and also to make sure the current strategic direction and priorities are clearly understood in the team.

This work will normally include some or all of the following elements.

2.4.1 Senior management workshops

These should help those involved to understand the current performance as well as any concerns and issues. They will also be useful in agreeing the information to be provided to the team.

2.4.2 A start-up workshop

The background, objectives and structure of the assessment process can be introduced to representatives from each relevant department or business unit. This helps to build a common view of the objectives for the work, as well as allowing agreement on who does what.

2.4.3 Individual interviews

These are held with staff members throughout the organisation. The team might talk to the CEO, board members and then a range of individuals from each of the departments.

This should be a detailed enough discussion to understand:

- their roles and responsibilities;
- the skills, learning and experience they bring to the role;
- their understanding of the company strategy (illustrating how well the strategy translates from the board level down into the organisation);
- the measures that are used to measure their work and the work in their part of the organisation;
- their views on current performance; and
- issues they believe exist at present for the organisation.

Once you've gone through a number of interviews, you'll start to have a picture of how well the current strategy is understood both across the organisation and also down the hierarchy. It also becomes clear where (or if) the understanding of the strategy becomes distorted or disappears entirely. At the same time, this work will also help to highlight where the performance measures and rewards are inconsistent with the strategy.

2.4.4 Process mapping

Mapping is used in both workshops and also one-to-one sessions to understand and trace the key processes in the organisation. One methodology used is IDEF0[3] which enables processes to be broken down into progressively more and more detail – describing the inputs, outputs, controls (what governs what happens in the process) and mechanisms (who or what does the work).

Processes can be very useful for a number of reasons. Once a process has been established, it provides a baseline for how particular parts of the organisation will operate. Even if someone is not available on a particular day, tasks can still be carried out in the same way.

The different generic types of processes that you can encounter are described in more detail in Table 2.3.

Table 2.3: Different types of processes

Type of process	Description	Comments
As Is	The current process that is *what actually happens*	–
As Intended	The formal description of the process from manuals, process charts, etc. – in other words, what is supposed to happen	Not necessarily the same as the 'As Is' process
To Be	Normally comes as a result of process improvement activities and is a new version of a process to be implemented	Reflects a better way to run the process after a group has considered the difficulties

Mapping processes allows the team to recognise issues and devise potential improvements.

The team will look at the processes and decide if there are underlying problems within them. Issues may include variation in how some processes are run, 'As Is' processes that are not fit for purpose, or processes that take too long to complete because of bad design.

A key strength of well-constructed processes is that they include criteria for decision making at relevant points. This means defining the rules for who is able to do what at particular points in a process. This allows for effective devolution of authority into the organisation and removes the sometimes random decision making that can occur without clear guidelines.

If there are no criteria for decisions, this can lead to senior management being involved in making relatively trivial decisions. At the other end of the spectrum, there can be cases where management approval is not sought early enough in a major process and significant resources are expended before management has a chance to sign off on what is being done. When the manager does not sign off, that effort has been wasted. It's much better to capture their opinion earlier in the process.

Another common characteristic of processes is the rework loop. This is a point where the process loops back on itself while some action is repeated before the process can continue. While you do want to avoid these as much as possible, there are points where you may *have* to redo some of the process due to a lack of information, change in circumstances, uncertainty around key information or even just a simple mistake.

However, where the organisation runs a process and the number of rework loops starts to creep up, something may be going wrong. The key is to examine whether the rework loops are necessary: eliminate them if not and also reduce down.

SNAPSHOT

Creating the mould for injection moulding of plastic components in a medical device manufacturer can occasionally be right first time, but can take up to 16 iterations to get right. Each minor adjustment requires further tests before it can be seen if the plastic components produced using the mould are within the right tolerances.

The variation in the number makes it hard to plan an exact duration to get the mould right. When the number of adjustments required creeps up, the organisation needs to review its practices and adjust the initial manufacturing assumptions.

2.4.5 Benchmarks and questionnaires

Benchmarks are used to assess the maturity of different aspects of the organisation such as resource management, project management and R&D (if applicable).

Criteria-based benchmarks are used where individuals score the maturity of detailed activities. The criteria range from 'immature' through to 'world-class'. Depending on the organisation, the 'right' answer may not be to be world-class in every category. There will be an optimal position for the organisation in each category. However, this first step is simply to understand variations in practice within and between different departments, sites and business units.

If a whole group strongly disagrees about how well the organisation executes a particular activity, this is interesting and should be explored further. Does this represent a simple misunderstanding or a significant variation of practice across the organisation?

SNAPSHOT

The criteria in the table below are from work in a government commission in Baghdad on behalf of the United Nations Development Programme. For each category on the left, participants ranked the commission by finding the criteria that best matched their current performance.

	Immature	Poor	Satisfactory	Good	Excellent
Clarity of scope and powers	Unclear – changes often based on ad-hoc political decisions	Goals may be clear but actual practice and extent of actions/ powers not adequate	Clear and stable remit defined in law and appropriate and stable in practice	Clarity with periodic review and improvement every few years in order to take account of changes in the sector	Clear and stable remit defined both in law and in practice with clear rational policy for evolving or dismantling elements of regulation over time

SNAPSHOT continued

	Immature	Poor	Satisfactory	Good	Excellent
Separation of powers	Few or too limited powers to achieve objectives	Limited powers or over-lengthy processes or too easily challenged means ineffective	Appropriate powers to fulfil remit and enforce decisions	Appropriate powers and decision-making capability	Appropriate powers, effective analysis and decision making, and able to enforce decisions rapidly and effectively
Independence of action	Unable to act, perhaps not even take decisions	Lack of direction and strategy means uneven progress and subject to influence in contentious areas	Effective leadership with reasonable safeguards. Fair degree of financial and intellectual independence	Effective, independent, leadership and drive at departmental level	Effective and independent leadership at all levels and enduring good governance with budgetary autonomy

If everyone agrees with how they rate performance in one category, this shows consistency but doesn't necessarily mean it's the best approach.

These workshops are most useful when they incorporate employees as well as relevant 'customers' of the organisation's products/services.

2.5   Identifying the real strengths and weaknesses

This second stage builds on the information about the organisation's capabilities to define its real strengths and weaknesses within the environment it is facing.

2.5.1 From SWOT to TOWS analysis

The problem with some management tools is that they can become so familiar that we don't give them enough thought. Most people in business have heard of SWOT analysis – the assessment of Strengths, Weaknesses, Opportunities and Threats. However, fewer are familiar with the argument that the analysis is better tackled in a different order.

As mentioned in Chapter 1, you have to know where you are to be able to understand what is a strength or a weakness for the organisation. So in doing this type of analysis, you would ideally consider the threats and opportunities first before considering how well the organisation is positioned to respond to these. We'll therefore use an alternative approach and look more deeply at the steps behind a TOWS analysis.

2.5.2 The TOWS elements

Threats

Threats are important to understand and you need to quantify both the potential impact of the threat as well as the probability that it will occur. Much like in a formal risk assessment, you need to make intelligent choices about which threats you respond to, as some may be incredibly serious but also very unlikely to occur.

(Note – we will look at tools for quantifying risks/threats in more detail in Chapter 11.)

Opportunities

For opportunities, you need to appreciate the potential upside and then the implications for the business in terms of what might be required to take advantage fully of the opportunity.

Categorising changes in the market as opportunities or threats can be difficult. If there is a new trend in the market, it may risk reducing your current revenues. However, it also provides you with the chance to adapt and increase revenues. Does that constitute a threat or an opportunity?

In reality, it's not important whether the category is correct as long as the impact has been considered, the right level of assessment has been carried out and a decision has been taken about how to respond.

Weaknesses

Weaknesses are the specific gaps and deficiencies within the organisation relative to the opportunities and threats it faces.

Strengths

Strengths are the areas of superiority the organisation possesses in addressing opportunities and threats.

These positions are rarely static. Strengths at one point may end as weaknesses as the environment changes:

- Filofax sales were based on widespread availability and strong brand image. However, the first PDAs – and now smartphones – have eroded sales.
- Dedicated digital cameras are being replaced by smartphones.
- Electronic calculators replaced slide rules but will themselves be replaced by smartphones for casual usage.

Let's put these categories into context with a real-world example we can all understand.

CASE STUDY

McDonald's TOWS

Since its foundation in 1955, McDonald's has grown to be a globally recognised provider of fast food. The following TOWS analysis provides an overview of the situation for the company in 2012.

Threats	Opportunities
• Move to healthier lifestyles and food choices • Greater awareness of nutritional values of foods (labelling) • Media pressure on eating habits • Increasing competition • Fat taxes (introduced in Denmark[4] in 2011 and threatened by David Cameron in the same year)[5] • Lawsuits concerning inducement of children to eat Happy Meals by including toys with the food • Environmental pressures on packaging and recycling • Competitors breaking out into this market (e.g. Starbucks expanding food line) • Competitor expansion (e.g. companies such as KFC)	• Consolidation of healthier meal options including salads • Continuation of freshly prepared meals • Expansion of franchised and own restaurants • Further expansion into coffee market (McCafe) • Recession squeezing consumer spending power and so leading to increased sales in fast food sector • Push into emerging markets • Exploration of further sub-brand opportunities (like McCafe)
Weaknesses	**Strengths**
• Seen as provider of unhealthy food[6] • Limited product line (burger-centric)	• Brand recognition and loyalty • Economies of scale (32,000 restaurants serving 64 million customers per day)[7] • Strong financials (net income figure of 30.4 per cent in 2010) • Consistency of product and quality across operation

EXERCISE

The output of work looking at the external environment (e.g. a PEST analysis) is required before moving on to TOWS. Otherwise you have no context against which to carry out the analysis. The steps are as follows:

1. Bring together a group that understands both the external environment and the results of the internal assessment. Add individuals responsible for commercial and strategy if possible.

EXERCISE continued

2. Brainstorm possible threats and opportunities.
3. Rate the threats and opportunities as follows:
   - Threats: severity of impact; likelihood of occurrence; high level estimate of costs/resources to defend against the threat; and
   - Opportunities: upside potential for the organisation; fit to strategy; ability to exploit; high level estimate of costs/resources to exploit.
4. Prioritise the opportunities and threats, given the ratings and the potential impact on the organisation.
5. List the strengths and weaknesses of the organisation considered against the threats and opportunities facing the organisation.
6. As a final step, match the strengths and weaknesses against the opportunities and threats to which they refer. Some may not relate to either at this time for the organisation, but at the end of this activity, you should have greater understanding about how the organisation is facing opportunities and threats – as well as a prioritisation of which need to be dealt with or responded to first.

Let's now turn to the different combinations of threats/opportunities and weaknesses/strengths to show how the thinking processes change from one pairing to another. We will also look at a couple of real-world cases and see what became of the companies facing the particular situation.

2.5.3 O–S: Opportunity–Strength

Here we are considering how to use strengths to take advantage of opportunities.

The default assumption is that the organisation will pursue opportunities that match its strengths. This seems logical but care should be taken as organisations will not necessarily have the resources to exploit every opportunity effectively. There may be a limited amount of finance available or the technical/human resources needed may be severely limited. Similarly, the management team in an organisation only has a finite amount of time and attention it can apply, and so care should be given in taking advantage of a new opportunity.

The right approach is to go beyond whether the organisation can exploit an opportunity effectively and to consider the following:

- How long will any advantage last?
- What is the overall financial benefit (revenues generated and/or costs saved by taking advantage of the opportunity less and costs to pursue it)?

In this way, you should be able to prioritise opportunities and make rational choices about how to use limited resources. You figure out the size of the opportunity and what it would entail before you make a decision.

SNAPSHOT

Samsung has long held a leading position as a manufacturer of display panels for different devices including TVs. Their expertise has been shown with their development of the world's largest LCD TV and the largest active matrix organic LED (AMOLED) display panel. This capability, as well as their expertise in consumer electronics, made the opportunity to move into the mobile phone market a logical step. Their in-house manufacturing expertise and economies of scale helped them to enjoy better margins than handset makers who needed to buy in all the components (rather than making them in-house like Samsung).

The company went on exploit this opportunity and their strength helped them to sell 50 million touchscreen phones in their first two years.[8]

2.5.4   O–W: Opportunity–Weakness

This combination describes an opportunity where the organisation's ability to exploit it is weak.

It's very easy to say no when faced with an opportunity that doesn't quite fit the business. In many instances that will be the right answer, but it shouldn't be a knee-jerk response. Each opportunity should be evaluated and, if it is exceptional, the organisation might justify the effort to turn the areas of weakness into strengths. That might be achieved through partnering with or acquiring another company, bringing in staff with different skills, extra training, gaining external finance or whatever is needed to overcome the weakness.

As before, the potential upside of the opportunity should be considered before any decision is made. It will be exceptional that an organisation chooses this course of action, as the investment needed to turn the weakness into strength may be significant and so the profitability of such a venture may be far lower than for companies which are already strong in the area. However, companies whose core markets are disappearing will perhaps consider this approach as the alternative may be going out of business.

2.5.5   T–S: Threat–Strength

Unlike the previous opportunity-based combinations, managing threats is essentially a defensive activity. Serious threats cannot be ignored and so there is little or no choice about whether you respond or not.

If you have a strength that matches up to a significant threat, you still need to make sure that there is a good fit. It's not a case of assuming you've got the threat covered – you have to do the homework and make sure.

2.5.6   T–W: Threat–Weakness

Having a weakness in the face of a significant threat is the easiest category: whatever choices are available to mitigate the threat, you have little choice but to respond.

SNAPSHOT

AOL once dominated the internet access business, but it did this using dial-up connections. The threat for them was from operators that could effectively cut them out of the business as new dedicated forms of connection appeared (e.g. DSL and cable). AOL reacted with the extraordinary merger with Time Warner to try to reposition itself – a combination of the old and new in the media world. However, this merger has since been dubbed 'a marriage from hell' by CNBC[9] and described as the worst merger ever.[10] AOL has since been sold and its future is far from secure.

AOL reacted to the threats to their original business model, but sadly the pairing with Time Warner did not convert their underlying weaknesses to sufficient strength to respond to the threats facing them.

Summary

Understanding the capabilities of an organisation is a vital step to deciding what direction it should take in the future. It is important that any assessments are carefully structured to provide a complete and accurate picture of the situation.

The areas that we look at in an organisation can be summarised in a number of ways including by using McKinsey's 7S approach.

Table 2.4: McKinsey's 7S Framework

Factor	Description
Strategy	The direction and scope of activities in the company
Style	The management style used within the organisation
Skills	Specific skills and experience of the staff
Staff	The people working in the organisation and their high-level capabilities
Structure	The way the different parts of the organisation are structured for management purposes – reporting lines and responsibilities
Systems	Processes and systems supporting day-to-day operations
Shared values	The underlying common set of values that drive the culture within the organisation

Alternatively, you can look at the processes, performance measures, roles and responsibilities, personal attributes and systems within the organisation. This approach provides tangible areas to examine.

The next step is to run a TOWS analysis that considers the external threats and opportunities before deciding if the organisation's capabilities constitute strengths or weaknesses in relation to these.

What's next?

In the next chapter, we will use this understanding of the organisation and proceed with more detailed thinking about the direction for the organisation and continue to explore this idea of strategy.

Notes

1. *Research In Motion (RIM) Year-End And Fourth Quarter Results For Fiscal 2012*, RIM Investor information.
2. 'Structure Is Not Organization', Tom Peters, Bob Waterman and Julien Philips, *Business Horizons*, 1980.
3. 'ICAM Function Modelling Manual – IDEF0' – US Air Force Systems Command – June 1981.
4. 'Fatty food tax introduced in Denmark', BBC, 2 October 2011.
5. 'UK could introduce "fat tax", says David Cameron', Guardian Online, 4 October 2011.
6. *Supersize Me*, directed by and starring Morgan Spurlock, 2004.
7. *2010 Annual Report*, McDonalds.
8. 'Samsung Corporate Profile, History', Samsung corporate website.
9. 'Top 10 Best and Worst Merger of All Time', CNBC.com
10. 'AOL – Time Warner: Worst Merger Ever?', Michael Hickins, *Information Week*, 28 May 2009.

Part B

Setting the direction

3
Developing strategy

3.1 The context of strategy

Developing a strategy doesn't happen without conscious effort. In the absence of a new or refined strategy, an organisation will be at risk from decision making based on increasingly out-of-date thinking and assumptions.

3.1.1 Strategic drift and gaps

When there is a perceived lack of clear strategies in an organisation, this may reflect either the absence of a strategy or a failure to communicate it clearly if one does exist. An absence of strategy may be due to the difficulty of trying to forecast in a turbulent environment or a lack of management competence and leadership.

A further challenge is the tendency towards incremental evolution of strategy in response to what is going on around an organisation at the time. Strategy is tweaked a little over time, and evolves very slowly but this is actually closer to simple, long-term planning than real and significant strategic thinking. This approach can help you get to a destination you have predetermined through minor course corrections, but it can miss the need to change direction radically sometimes.

When this type of strategic gap opens up (i.e. where a company is a long way from where it should be), the investment to get back on track can be significant and many companies will fail to recover.

3.2 The strategic planning cycle

The creation of strategy is a carefully structured and iterative process. You need to get the right strategy, monitor the performance against that strategy and then update it on a regular basis (e.g. yearly) or when circumstances change dramatically for the organisation.

The starting point is normally the current vision/mission (see Figure 3.1).

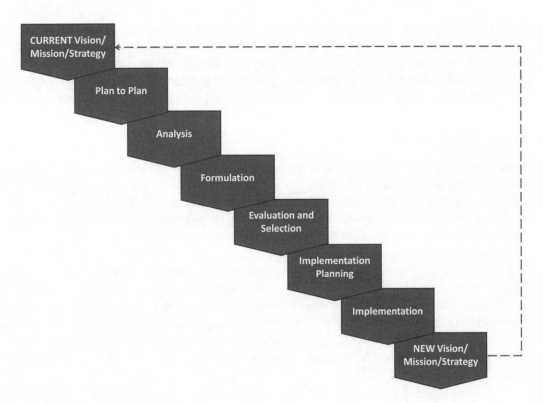

Figure 3.1: The strategic planning process

3.2.1 Plan to plan

Before you begin thinking about potential directions for the organisation, you need to figure out who should be involved in the decision-making process. This might include people inside the business but may also involve suppliers, buyers and external analysts. They won't necessarily be available without notice, so you need to create a plan that carefully schedules in whatever workshops and meetings you need. All this has to happen while also including enough time between meetings to gather data, communicate findings, gather feedback and share that with the various other relevant stakeholders.

3.2.2 Data gathering and analysis

Once you start the strategic planning process for real, the first stage is to gather and analyse relevant information.

The PEST and TOWS analysis results will be important in understanding the external factors influencing the organisation as well as any significant opportunities and threats. Although this type of analysis may have been done in developing the existing strategy, it must always be repeated at the start of each new strategy development process.

Data should also be gathered about performance against targets and the general health of the organisation. This might include sales figures by segment, product line and geography through to financial performance metrics (e.g. profit margins, progress on cost-reduction measures, etc.). However, it will also reflect findings from any organisational assessments that have taken place. The results will provide information across both the hard and soft variables in the organisation.

3.2.3 Formulation

A number of scenarios are then formulated based on the work in the data analysis stage. These scenarios describe the different paths that the organisation can take and they are honed down to a small number of promising scenarios that will be fully evaluated in the next stage.

At this point it is worth stressing that one of the scenarios taken forward for evaluation should always be 'do nothing'. The 'do nothing' option provides a vital baseline against which you can compare each of the other scenarios. For example, one scenario might cost £50 million more than the 'do nothing' base case. However, the incremental profit over the next few years may be £150 million. You can only work that out if you have the baseline of the 'do nothing' case for comparison.

Another reason for including a 'do nothing' base case is that although members of the management team may understand exactly why doing nothing is unacceptable, there may be those on the board or in other stakeholder groups who do not. If you don't justify why a change is required (by showing the flaws associated with the 'do nothing' approach), then these people may not support your proposal.

3.2.4 Evaluation and selection

When the scenarios have been formulated, the next step is detailed evaluation and selection.

The first part of the evaluation involves defining the full set of implications for the organisation for each scenario. There should be the elements of a traditional business case for each, which means considering the financial benefits against changes in operating expenses and capital investment. This work should also include risks and issues in pursuing the scenario and potential mitigation to reduce down the potential impact of those risks.

However, there should also be a detailed analysis across the 7S Framework within the organisation to see which areas will need to evolve; you need to ensure that they have been adequately considered within the evaluation of the scenario.

This work provides a view of the pros and cons of each scenario, but the next stage is to compare them. At this point, the specific constraints in the organisation will help to shape the decision. For example, if the company is low on money to invest, then some costlier scenarios may be discarded even if they appear attractive. Similarly, some scenarios may be considered too risky for the organisation to pursue.

The impact of introducing radical products, services or significant changes to an organisation are hard to quantify and can lead to serious errors in forecasts. This means you need to consider very carefully the underlying logic behind any possible radical changes. It's always a gamble to some extent but, when you're betting on a company's future growth and success, you need to do your homework thoroughly.

CASE STUDY

Apple disrupts a new market

At the Macworld event in January 2007, Steve Jobs announced the company's name would change from Apple Computer Inc. to Apple Inc., reflecting the company's move away from being solely computer-based to a wider range of consumer products.[1] This in itself was a radical move. Jobs announced on the same day the launch of Apple TV and the iPhone.

Entering the mobile phone market was extraordinary in some ways as this was a market in which Apple had no previous experience. The CEO of Microsoft was even moved to laugh at the launch of 'Apple's $500 phone that doesn't even include a contract'.[2]

The markets, however, reacted very positively to this change in direction and Apple's shares rose 13 per cent with the announcements from US$85.47 the day before to US$97.00 the day after the event.

However, Apple was not just entering the market, it was redefining it. The traditional business model for handset manufacturers was simple: they sold their phones to operators who then provided them for free or at a cost to their subscribers. In addition, the operator could make additional revenues by selling applications to subscribers.

Apple changed these rules with the original iPhone in that they would receive part of the monthly contract payments made by subscribers to the mobile operators. In addition, there was the Apple App Store, which is essentially a closed system that cuts the operator out of the value chain for software applications and content. Users buy direct from the store and operators receive no part of this transaction.

Apple initially only worked with one operator per territory, creating a great opportunity if you were the sole company providing iPhones, but also allowing Apple to negotiate very hard with the operators for the exclusive rights. For example, in the UK, the iPhone was exclusively on O2 for some time.

Latterly, Apple has moved from this approach to serve multiple operators in the same territory and it even sells unlocked phones that can work on any network. This helps Apple to achieve greater unit sales of the device and therefore have more potential customers to buy apps and content from the Apple App Store. The revenue share model has also evolved with most revenue-sharing agreements changing to pure handset purchase by the operators.[3] Apple sold just over 37 million iPhones in the final quarter of 2011 alone as well as 15.43 million iPads.[4] The App Store itself reached 25 billion downloads in March 2012.[5] Apple has entered and fundamentally changed a market it was not previously part of as well as achieving extraordinary sales and download numbers. This was a big gamble but it has certainly paid off.

3.2.5 Implementation planning

When the strategy has been developed, the extent and details of the changes required can be fully understood. Minor course corrections are relatively simple, but major fundamental changes to the organisation will need carefully structured plans and time to implement them well.

This structuring process involves a logical breakdown from the strategy to smaller chunks of work until eventually arriving at individual tasks and actions. For example, for each organisational strategy, one or more objectives will be set to deliver the strategy. For each objective, there will be one or more tasks to do to achieve the objective.

One approach to this breaking-down process is known as a GOST: Goals, Objectives, Strategies and Tactics. Unhelpfully, this acronym includes the word strategies to describe sets of activities designed to deliver the objectives. The strategies/approaches referred to in this context therefore only form a small part of the overall organisational strategy that we have been thinking about up to this point.

The table below shows the theory behind the GOST approach with the levels within the GOST structure shown in the left-hand column and then a definition next to it. To illustrate the approach, there is also a real-world example in the right-hand column to show how these factors relate to one another.

Table 3.1: GOST theory

Level	Definition	Example
Mission	Stakeholder-driven view of the long-term premise of the business	Be considered the 'best' car company according to customer surveys of quality
Goal	General statement of aim or purpose	Improve quality
Objective	Specific and quantified restating of all or part of the goal	Improve defect-free rate to 99.8 per cent
Strategies/ Approaches	Strategies to deliver all or part of the objective	Toughen quality standards for suppliers
Tactics/ Actions/Tasks	Breakdown of the activities necessary to deliver the particular strategy – may be at several levels of detail (work breakdown)	Renegotiate all component supply contracts, improve testing of inbound components, increase penalties for supplier failures

As you can see, being the 'best' car company for quality translates through the goals, objectives and strategies down to tasks. However, remember that each factor (such as a goal) can spawn multiple things to do at the level below. So there will be many tasks at the bottom level to help deliver the top-level mission to be the best car company.

EXERCISE

We have discussed how important it is that the understanding of the strategy (and appropriate measures) is spread down into the organisation. Consider your own organisation in terms of the GOST breakdown. Think about your major areas of work for a moment and write them down. Once you've done that, ask yourself: Is there a recognisable goal or objective they relate to? Do you understand how the work fits into the breakdown from goals down to tasks or not? Are there major areas of work where you are unclear what the associated goal or objective might be?

Does your team understand this in the same way that you do?

Organisations may have different terminology for these different levels of detail, but there should ideally be clarity about how the work you and your team are doing fits into delivering the overall strategy for the business.

3.2.6 Monitor

Finally, the impact of changes should be assessed as part of the ongoing measurement of performance. This is particularly important: unless you understand how you are performing against targets, you won't know if what you are doing is working as expected or if further changes may be needed.

As noted previously, defining strategy is not a static event that happens once and is forgotten for a few years. It should be a regular (e.g. yearly) refresh of approach across the organisation and should reflect the performance of the business relative to the current strategy. When the situation for the organisation alters suddenly, with serious changes in the environment or a new opportunity, then this may warrant an immediate re-evaluation of the strategy.

3.3 Strategic analysis – tools for formulation

Up to now, the assessments have considered the external environment and the capabilities of the organisation before defining strengths and weaknesses in the face of opportunities and threats. The next stage in the formulation step described earlier is to look at current and potential future trends in the markets the company serves. These changes may relate to the way the market operates overall or the organisation's relationships with the companies that supply it with goods and services and those that buy from it.

The challenge in trying to understand the external environment is the complexity of influences acting on an organisation at any given time. Michael Porter, widely considered one of the most influential global thinkers on strategy, developed a very useful approach to dealing with this complexity with his Five Forces Model.[6]

3.3.1 Porter's Five Forces

Porter created the model shown in Figure 3.2 as a first step to devising appropriate actions.

The model shows that a company is influenced first by the actions of competitors in their chosen markets. The vertical axis shows how the competitive balance can be altered by new players entering the market or products/services acting as substitutes for the customer's money. The horizontal axis reflects how the other players in the supply chain can exert their power to influence the situation.

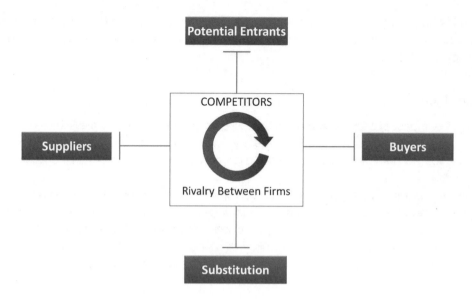

Figure 3.2: Porter's Five Forces Model

The Five Forces are therefore the competitive rivalry with the four other major power influences – buyers, suppliers, potential entrants into the market and the potential for substitution.

Competitive rivalry

Competitive rivalry will be affected by many factors, including:

- number and size of competitors;
- market share;
- maturity of the market;
- costs to exit the market (this could be financial but could also be loss of face, keeping the company in a market it should really leave);
- profit margins;
- cash flow;
- capacity utilisation; and
- strategies and ambitions.

Buyer power

This is the amount of power that buyers can exert on an organisation in terms of the price they pay, terms they will agree to, service agreements and specifications.

The power is higher when:

- the buying group is concentrated (only a few buyers);
- purchases are made in volume; or
- the purchase doesn't save money for the buyer or provide any other perceived value (i.e. is essentially a commodity).

A potato farmer might find that the pool of buyers has reduced over time with local greengrocers closing down in the face of competition from supermarkets. The farmer may find that those same supermarkets are actually their only potential buyer – limiting the farmer's power to negotiate and allowing supermarkets to aggressively dictate their own terms.

SNAPSHOT

As an example of the buyer power of retailers, consider Wal-Mart. Revenues of US$422 billion, net income of US$15.4 billion[7] in their 2012 fiscal year and a global footprint make Wal-Mart a very attractive company to sell products to. Their reach provides a significant platform for a company selling to them. However, their financial power gives them the ability to negotiate exceptionally hard with their suppliers.

CASE STUDY

Amazon vs. Apple – The book market transformed

The history of Amazon in the book market is an excellent example of buyer power changing a market. Amazon's extraordinary success, coupled with their desire to sell e-books at low prices, has led some major players in the publishing industry into an agreement with Apple to try to maintain higher prices.

Amazon is a company that disrupted the retail industry for print books and then quickly went on to do the same across a swathe of other retail business models. In parallel, the company continuously innovated with the addition of external suppliers and a second-hand marketplace to their site.

Amazon took what appeared to be a very brave leap into the technology arena with their original Kindle e-book reader, which launched in late 2007. By July 2010, sales of Kindle e-books outstripped hardback book sales through the company. It was six months later that Kindle e-books overtook paperback sales[8] and then in May 2011, Amazon announced that for the first time they were selling more Kindle books than print books.[9] That's less than four years from the launch of the Kindle compared to 15 years of traditional book sales for the company.

Amazon uses a traditional wholesale model where they buy at a percentage of the recommended price but are then free to sell at whatever price they choose. This means they control their own margin and can reduce prices to encourage take-up of the Kindle, for example. Publishers normally sell to Amazon at around 50 per cent of the recommended retail price for a book.

Amazon's habit of discounting e-books created concern in the publishing industry that this approach would set an expectation of low prices in the mind of the public.

Apple, the big player in content download, clearly saw the potential of e-books as an attractive driver of sales for the launch of their iPad. To attract publishers, Apple chose an agency model whereby the publisher sets the final sales price and Apple takes a 30 per cent cut. However, they also insisted that publishers offer Apple the lowest prices in the market.

CASE STUDY continued

This 'most favoured nation' approach means publishers have more control over pricing to the consumer and can limit discounting in at least part of the market.

The Department of Justice in the US has been investigating whether this has been keeping prices artificially high and whether there was collusion between the five publishers in the agency agreement with Apple.[10] The charge is that the group acted together to enforce high prices. However, the publishers will argue they were trying to prevent Amazon from becoming a dominating force in the industry.[11] If this was the aim within the group, it may already be too late.

Amazon is moving aggressively up the publishing food chain by signing up authors directly and therefore cutting traditional publishers out completely.[12] The impact of this move by Amazon can be seen with 16 of the top 100 paid e-books on Amazon in April 2012 actually being exclusive to the company.[13] The theory is that publishing electronic versions of books means very few associated costs for production for Amazon and there is no royalty to pay to a third party as they are also the publisher. This means Amazon can theoretically pass on bigger advances and royalties to authors who choose to publish direct with them.

In parallel to this move up the value chain, Amazon has also made it possible to buy books either new or second hand from third parties but using the Amazon platform as the front end for vendors. The latest move has been the introduction of the lending library where authors are paid a cut when a Kindle user 'borrows' their book – essentially gaining access to the book for 14 days.[14]

Amazon's transformation of the market demonstrates the power they wield as a buyer and how this has provoked defensive reactions from their competitors.

Supplier power

This is the power that suppliers have in negotiating terms and conditions with the potential purchaser. This is about the balance between a supplier's ability to drive prices up against the buyer's ability to change supplier.

Suppliers are more powerful when:

- the product/service is highly differentiated;
- the costs to switch to an alternative are high (e.g. in the car industry where a part may be designed for a seven-year life and switching may mean safety tests have to be redone or require redesign of other components);
- the market is not important to the supplier (e.g. low margins or turnover);
- there is no competition or only few competitors; or
- they could enter the market of the companies buying from them (this threat of entry makes it harder for buyers to exert much power on suppliers).

STOP AND THINK

Think about launching a new manufacturer of laptops. You would need to source almost all the components from other companies, including the processor that lies at the heart of the machine. This processor could come from Intel or AMD, but there are no other major providers of this component.

1. What is your power in this negotiation with one of the two companies?
2. How will these negotiations differ for you compared to an established industry giant like Dell?
3. Is there going to be true competition between these two suppliers?

Stop and think about that for a moment before reading on.

This negotiation is likely to be very difficult for a new player as both suppliers know there is limited scope to buy elsewhere and volumes are unlikely to be significant to start with. A further complication may occur if your strategy requires you to select one vendor over the other (e.g. choosing Intel for a higher-priced, higher-performance range or AMD for a more mass-market product).

Let's look in more depth at the case of two competitors in a market as it illustrates some interesting thinking about how they might behave.

Duopolies

As a rule of thumb, two companies in a market do not create true competition. It creates a duopoly. If there is potential to differentiate the products in some way, then one company may be able to outperform their competitor. However, there are also several ways in which a form of equilibrium can occur between the two.

- If the product is nearer to being a true commodity with little differentiation between products, then a natural equilibrium may occur where performance is broadly similar (e.g. Mastercard and Visa).
- A larger company may choose to allow the smaller competitor to remain in a market. The larger company may have the resources to destroy the competitor (e.g. by reducing prices for a period) but may choose not to because being left in a monopoly position might attract attention from law makers and regulators. It may therefore 'tolerate' the smaller company having a part of the market. Microsoft have fallen foul of anti-trust laws repeatedly because of their market dominating position and were even fined £691 million by the EU for failing to comply with a previous ruling.[15] The lack of a credible competitor for Microsoft has hurt them in this case.
- The smaller company may undercut the prices of their larger competitor by a certain amount, but there is then a danger of entering a price war which they would almost certainly lose.

The end result can be that even without any formal discussions between the two about fixing pricing (as this would be illegal), the situation can stabilise with the large company 'allowing' the smaller one to exist and the smaller one accepting that actions to increase its market share might not be a good idea.

There are, of course, exceptions. The fight between Boeing and Airbus illustrates that sometimes two competitors do go all out in the same market.

CASE STUDY

Boeing versus Airbus

The jet age for commercial travel began in 1949 with the launch of the first jet airliner, the De Havilland Comet. The market quickly began to fill with competitive aircraft produced by companies that had previously been making propeller transports and airliners.

The challenge of smaller countries competing with the might of the Americans led to the formation of Airbus in 1967, bringing together France, Germany and Britain to build aircraft jointly. In the US itself, the battle for dominance between Douglas, Lockheed and Boeing was slowly won by the latter. Douglas merged with McDonnell to try to benefit from economies of scale and to support the cash flow required for major aircraft development, but they ended up merging with Boeing in 1997.[16] Lockheed fell away by refusing to build a wide-bodied, small twin-engine aircraft, but this is the very format with which Airbus started.[17] The Airbus A300 essentially provided the new consortium with a foothold in the market.

From the mid-1980s onwards, the commercial airliner battle slowly evolved to being about Boeing versus Airbus. Airbus began to catch Boeing, which was seen as risk-averse and somewhat complacent to their marketplace. By 2004, Airbus had received their 5,000th order and they had overtaken Boeing.[18] It only took another six years for them to register their 10,000th.

Development paths

The companies are taking ambitious paths for their newest aircraft. While Boeing took an advanced design approach with their new 787 Dreamliner, Airbus was criticised for just going to a bigger design with the double-decker A380. For the Dreamliner, orders stand at 870,[19] but delivery has been delayed by several years due to the complexity of the design.

To counter the A380, Boeing has created the stretched 747-8 Intercontinental – the latest version of an aircraft that dates from 1969.

Airbus has responded to the Dreamliner threat with the A350. Orders stand at 555 aircraft in early 2012 and deliveries hopefully in 2014.[20]

Delivering the Dreamliner on time would have led to more orders and the delays have allowed the A350 to partly catch up (assuming it is delivered on time). However, the complexity and challenge of this type of project can be judged by the A380 programme that involved 1,000 different suppliers.[21]

Incredible numbers but limited threat of entry by new players

New and replacement airliners from 2011 to 2030 will total 26,921 – worth $3.2 trillion.

Seventy-one per cent of new deliveries to 2030 will be single aisle through to very large aircraft being 5 per cent of new deliveries but representing 14 per cent of the value.[22]

North America and Europe are forecast to take 22 per cent of these aircraft showing the 'home' markets for these two strong competitors will not particularly favour one side or the other. Those are incredible numbers and you might imagine that they are so tempting that a new entrant could come in to try to take a part of this enormous potential. However, the huge

CASE STUDY continued

development costs coupled with technology and market risks make a new entrant unlikely to appear in the near future.

Continents in competition

This duopoly is still fighting hard for market share and survival. A clear cause of friction is in the level of subsidies they are given by their respective governments.

The US government's financing guarantees for aircraft hit $11 billion in 2011.[23] In Europe, Airbus has historically received a third of development costs from governments. In the case of the A350 the total development cost was estimated at £9–£10 billion. By 2012, cost overruns were estimated at several billion more.[24] The latest loans for Airbus have been referred to the World Trade Organization following complaints and are on hold as of May 2012 until a decision is made.

Threats from potential new entrants into the market

This threat relates to the ability for new players to credibly enter and disrupt the market. In particular, this forces a company to consider the barriers to entry that exist (or could be erected) to prevent another company entering their market.

CASE STUDY

Fisker uses the economic downturn to create a new car company

The economic crisis created the right set of circumstances for the creation of a new car maker. Henrik Fisker, a former Aston Martin designer, started doing bespoke coach building in California until circumstances allowed him to make an audacious entry into the car market.

The first car, a beautiful £80,000 hybrid sports car, is now on sale barely four years after it was first shown to the world. Fisker has been able to achieve his aim directly as a result of the crisis in the US car industry.

Normally, the investment finance would be hard to come by and would need to be considerable to buy manufacturing facilities. However, the company was contacted by the US Department of Energy, which backed the company to try to reduce the potential downside of the troubles being experienced by the big-three makers in the US. Eventually, the DoE promised around £332 million[25] of funding and Fisker's company is rumoured to have up to £650 million of private equity money at its disposal.[26]

Fisker was also able to acquire a former General Motors plant in Delaware for £13 million, which would have been worth multiples of that price a few years previously when the industry was in better health.

The traditional car companies were therefore surprised by the path that Fisker had taken through all the pitfalls. The aim is to produce a range of £35,000 hybrid models by 2013.[26]

Unsurprisingly, the company has been facing significant challenges and as of early 2012, the future of the company is not certain. Will it become an established manufacturer or go the way of the UK government-backed project to build the DeLorean sports car in Northern Ireland?

Fisker shows that even an industry 'defended' by high investment requirements to enter can be attacked from the outside if circumstances are right. The following example shows how even charities that have been in existence for many years can suddenly come under threat.

CASE STUDY

Help for Heroes

The UK charity Help for Heroes was started by Bryn and Emma Parry in 2007 – raising £12 million in the first year, £18 million in the second[27] and a total of £130 million by mid-April 2012.[28] From 2009 to 2010, the period when Help for Heroes was becoming very well known, income for the Royal British Legion (RBL) fell by around £10 million to £115 million.[29] This may have been purely the impact of the economic climate, but charitable income during the year to 2010 actually rose by 6.5 per cent in the UK.[30] The question is whether the newcomer is taking donations that would otherwise be going to the long-established charities (the Royal British Legion was founded in 1921) or whether it is finding new sources of income. It seems strange to think of charities acting in competition with one another, but essentially their job is to maintain and grow the sources of revenue to carry out their objectives. That means defending against new entrants to the sector and also responding to changes they create in the market. The Director General of the Royal British Legion is on record as saying the RBL has had to update itself, in part because of the impact of Help for Heroes.[27]

Potential for substitution

In simple cases, this involves like-for-like substitution (i.e. similar product types). The threat is simple and the alternative choices are easy to identify. For example, an executive might switch from a BMW to a Mercedes-Benz. However, in some cases the threat of substitution can be trickier to understand. Discretionary spending is far harder to assess in terms of substitutes as the substitute use for the money is unrelated – someone decides against purchasing one product and instead spends the money on something completely different.

A summer holiday might be replaced by a skiing break in winter. However, the money earmarked for the holiday could equally be used to pay for a new bathroom, a motorbike or anything else the buyer wants. Where the spending is on something that is 'nice to have' rather than a 'must have', it's difficult to predict exactly where the money might go.

EXERCISE

Carry out a Five Forces assessment on your own organisation or one that you know well. This might be a competitor, a client or a company you wish to do business with in the future. This exercise can be done on your own but the outline below shows the approach when working with a group.

- Use one flipchart page for each of the five forces and position these on a wall with a title at the top.

EXERCISE continued

- Using the diagram in Figure 3.3 as a prompt for relevant questions, brainstorm factors for each of the five forces for the organisation you are considering and ask people to capture their ideas on Post-its first.

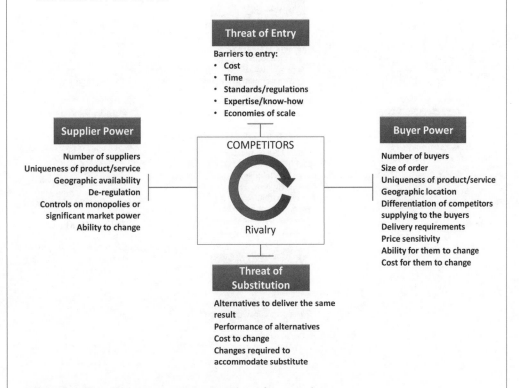

Figure 3.3: Five Forces – prompt questions for exercise

- Transfer the Post-its on to the relevant flipchart sheet, eliminating any duplicates and clarifying understanding as you proceed.
- Next, draw a line down each flipchart sheet and then move the factors for each force to the left or right of the line. Place each one to the left of the line if they are affecting the current situation or to the right if the factor is more about the future.
- Now consider each force with the group and ask if you have identified all the relevant current factors and then future factors. Fill in the gaps as necessary.
- If you have the time, you can also prioritise which areas you do more work on next. Ask the group to vote on whether each individual factor needs further investigation and/or action either now, soon or when possible. You can mark those that need work now with a red pen, soon with amber and the when-possible factors with green.
- Define next steps for the red items and plan on how and when you will address the amber items.
- Capture the output from the session.

The Amazon vs. Apple case study earlier in this chapter discussed the way that Amazon has grown to be a threat to traditional book publishers and how some have responded with their deal for Apple's iBooks service. The example in Figure 3.4 shows how the broader set of Five Forces might look for a traditional print book publisher.

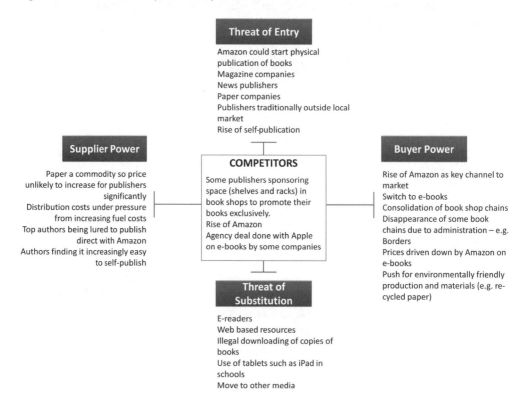

Figure 3.4: Porter's Five Forces applied to a traditional book publisher

3.4   Understanding where to invest

Many of the approaches discussed so far have involved looking at the current situation. We're now going to move on to assessing different options at a more detailed level.

3.4.1 Ansoff Matrix

Igor Ansoff developed a matrix to describe the choices an organisation can take when considering options to increase revenue.

Figure 3.5 shows the combinations of new or current products and markets. The notes in the boxes show the main activity needed if you are trying to increase revenues.

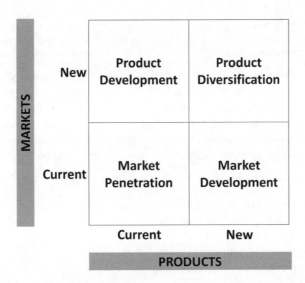

Figure 3.5: Ansoff's Product Development Matrix

Table 3.2 describes the matrix in more detail and some of the choices in each area.

The top right position is the most difficult to get right as, by definition, the company is changing to both a market and product/service that it does not necessarily understand.

You will hear people quote how Sony invented the Walkman market out of nothing or how Apple moved into the mobile phone market to justify their own ideas in this new product/market area. The problem is that there are always exceptions. For every product that has succeeded with such bold moves, such as those of Apple or Sony, there are many, many more that have perished for trying precisely the same thing.

The Ansoff Matrix is a little black or white in its distinction between current and new products/markets. It is useful to consider a stage where the product or market is modified rather than completely changed. For example, Product Extension is the creation of new variants of a product rather than something completely new. Coca-Cola extended their product line by creating numerous versions of Coke including diet, caffeine free and Cherry Coke variants as well as ones with added lime or lemon.

The subtle differences of approach are shown in Figure 3.6.

Table 3.2: The Ansoff Matrix

	Current product	**New product**
New market	When taking the current product to a new market, you understand the capabilities and limitations of the existing product, but you don't necessarily understand what is needed in the new market. You might consider: ● new territories; ● making a move from retail to wholesale channels; and ● looking at different demographic groups.	This is pure diversification. 　You are moving to a market you potentially don't understand with a product/service that is also not familiar. 　This can be a very dangerous place for a business.
Current market	This is where all or part of your business currently operates. Choices here include: 1. Do nothing. 2. Consolidate. 3. Withdraw from the market. 4. Grow through acquisition or another company or business unit. 5. Increase penetration by marketing actions: 　● bundling; 　● discounts; 　● special promotions; 　● changing warranties; 　● increase advertising and/or change media channels used; 　● take on new distribution channels (e.g. online); 　● increase the sales force; or 　● new brands.	This involves taking a new product to your existing market. 　You know the customers so should understand their needs and the existing relationships should enable you to explore different ideas for new products/services with them. This might involve: ● offering accessories to the core product – e.g. cases and power adaptors in a mobile phone store; ● complementary services – e.g. an accounting firm adding an auditing service; or ● vertical integration – e.g. a delivery company also taking on the storage of products they deliver

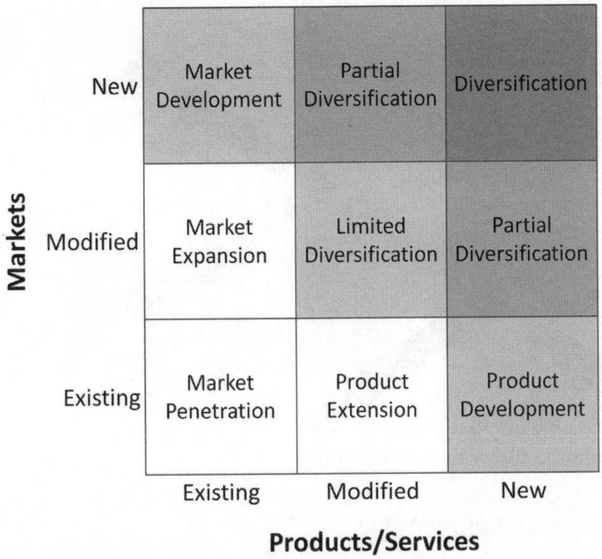

Figure 3.6: Potential product and market evolution strategies and risk

The risk in following the particular strategy shown in each box is represented by the shade of grey. The darker the box, the greater the risk will generally be in pursuing the approach.

3.4.2 Bowling pin strategy

Another way of considering how to increase revenues is bowling pin strategy.[31] It is an approach to growing a new business that suggests it is best to take a new product to an existing customer or find a new customer for an existing product.

At any point, you have a choice of what to do as shown in Figure 3.7. If you think of a set of bowling pins from above, you start at the first pin (the kingpin) and then at each point are confronted by two pins to hit. Unlike in ten-pin bowling, the objective is specifically not to try to knock every one down but to pick a carefully considered path at each point.

The choice is whether you try to find a new customer for your product or service. This may involve:

- geographic expansion;
- customisation for customers who don't wish to or cannot use the standard product; and
- modification to meet the needs of a similar market.

Alternatively, you may wish to address your existing market with a new product.

Figure 3.7: Bowling pin strategy – example

Figure 3.7 shows the logical progression with an initial market and product combination, leading to pursuit of a new market and then development of new products for that current market.

Bowling pin strategy is relatively simple and the thinking can be applied from a large market through to specific niches in the market. However, it is best used as a way to provoke thinking and it should be noted that it essentially eliminates the most dangerous diversification option in the Ansoff Matrix (new product, new market).

CASE STUDY

What threatens your business may not be what you expect

The ferry companies operating from the south coast of England to France expected the Channel Tunnel to hurt business – particularly for those operating the same Dover-to-Calais route. The Eurotunnel opened for freight and passengers in 1994. Eurostar train passenger numbers for the tunnel have grown year-on-year to reach 9.7 million on Eurostar, and 7.8 million used the tunnel to travel in cars or coaches in 2011.[32] At the time the tunnel started operations, ferry traffic via Dover stood at 19.1 million passengers (excluding car and coach passengers). By 2011 this had fallen to 12.7 million.[33]

It is logical to assume the tunnel had an impact on the ferry businesses. What was less expected but very significant was the advent of low-cost air travel. Ryanair carried only 5 million passengers in 1999[34] but this had risen to 76.4 million by December 2011.[35] Similarly, Easyjet carried 50 million passengers in the year to January 2011.[36] The ferry companies may have feared the tunnel, but in the longer term the rise of budget travel may have had a greater impact.

3.4.3 GE Matrix

We've looked at choices at an organisational level. This model from McKinsey (developed on behalf of General Electric, or GE) is interesting as it maps the strength of a strategic business unit (SBU) or company within a particular industry against the attractiveness of that industry. It is unlike the previous tools which considered moves into new or adjacent areas. This model considers how strongly the parts of an organisation are placed within different industries.

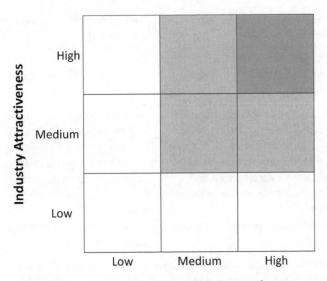

Figure 3.8: The GE Matrix

The axes in Figure 3.8 are relatively straightforward on the surface, but the challenge is to come up with a way of measuring the industry attractiveness and business unit strength that is meaningful. Otherwise, high, medium and low could become very subjective. The good news is that the information required to measure these attributes should have been at least partially defined while looking at the PEST factors, Five Forces, TOWS and other analysis to date. The missing elements might be the more numerically based information relative to the company's performance and the overall size and evolution of the market.

In this case, rather than plot the business units on the matrix as a single point on the matrix, further information is added to help understand the overall situation. The size of the market in question is represented by a circle (centred on the coordinates representing the score on each axis for the business unit and where the area of the circle is proportional to the market size – see Figure 3.9 on page 55). The current market share for the company or business unit is represented as a sector where the area (shown in white in this example) represents the share of the total market.

EXERCISE

Developing this matrix requires a number of steps that will yield the best results when carried out with the right group of people. That group may be the same when considering the industry and business strength or may vary slightly as you bring in experts in a particular area.

	Industry attractiveness	Business strength
1	Identify the people needed for this assessment.	Identify the people needed for this assessment.
2	Carry out a brainstorm with them to identify factors contributing to **Industry Attractiveness**.	Carry out a brainstorm with them to identify factors contributing to **Business Strength**.

3	Rank the factors by importance and agree a score for each from 0 to 10 (where 0 is unimportant and 10 is vital).
	  Add the scores up and then calculate the percentage for each factor's score divided into the total of all the individual factor scores.
	  This provides a percentage weighting for each factor.
		Rank the factors by importance and agree a score for each from 0 to 10 (where 0 is unimportant and 10 is vital).
		  Add the scores up and then calculate the percentage for each factor's score divided into the total of all the individual factor scores.
		  This provides a percentage weighting for each factor.

4	Score the attractiveness of each factor in this category to the business unit(s) – 0 is completely unattractive to the SBU, 5 is average and 10 is incredibly attractive to the SBU.	Score the strength of the business unit(s) with respect to each factor in this category – 0 is weak, 5 is average and 10 is very strong.

The next stage is to combine these together in a weighted factor analysis.

The individual weight factors are multiplied by the corresponding score and then added together to provide a total score. So, for example, in the table below, multiplying the individual Weight scores in the column marked 'a' by the corresponding scores for Business Unit A in column 'b' gives a total of 6.55 out of a possible 10. The same approach gives a score of 4.5 out of 10 for Business Unit B.

	a	b	
Attractiveness factor	**Weight**	**Business Unit A**	**Business Unit B**
Market growth	25%	8	2
Market revenues	10%	6	3
Margin	15%	4	2
Competition	35%	7	8
Low cost to enter	15%	6	4
TOTAL	100%	6.55	4.5

EXERCISE continued

The same approach is followed with the strength of each SBU relative to the market being considered, as shown below.

	a	b	
Business strength	**Weight**	**Business Unit A**	**Business Unit B**
Fit to current skills	35%	8	2
Existing relationships with market	20%	6	6
Channel fit	30%	4	5
Capacity requirements	15%	7	4
TOTAL	100%	6.25	4

The final step is to plot this information on to the matrix as shown in Figure 3.9.

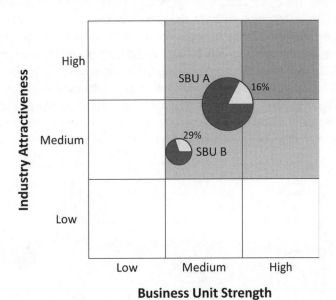

Figure 3.9: GE Matrix example

This approach can be used to look at existing business units or to consider entry into new markets or potential acquisition targets.

SNAPSHOT

Jack Welch, former CEO of GE, provided a simple rule for his business units that really underlined the approach shown above. A business unit had to be first or second in its market or it had to leave. That might mean selling it, shutting it down or working out how to get to be number one or two, but it was clinically simple.[37]

Limitations of the GE Matrix

Although very useful as a comparison tool, the weightings and concepts like 'attractiveness' are somewhat subjective. The better the thinking in setting up the measurement criteria, the better the result will be.

3.4.4 Product/market evolution

The model (known as the Hofer-Schendel Matrix)[38] combines the elements of competitive position within the lifecycle of a product. The life covers from development through growth, to where weaker competitors are either bought by other players or give up (known as the shake-out phase). For the players reaching maturity, the growth in the market is limited but this stability offers the chance to earn good profits. Finally, the market may move into a phase of decline.

This model can be very useful to view the current portfolio of products/services and how they are likely to develop over time. What will be growing? What will be declining?

Consider the following two different portfolios of products/services. Each product is positioned to show the respective competitive advantage against the vertical axis and also the place in the product lifecycle. The area of the circles show the total market revenue and the company's share of the total market for each product is shown by the white sector within the circle.

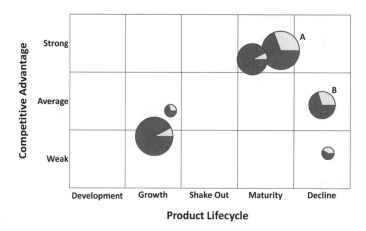

Figure 3.10: Product/market evolution – Example A

The portfolio shown in Figure 3.10 includes good market shares in largish markets for some products (e.g. A and B), but overall most of the revenue is in markets about to decline or already declining. The large market in the growth phase only shows low market share for the company and weak competitive advantage. It may be difficult to change this level of market share and the implication is that future revenues are likely to go down once the products shown (A and B) decline and the weaker newer products replace them.

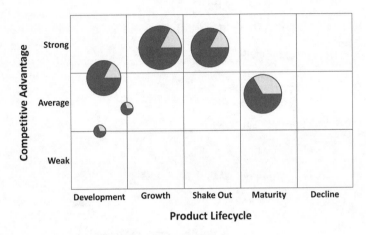

Figure 3.11: Product/market evolution – Example B

The portfolio in Figure 3.11 is more attractive in the long term. The markets are generally large and the company combines reasonable market share with average to strong competitive advantage. In particular, the company appears to be looking good overall, as the products are doing well and are competitive in the growth or shake out stage. This will give them a good chance to remain competitive into the important maturity phase (where profits are typically highest).

Overall, the portfolio in Example B is much better than the ageing and weaker portfolio in Example A.

You can use this approach to compare products within a business unit or across the complete organisation (if what they do can be summarised within the context of just one market).

3.4.5 How to respond to competition

As a first step to formulating a response to the position and strength of competitors, you can consider your own relative strength or weakness against them on a product-by-product basis.

If you understand the relative strength or weaknesses (as shown in Figure 3.12), then the next step is to work out what to do.

In their book *Product Juggernauts*,[39] Deschamps and Nayak proposed options for companies to consider in responding to competition as follows:

- Target and beat.
- Target and emulate.
- Monitor carefully.
- Cooperate.

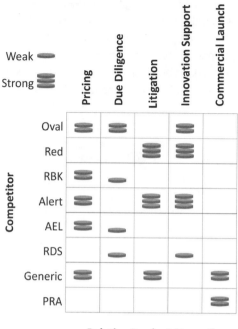

Figure 3.12: Relative product strength compared to competition

You can define an option relative to each competitor. This can be at a generic level – say a car company wanting to emulate BMW – or could be based on product groups. So in one area (e.g. hybrid engines), two competitors could cooperate for mutual benefit. In another area, these two companies may remain bitter rivals and so the response to them will be different (e.g. target and beat).

STOP AND THINK

For your main products/services, think about the different competitors. Who are you emulating? Who are you beating? Who are you cooperating with?

   Now look at each current situation. Is each one correct? Which would you change and why? In other words, where is your current competitive approach wrong or in need of modification?

3.4.6 The value of hitting a market on time

It's not just important to have the right product, it's also vital to launch at the right time. The financial penalties for being late to a market can be severe as your competitors grab market share and volume that will enable them to take advantage of economies of scale. Though being first isn't always ideal, being late to a market is almost always serious.

CASE STUDY

The cost of being late to the market

The Go Telecoms company in Saudi Arabia was awarded a licence to operate a wireless broadband service as one of three new competitors to the incumbent operator. In this situation, there was a race to be first to launch to capture significant pent-up demand across Saudi Arabia and work done to understand the impact of any delay.

The issue created by any delay was that other competitors would be launching at the same time and would be signing up subscribers. Once customers were lost to the competition, the assumption was they would never return in meaningful numbers.

The approach considered a five-year period of revenues from the business. Delays naturally mean that the revenues will be hit because the:

- network is not as extensive as the competitors and so fewer customers will be able to sign up for the company's products (as they are not covered by the service);
- revenue per subscriber reduces over time (and so you would acquire the subscribers on marginally lower revenues per month due to the delay); and
- ability to win new subscribers diminishes as more and more subscribers are taken by competitors (and you'll struggle to convert them later).

The result

Looked at simply, if each lost subscriber is worth £30 of revenue per month, then over five years, that adds up to £1,800 of lost revenue per subscriber (ignoring price erosion and inflation). Each month of delay would actually result in thousands of the company's potential customers going elsewhere.

The detailed comparison between the base and delayed cases did not seem to show a large difference in revenues at a particular point, but over five years, the impact was an accumulated loss of around £30 million of revenue.

Does your organisation consider the impact of delay when negotiating any major investments? If you're not careful, the amount saved in protracted negotiation can easily be lost in delays to launch.

SNAPSHOT

In September 2010, Nintendo was forced to admit its 3DS handheld games device would not launch in time for the critical Christmas sales period. By its own estimate, this would result in a reduction in profit of around £900 million, which was the loss on the device as well as the games.[40]

3.5 Where should the focus be?

Organisations can set themselves up to deliver in a variety of ways to their customers/clients. The focus can be moved from production through to sales – as described below.

- **Production-focused** companies assume customers will want products that are available widely and at a low cost. This approach is valid if demand outstrips supply or where reducing the unit cost will stimulate demand.
- **Product-focused** companies assume customers look at the quality, attributes, and performance of a potential purchase and can recognise, understand and value the particular features of the product.
- **Selling-focused** companies assume customers could buy more of the product and aim to make this happen through sales and promotional activities. These companies focus on selling what they can produce rather than necessarily producing what customers want.

This selling-focused approach assumes the market will accept this situation and won't react. In the past, the classic marketing wisdom dictated an unhappy customer would tell 11 people. This related to simple word of mouth. However, the advent of social media and widespread access to the internet means people can share their experiences easily and instantly with their friends. It is therefore harder to succeed with a selling focus than in the past, as potential customers may be more aware of the tactics of companies doing this as well as being able to compare products and services easily.

3.6 Markets will change

Sometimes companies have adopted strategies that imply they think the 'good times' will carry on indefinitely and subsequently have failed to adapt to changing circumstances. Every company, no matter how successful it is, will need to keep thinking about its markets and how it delivers to them because of the following:

- **Markets evolve and transform** – driven by changes in technology, demographics, spending power, competition, and usage habits.

SNAPSHOT

The markets for voice recorders, digital cameras, calculators, navigation systems, video cameras, maps and even guitar tuners are being impacted by the take-up of smartphones which incorporate these functionalities (or can add them as applications). The most popular camera used for uploading images to photo sharing site Flickr is now the iPhone 4.[41] Analyst company the NPD Group suggested that, at the end of 2011, one in four photos and videos is now taken with a smartphone in the US. It contrasted this with US sales of digital cameras, which fell 17 per cent in the year to November 2011.[42]

To underline the importance of the smartphone camera market, Facebook announced in April 2012 that it would buy the smartphone camera app company Instagram for US$1 billion.[43] This for a company that had zero revenue to date.

- **Markets will be redefined by competition** from wider and/or complementary product groups. For example, the Automobile Association has been providing assistance to motorists who have broken down since 1905 and more recently has offered that assistance at members' homes at a small extra cost. Having a fleet of mobile engineers serving clients at home has now been extended with the AA taking their 'fourth emergency service' positioning further to provide cover for home emergencies such as problems with plumbing. Food retailers such Tesco have created internal fishmongers, added pharmacies into their stores and then gone a step further with opticians. Budget airlines now try to sell hotel accommodation, car hire and transport from the airport to nearby cities to their travellers.
- **Channel changes will affect how some markets operate.** (See Snapshot below.)

SNAPSHOT

Many of the traditional functions of the British Post Office can now be done online. Previously you would go to the Post Office to do a number of important things that have been undermined steadily over time. For example:

- More parcels are delivered directly now and Amazon has taken a huge chunk of traditional Post Office delivery business into its own systems that are to the door.
- Applications for a tax disc for a car can be done online now.
- Many pensioners and benefit claimants would get their money as cash from the Post Office. The advent of internet and telephone banking, not to mention the problems of robberies on days when the Post Offices had the most cash, have meant many payments are now made direct into accounts.
- Application for a passport can be done online or at a Passport Office. The Post Office has a service where they can 'check' your application to ensure you haven't made any mistakes, but this is hardly a strong business model.

3.7 Strategy to action

The start of this chapter described the strategy process. We have also discussed the challenges for an organisation where the strategy is unclear or misunderstood. To finish this chapter, we will therefore look at some pragmatic methods for sharing strategy throughout the organisation.

3.7.1 PORTS

A variant of the GOST structure introduced earlier, PORTS is a way to structure the overall purpose of a department, business unit or organisation. It then breaks this purpose down into the different objectives and tasks that support it. The acronym stands for:

- **P**urpose
- **O**bjectives
- **R**esponsibility
- **T**asks
- **S**chedule.

PORTS differs from a complete work breakdown structure as used in project management. In particular, there is no structuring of the relationship between tasks or timeline included (as would be seen in a Gantt chart). The PORTS chart is a tool that helps to show the structure of who is doing what task when – and how they relate to the top level purpose of the group etc. This can be seen in Figure 3.13.

Purpose	Objectives	Results	Accountability	Tasks	Responsibilities	Schedule
Purpose of business unit or function	Objective One	Target with date	J. Jeffcock	Specific task	JG	Xx/xx/12
		Target with date	F. Tucker	a. Sub task	GH	Xx/xx/12
				b. Priorities list	GH	Xx/xx/12
				c. Time line / production	EF	Xx/xx/12
				d. Allocate who does what	EF	Xx/xx/12
		Target with date	P. Jaques	Permanent meeting agenda	AB	Xx/xx/12
		Target with date	William Patrick	a. Specific task	EF	Xx/xx/12
				b. Specific task	GH	Xx/xx/12
	Objective Two	Target with date	Harry Alastair	Specific task	EP	Xx/xx/12
		Target with date	J. Sunley	a. Sub task	HJ	Xx/xx/12
				b. Priorities list	SR	Xx/xx/12
				c. Time line / production	EF	Xx/xx/12

Figure 3.13: A PORTS chart

The left-hand column shows the overall purpose. This could be one of many. To the right are two objectives defined that support that purpose. For each objective, there is a person under Accountability. That means they are there to ensure the work is done. They are directing but not normally carrying out the work themselves.

To the right of each objective, there are one or more tasks relating to the objective with the responsible person(s) or group defined. These are the people actually doing the work. Finally there is a scheduled date for completion of each task and a column (third from left) that defines the desired results.

3.7.2 RACI

The RACI Matrix is a useful way of understanding who is involved in a task and how they are involved. Those involved are defined very simply with a letter that shows their role.

The inclusion of the person who signs off the work is a useful addition and leads to this method sometimes being called RASCI.

Table 3.3: RACI Matrix

Ref.	What it means	What they do
R	Responsible	Does the work
A	Accountable	The person/group making sure the work gets done – supervising the quality, etc.
C	Consulted	Involved in two-way discussions
I	Informed	One-way communication of results to these people/groups
S	Signs	Is the person/group that needs to sign off the work

3.7.3 Combining PORTS and RACI

You can take the best of these two approaches to create a hybrid way of sharing tasks and responsibilities with people in the organisation. You do this by creating a detailed matrix of tasks and responsibilities that essentially combines PORTS and RACI into one matrix.

The matrix enables assumptions to be shared about:

- how things fit together – the relationship between purposes, objectives and tasks;
- who is accountable for what;
- who is responsible for what;
- who is involved through consultation; and
- who receives information about task outputs.

This information is very useful as it enables people to look at the overall assumptions and identify any gaps or errors about who is going to do what. This may be a problem with the way their own work has been defined or they may be able to help spot problems in the definition of work in other areas of the organisation.

This matrix is particularly helpful in clarifying roles and responsibilities in new organisations or where there has been significant change. For example, I used this to good effect in a change programme on behalf of the United Nations in Baghdad.

EXERCISE

It is probably easiest to create this content in a spreadsheet using the merge function to show that, for example, one objective has multiple tasks (as illustrated in Figure 3.13).

The content for this matrix will be derived from work done to this point to define the overall strategy and the GOST breakdown beneath it. However, it is rarely exhaustive and you should review the GOST output during the creation of this matrix with a team representing the different groups covered in the matrix.

Create a first draft document with columns as described in the following list.

EXERCISE

Column	Usage	What you do
Department or business unit	Helps identify tasks relating to a specific part of the overall organisation	Define the different departments/ groupings to be addressed in the matrix
Purpose	One of a number of objectives relating to the department, business unit or company	List the different purposes (or goals) for the groups defined above
Objective	Define each objective that builds to deliver the purpose defined above	Take any objectives defined in the GOST process and capture them in the matrix next to the purpose to which they relate
Tasks	Define the tasks required to deliver each objective defined above	List any tasks from the GOST process and other work – listing these next to the objective to which they relate Do not forget external partners, suppliers and/or clients if these are important in delivering tasks

Summary

Developing strategy is an iterative process that an organisation needs to engage in on a regular basis to avoid gaps occurring between where the organisation is and where it needs to be. Attempting to correct the position when a large gap has opened up can take significant time and money, and will not always succeed. It's easier and cheaper to stay on track and react to significant changes as and when they occur.

Porter's Five Forces model provides a good way to understand the competitive situation further, and tools like the GE and Hofer-Schendel models help illustrate the competitive position of business units down to individual products and services. Using these to consider how the portfolio of products/services will evolve over time is vital to understanding future problems that may drive the organisation to change now.

Finally, we looked at one way of sharing, from the goals in an organisation down to the detailed tasks that will deliver these – enabling identification of any errors and/or omissions.

What's next?

Now we've seen how we can structure the breakdown from strategy to individual tasks, we'll get back to figuring out the decisions that get us to that level of detail. The next chapter goes through marketing – understanding the products, services and markets that an organisation can and should deliver.

Notes

1. 'Apple drops "Computer" from name' by Mathew Honan, MacCentral, 9 January 2007.
2. Microsoft CEO Steve Ballmer interview with USA Today's David Lieberman at the sixth USA TODAY CEO Forum, in conjunction with the University of Washington Business School, 29 April 2007.
3. 'United States Securities And Exchange Commission Form 8-K Pursuant to Section 13 or 15(d) of the Securities Exchange Act of 1934', 9 June 2008.
4. 'Apple Reports First Quarter Results', Apple.com, 24 January 2012.
5. www.apple.com/itunes/25-billion-app-countdown.
6. *Competitive Strategy* by Michael Porter, Free Press, New York, 1980.
7. Wal-Mart investor information, press release, 21 February 2012.
8. Amazon press release, 29 January 2011.
9. Amazon press release, 19 May 2011.
10. 'Justice Department Threatens Lawsuits, Alleging Collusion Over E-Book Pricing', Thomas Catan and Jeffrey A. Trachtenberg, *Wall Street Journal*, 2012.
11. 'Apple's struggle to defeat Amazon set to be exposed by European eBook inquiry,' Juliette Gartside, 19 December 2011, Guardian.co.uk.
12. 'Amazon Signs Up Authors, Writing Publishers Out of Deal', David Streitfield, 16 October 2011, *New York Times*.
13. Amazon press release, 4 April 2012.
14. www.amazon.com.
15. 'Antitrust: Commission imposes €899 million penalty on Microsoft for non-compliance with March 2004 Decision', 27 February 2008. EU Commission decision reference IP/08/318.
16. Boeing.com, corporate chronology 1997–2001.
17. *Boeing Versus Airbus: The Inside Story of the Greatest International Competition in Business*, John Newhouse, Vintage Books, 2008.
18. Tom Enders, Airbus President and CEO quoted in Airbus Press Release, 17 January 2011.
19. www.boeing.com.
20. Airbus Order Book, February 2012, Airbus.com.
21. Tom Enders, Airbus President and CEO quoted in Airbus press release, 17 January 2011.
22. 'Airbus Global Market Forecast 2011 – 2030', Airbus.com.
23. 'Fears Of An Aircraft Order Bubble', *Aviation Week*, 2 April 2012.
24. 'Airbus A350 Government Loans to Total $4.6 Billion', Bloomberg, 15 June 2009.
25. 'Fisker CEO revamps business plan amid Karma woes', Reuters.com, 4 April 2012.
26. 'The highs and lows of starting a car company' by Steve Cropley, *Autocar*, 2011.
27. 'How Help for Heroes charity became a £100m fundraising phenomenon', Patrick Barkham, the Guardian, 28 November 2012.
28. www.helpforheroes.org.uk.
29. *The Royal British Legion Annual Report 2010.*
30. 'Facts and Figures – Recent History 1999 – 2011', www.charity-commission.gov.uk.
31. *Crossing the Chasm: Marketing and Selling High-Tech Products to Mainstream Customers*, by Geoffrey A. Moore, HarperBusiness, New York, 1999.
32. Eurotunnel corporate information. Traffic figure history 2005 to 2011: www.eurotunnelgroup.com/uk/eurotunnel-group/operations/traffic-figures.
33. Port of Dover annual traffic statistics: www.doverport.co.uk/?page=AnnualTrafficStatistics.
34. *Ryanair Annual Report – 1999.*

35. Ryanair investor relations information, www.ryanair.com.
36. 'Easyjet passenger numbers rise to 50m each year', Easyjet press release, 4 February 2011.
37. *Winning: The Ultimate Business How-To Book* by Jack Welch and Suzy Welch, HarperBusiness, New York, 2005.
38. *Strategic Management: A New View of Business Policy and Planning* by Dan Schendel and Charles Hofer, Little, Brown and Company, New York, 1979.
39. *Product Juggernauts*, Deschamps and Nayak, Harvard Business Press and Arthur D. Little Inc.
40. Nintendo press briefing, 29 September 2010.
41. www.flickr.com/cameras, 11 April 2012.
42. 'Consumers now take more than a quarter of all photos and videos on smartphones', www.npd.com press release, 22 December 2011.
43. BBC News, 10 April 2012.

4
Marketing

If you don't have a competitive advantage, don't compete.

Jack Welch, former CEO of GE[1]

4.1 What is marketing?

There are many definitions of marketing, although it is hard to find one that covers every aspect. A common misconception is that marketing and selling are the same thing – they're not.

- **Selling** concentrates on generating cash from a product.
- **Marketing** aims to satisfy the needs of a customer with a product/service and all things the customer experiences in it being purchased, delivered, used and supported.

SNAPSHOT

Theodore Levitt provided a description of this difference in his classic Harvard Business Review article, 'Marketing Myopia'.

Selling focuses on the needs of the seller, marketing on the needs of the buyer.[2]

What was, and still is, important in this article was his description of the dangers of focusing on products rather than buyers. His view was that companies that fall into this myopic trap may fail to keep up with changing customer needs and be badly prepared when major shifts occur in an industry.

Marketing is based on three different levels of requirement:

1. **Needs** – There are the things individuals or groups must have. We need food and water to survive and a warm place to shelter from cold weather. Needs can be extended beyond these most obvious examples, but the key distinction of needs should be that they are not optional.
2. **Wants** – Wants are the longing for a specific something to satisfy a need. Wants are optional so although you *need* food, you may *want* that food to be Chinese or Italian or even chocolate. Wants are things we are wishing or hoping for.
3. **Demands** – These occur when there is the ability to pay for something that is a want.

From a marketing perspective, there is little sense in spending money to educate or persuade a market to take products or services that serve their needs. These things are not optional so, for example, an advertising campaign for the virtues of electricity would almost certainly be a waste of money. However, marketing could and should operate to influence buyer's preferences towards a particular supplier of electricity.

Companies will seek to find different approaches to the delivery of products and services to their market.

In order to understand the different parts of marketing fully, we'll start with those higher-level aspects that lead on from (and in part overlap with) strategy.

A good first step is to look at the marketing concept.

4.2 The marketing concept

The marketing concept has some fundamental elements that describe basic requirements in delivering to the market. These include the following:

Table 4.1: Elements of the marketing concept

Element	Description
Market focus	Companies cannot hope to succeed everywhere and the finite resources at their disposal should be used carefully. This means monitoring with care the markets to be in, including entering new markets, or leaving existing ones, at the right time.
Customer orientation	Rather than companies looking at customers as recipients of whatever they happen to produce, customer orientation demands understanding the needs of the customer *from the perspective of the customer.*
Coordinated marketing	This goes further than just the marketing department. This is about the whole company understanding and delivering against the commitments and targets relating to customers.
Profitability	Marketing aims to find and exploit profitable opportunities. While it could be argued that marketing functions don't always succeed in this regard, the intention is clear – find new and improved ways to deliver value to customers and profit to the organisation.

In general, it is harder to win new customers than retain existing ones, so understanding what they need and delivering to them will save you considerable acquisition costs trying to fill gaps in revenue created by customers you have lost. Satisfied customers buy from you again, may recommend you to others and will be less likely to consider alternative offers while they remain satisfied.

4.3   Assessing strategic alternatives

You need to understand how the markets you are serving are segmented and also how they are evolving. In particular, consider the changes that are happening or might happen in the near future, in areas such as:

- new primary demand;
- new technologies;
- redefinition of the market; and
- changes in the channel to market.

However, where should the company focus? It is a tricky question but the company should:

- consider all the markets that appear to have potential (for revenue and/or market share growth or new markets to enter);
- target homogenous markets (ones where there is a group of buyers with a common set of demands and expectations from the product); and
- define what it will take in terms of resources, time and investment to improve the company's products/services to better match the market.

It is not always simple to identify what is the best fit between the existing/potential markets and the strengths and capabilities of the company. However, the type of organisational assessment described earlier provides a context for these decisions – giving the baseline for what the organisation can do now (and what it cannot). When complete, this work will define the resources needed to succeed and what may be significant changes to the organisation to meet the needs of new markets and/or to leave existing ones.

4.4   Generic marketing strategies

Prior to looking at more detailed decision-making techniques, it's useful to look at some generic approaches to serving a market and the respective pros and cons.

4.4.1 Porter's generic strategies[3]

Michael Porter suggested three generic factors to describe how an organisation addresses a market.

Table 4.2: Porter's generic strategies

Strategy	Description
Differentiation	This is a market-based approach that creates: • one or more aspects of the product/service that is perceived as unique or of higher value than competitive offerings; and • reasons for customers to choose the product instead of a competitive offering.
Cost leadership	Here the company aims to achieve: • the lowest costs for production and distribution; • economies of scale (actively managing the supply chain to drive prices down as volumes increase); and • cost minimisation across the company.
Focus	The level of focus refers to the breadth of the market that the organisation will address. This may be from a narrowly defined niche through to mass market coverage. Within the scope defined, the organisation can then deliver to the market via either of the two strategies described above – differentiation or cost leadership. A focus strategy is therefore actually one of two variations – cost focus and differentiation focus.

Porter stressed the importance of not attempting to follow all strategies at the same time, as the demands on the organisation are very different. However, he suggested that companies that fail to aggressively follow any of the three generic approaches would be 'stuck in the middle' and might struggle to compete effectively.

4.4.2 Risks of Porter's generic strategies

Although following one of the strategies appears to be sensible, they are still not without their own risks.

STOP AND THINK

Consider the way your own organisation operates in one particular market.
• Which of the generic strategies do you think is being followed?
• Is it clear that one strategy is being targeted or are you more geared towards being stuck in the middle?
• How well do you think that the approach is working?
• Which approach are your competitors taking?

Table 4.3: Risks of Porter's generic strategies

Strategies	Potential risks associated with following the strategy
Differentiation	• Competitors imitate the differentiation. • Differentiating factors become less important for current buyers or new buying groups are less impressed by the company's offerings. • Costs increase to deliver the differentiation – reaching a point where buyers do not value the differentiation enough to buy the product once it becomes more expensive.
Cost leadership	• Cost advantages are eroded by competitors – you lose your edge. • Technological change – leading to the product being outflanked suddenly. • High competitor differentiation – meaning cost is not the most important criteria for potential buyers. • Spending on R&D too low – leading to an inability to maintain differentiation.
Focus	• Segments may become less attractive over time as the market changes and competitive strategies take effect. • Competitors may re-segment or sub-segment the market. For example, consider the traditional market for large estate cars which was dominated by Volvo and Mercedes. It has recently been sliced into numerous sub-segments including people carriers of all sizes (e.g. SUVs and 4x4s). • Competitors may imitate.

4.4.3 Value disciplines

An evolution of Porter's strategies created by Fred Wiersema and Michael Treacy describes three value disciplines.[4]

1. **Product leadership** involves delivering differentiated and/or high-margin products, and so requires strength in skills such as innovation, product development, technology development and branding. The result of this approach will often be the ability to achieve higher margins for a more desirable product. Apple, BMW, Mercedes-Benz and Sony are companies that show product leadership.
2. **Customer intimacy** focuses on gaining a deep understanding of the customer and then delivering tailored products or services to them. This may be an individual product or a bundle of complementary offerings centred around the customer's desires or needs. MacMillan Cancer Support offer support for those affected by cancer with a very high level of customer intimacy. Their wealth of experience has shaped the care they offer and this includes nursing care in the patient's home but can also range from financial support through to a lift to the hospital. The care they provide is different in every case.
3. **Operational excellence** is where an organisation targets cost leadership in its industry. This is accomplished through the standardisation of processes to improve throughput, reduce errors and enable high levels of output at low costs. Economies of scale will help in this case and so in manufactured goods, standardising on parts across different products will assist by delivering higher volumes of a reduced number of components. The more you produce of the

same thing, the lower the unit costs should be. In service businesses, operational excellence will involve streamlining the operation by converting manual processes to automated ones – e.g. capturing customer information online and scanning correspondence.

Organisations need to have a certain capability in each of the disciplines to compete in the market. However, as with Porter's strategies, the danger is in attempting to be all things to all men. Clearly, the cost-cutting approach of operational efficiency will not work well alongside trying to deliver high levels of customer intimacy.

4.4.4 The challenges of targeting particular strategies

The different generic approaches outlined previously are all simple enough to understand but are more difficult to actually achieve. Let's look at some of the complexities in pursuing these strategies.

Aiming for cost reductions

Cost reductions do not happen automatically and so companies need to actively focus attention on one or more of the following areas:

1. Improving production efficiency – e.g. making larger quantities may enable a company to move from batch production (making a number at a time) through to something closer to a full production line.
2. Economies of scale – buying in greater quantities should allow a company to gain better discounts from suppliers. The suppliers can improve their own production efficiency, allowing them to pass on cost reductions if they are themselves making larger orders.
3. Increasing the utilisation of resources. For example, low-cost airlines aim to increase the time their aircraft are in the air. Legal firms will seek to increase the billable hours for their lawyers.
4. Advantages based on relationships to other SBUs such as production expertise, better-quality materials, advance notice of changes, etc.
5. First mover advantages. The first mover can sometimes gain exclusive access to a technology or other part of the value chain (e.g. sign up the number one supermarket in the country to act as a distributor). However, you need to be careful as history is littered with companies that have tried the 'leading edge' of a technology and discovered it is more of a 'bleeding edge'. This failure to perform may be because the technology and associated processes are not mature enough for production or the market does not take to the new technology.
6. Physical location. This may be to do with distribution costs (so being close to a major transport hub would be beneficial) or being close enough to customers to provide them with rapid after-sales support.

Diseconomies of scale

Diseconomies of scale are the logical reversal of economies of scale. Beyond a certain point, growing bigger can actually hamper the effort to deliver.

For example, small companies don't tend to be weighed down with complex IT and HR policies and don't need to have carefully defined processes for doing everything. The number of employees is low enough that everyone probably understands what needs to be done and roughly who does what. However, as you add people to a task, you find that the need to coordinate the efforts will start to become more and more significant.

SNAPSHOT

Adding people to the organisation also increases the number of potential lines of communication. Two people only have one line of communication to manage – with each other. Three people have three lines. By the time you get to 10, you have 45 potential lines of communication and with 40 people the number reaches 780!

4.4.5 Aiming for product differentiation

Differentiation can address different aspects of a product.

The **core benefit** represents a different/better way to achieve the basic requirements of the product or service.

The **tangible product** is the look, feel and performance of the product – so may relate from materials and packaging through to useable life, weight and usability.

The **augmented product** covers the rest of the purchase and ownership experience – including payment options, delivery options, after-sales support, ease of setup, guarantees, etc.

SNAPSHOT

In the 2011 J D Power Vehicle Ownership Satisfaction Survey, Honda was rated above Jaguar, BMW and Mercedes-Benz.[5] This does not necessarily mean that Honda's cars are more desirable but shows that Honda was doing a better job of understanding and matching the expectations of its customers with its augmented product.

There are a number of variables that a company can use to differentiate its offerings.

Table 4.4: Ways to differentiate products

Source of differentiation	Factors	Example
Style/design	Creating eye catching designs and/or excellence and simplicity in usage	iPhone Range Rover Evoque Sony Vaio laptops
Packaging	Protection against damage Storage under extreme conditions (e.g. cold, heat, fire) Storage density – i.e. can pack more of a given product into a space Safety of product in transit	Tetra Pak provide a range of strong, light and recyclable cartons that are food safe for drinks and soups
Distribution	Availability through different channels On-time delivery Overall speed of delivery Range and flexibility of delivery times Cost	One of Amazon's key differentiators is its delivery – customers trust they will get what they ordered when they are promised and in a state they demand (i.e. well packed and undamaged)
Promotion	Advertising – print media, online, TV, cinema, billboards Packaging Brand Sponsorship	Effective campaigns include: ● 'Compare the meerkat' – comparethemarket.com; ● the '1984' and 'Think Different' campaigns for Apple Computer; and ● Red Bull's sponsorship of extreme sports and two Formula One teams
Perception of quality and/or value	Usability Durability Materials used Weight Feel Touch points	Interior trim in a quality car (soft touch plastics, damped movement of grab handles) Jaguar XF's gear knob that rises from the dash when the engine starts
Pricing	Permanent lower pricing Temporary discounts Buy one, get one free Cash back Bundling	Supermarket's own low-cost brands (e.g. Tesco's Everyday Value)

In developing differentiators, an organisation must consider the longevity of the advantage. There is generally no point developing or launching advantages that only last a short time. The company should consider the:

- investment (financial, time) necessary to deliver the differential advantage(s);
- impact on costs;
- time competitors would need to imitate the advantage; and
- potential upside (increase in sales and/or margins – linked to the size of the target market).

4.5 Marketing at a more tactical level

Porter's strategies and the value disciplines describe broad options that an organisation can choose.

However, the more tactical approaches below describe how it positions itself against competition in order to advance or defend its position and interests. In other words, we're going to look in more detail at ways to fight competition once you have committed to a market.

4.5.1 Approaches for market leaders

Market leaders have significant power over the market but need to manage how they use this power. Certain industries (e.g. power and water utilities, telecoms) have laws and/or regulations that apply to companies that are monopolies or achieve market dominance.

In some markets, dominance might be defined as having more than a certain percentage market share (e.g. 40 per cent or higher). The problem is that being above this threshold (and so being defined as dominant in the market) may render a company subject to adverse terms applied by regulators or government. These terms might include things like imposing asymmetric regulation on the company (where the competition enjoys a better set of regulations than the dominant company).

The market leader has a couple of choices, as Table 4.5 shows.

Efforts to expand market share are obviously easier said than done, but there are reasons why this is sometimes difficult or even undesirable. As mentioned above, moving into or strengthening a monopoly position will create additional problems for a company. These may include price controls or the imposition of measures to increase competition. However, increasing market share is also a challenge as some customers will never buy certain products under any circumstances and others will take significant effort to convert. It becomes harder and harder to try to sell to these groups, and the law of diminishing returns will kick in with each additional per cent of market share costing progressively more to obtain.

Another option for a market leader is simply to hold market share.

Table 4.5: Market leaders' options

What?	How?	Example
Expand the total market	Expand the usage by current customers	The 'bet you can't eat three Shredded Wheat' campaign tried to get people to eat more of the product at a sitting
	Find new users	Expand to new geographies
	Find new uses for the product	New uses for plastics (as well as variations with new properties have appeared steadily) Thin display screens have moved from calculators to laptops and on to tablets, phones and TVs
Expand share of the market	Change the price, product, promotion or the channels to increase customer preferences for your product/service	Increase advertising spend so that awareness in the target market group rises Decrease price – if that will stimulate increased purchases
	Change and/or increase channels to make it easier for potential customers to buy your product	Mobile phone top-ups offered using cash machines/ATMs and at payment points in small shops
	Introduce new products to penetrate previously unserved parts of the market	Microsoft included their Internet Explorer browser with their operating systems to increase their control over the market Google is bundling new apps to increase the value of a Google account (e.g. calendar, mail and tasks)

STOP AND THINK

If you are limited in the share of the market you are allowed to have, then which customers would you aim to keep? Write a few down now, then read on.

The first question that affects this choice is how market share is defined. Is it based on the number of customers or revenues? So if you have to consider both scenarios (market share and revenue), which customers would you maintain?

Now consider for a moment. If you can only keep a certain percentage of customers, then presumably you've listed the ones that generate the highest revenues. If the information is in your head, then maybe you've been even smarter and listed the ones that produce the highest margins.

If you can only keep a certain percentage of the revenue in the market, hopefully you thought about minimising the number of customers that will deliver this revenue. This will minimise the operational expenses to pay for serving customers. If you already know which customers to keep to maximise the profit margin on a given revenue figure, that's very impressive.

Defensive strategies

Being a market leader means that frequently you will be defending that position of leadership. There are a number of strategies open to market leaders to defend against existing competitors and new entrants.

Table 4.6: Defensive strategies

Defence	What you do	What you think about
Static defence	This is the 'do nothing' strategy.	Keep doing what you're doing.
Mobile defence	Spreading the company's interests across new areas that could be future core markets or provide a base for counter attack.	Test new market areas.
Pre-emptive defence	This is the embodiment of 'the best form of defence is offence'.	Saturate the market with products to deter competitors.
Flank defence	Strengthen the areas around your market to discourage competitors.	Create products that are in market segments adjacent to current ones to prevent competitors forming a bridgehead they might exploit to enter your main markets later.
Counter-offensive defence	Keep the opposition busy and search for weaknesses through carefully controlled attacks.	Choose your battlegrounds but do not commit too much to any one attack. Exploit when weaknesses are found. Be ready to withdraw when you come up against strength or the cost to fight becomes too great.
Contraction defence	This is known as a hedgehog defence, as the implication is the company rolls itself into a ball and hopes for the best. It works well against minor attacks but is too static in the face of sustained aggression.	This has often been seen as a slow withdrawal from the market – where a company gradually has its markets taken from it. Be careful what you give up if you provide a bridgehead for another company to enter your market.

Of all of these approaches, the static defence is a particularly dangerous one to pursue in the longer term. As discussed in Chapter 3, markets do not remain static and the situation may evolve around a company and become untenable before they have the time to respond. The other risk is that slowly the static company loses parts of its market and the static defence morphs into a contraction defence.

A better approach is to:

- be open to change with a more mobile defence;
- ensure the competition knows your strengths (and hope that deters them);
- make the competition aware of what you will defend; and
- attack from time to time to keep the competition on the back foot.

4.5.2 Approaches for market challengers

The assumption is that a challenger in the market is not going to sit back and defend its position (unlike followers in the market, who we will discuss shortly). A market challenger is looking to take on the leader(s) and gain a significant part of the market. The strategies open to it therefore revolve around attack.

Attacking strategies

If a challenger is going to attack, it needs to understand what it's trying to achieve. Simply sparking a price war isn't very smart if everyone's margins suffer and you don't gain any market share.

Any attack, just like with a military strategy, should focus on the weak points of the competition, be carefully timed and be based on real advantages of the attacker.

Table 4.7: Attacking strategies

What attack?	What you do	What you think about
Frontal attack	Pick your target carefully. Going toe to toe using this type of attack on a vastly superior opponent is liable to be both painful and unsuccessful.	Target attack where: • there is low brand loyalty; • products are poorly differentiated; • the target has limited resources to respond; and/or • you have significant competitive advantage.
Flanking attack	This approach searches for territories where the target is weaker or there are unserved/under-served niches in the market.	Avoiding the main strength of your opponent means a smaller challenger can achieve things that would not be possible with a frontal attack. Attacks should be fast and decisive where possible. Make moves that the competitor will not automatically have to respond to – in other words, make them think hard first before they respond.

What attack?	What you do	What you think about
Encirclement attack	To avoid a full confrontation, a company swamps the market with products and/or expands across every segment and channel in the market.	Requires the attacker to commit significant resources and will work best where the segmentation is not strong.
Bypass/ leapfrog attack	Often led by a new technology or business model, this type of attack in a congested market can be very effective.	Changes the game and can be very effective if you are prepared to take the risk of, for example, the technology failing to deliver.

CASE STUDY

Frontal attack in the airline industry

Budget airlines have carried out a frontal attack by challenging the status quo of the main carriers.

From Southwestern Airlines in 1971 through Laker's attack on transatlantic travel and on to the strength of easyJet and Ryanair in Europe, this has been a difficult strategy to pull off and there have been many casualties along the way.

The business model normally revolves around decreasing turnaround time to maximise the time in the air for the fleet of aircraft. The aircraft themselves have typically been older models early on in the life of the airlines, with single class configurations designed to carry the maximum number of passengers possible. Food and drinks are sold on board and some operators offer a near continual stream of things to buy on some flights (e.g. duty free, lottery cards, transfer tickets).

To keep fares low, the budget operators in Europe have sometimes chosen to use secondary airports that may be some distance away from the city they serve. Municipalities have been keen to attract the tourists that come with the low-cost airlines and a number of new small airports have been upgraded especially to work with these operators. Charleroi (or Brussels South as it is optimistically called) is 30 miles from Brussels but is used by Ryanair in preference to the more expensive main airport.

In 2004, Ryanair was ordered to repay £2.8 million in illegal subsidies received from the regional government because of the favourable agreement made between the airline and Charleroi.[6] In return for guaranteeing a certain number of aircraft per day, Charleroi offered the airline a 50 per cent reduction in landing charges and a 90 per cent reduction in handling charges.[7] The 2010 landing charge[7] in this agreement would have been just over £1, while in comparison, the domestic landing charge at Heathrow was £20.25 in 2011.[8]

In February 2011, a German court gave two airlines leave to pursue Ryanair under EU anti-trust rules in relation to subsidies provided to it by two German airports.[9]

In response to the pressure from these low-cost carriers, some of the traditional airline companies have developed their own lower-cost sub-brand. These have had a very mixed success rate. Bob Ayling, Chief Executive of British Airways, drove the company to launch budget brand Go Fly under the leadership of Barbara Cassani. The operation took to the air in 1998, finally making a profit of £4 million in 2001, having lost £21 million the previous year.[10]

CASE STUDY continued

However, the budget airline actually competed on some routes with their own parent, creating a serious problem, as BA didn't want passengers converting from high fares to the low-cost alternative. In the face of poor results for BA, the new CEO Rob Eddington was not as enthusiastic as Ayling about Go Fly.[11] In June 2001, BA sold the airline in a management buyout (MBO) for £110 million. The MBO team sold the company to easyJet in 2002 for £374 million.[12]

In a similar vein, KLM created Buzz in 1999 to try to compete against the low-cost operators. Again it was not an outstanding success and it was sold to Ryanair in 2003 for a net cost of less than £4 million.[13]

Latterly, carriers such as Ryanair have been criticised for charging additional fees for essential items such as taking luggage and checking in, as well as adding fees for credit card payments that are disproportionate to the actual cost of processing the transaction. The credit card supplement is indicative of the drive to maximise revenues but will be made illegal in the UK by the end of 2012.

Around 75 million passengers a year now fly with easyJet and Ryanair, showing how the new budget entrants have changed the face of air travel in Europe.

4.5.3 Market followers

A market follower has chosen not to compete aggressively with the market leader. It recognises that an attack is likely to provoke counter-attacks that could destroy it and so particularly looks for segments unserved/under-served or completely abandoned by the leader.

A benefit of being a follower is that a company can avoid the risks of launching products or services themselves. It can copy or adapt what works and ignore what doesn't. This will reduce their development costs and minimise costs of failure.

A company may follow the market leader(s) in a number of ways and at differing distances.

Table 4.8: Following the market leaders

What distance?	How?	Comments
Close	They might stay very close to try to cover every move made by the leader. This will limit the distance between them in the mind of customers and may neutralise much of the benefit of being the leader.	Can be effective but may also result in a company following the leader down a blind alley. It is important to think at every stage whether this distance should be maintained.
At distance	Here there is a more considered approach with the market leader allowed to take a significant lead.	This will limit the danger of following the wrong technology or product choice, but introduces the risk that a killer blow by the market leader will somehow lock out the follower.
Selectively	Pick your battles and battlegrounds.	–

However, a follower can't just hope the market leader makes a mistake. The low market share companies need to use their resources very effectively as the leaders will (or certainly should) be taking advantage of better economies of scale and hence lower costs. If the follower does not have a clear and consistent drive to invest carefully and be ultra-efficient, their life is likely to remain difficult.

4.5.4 Market nichers

This approach means finding a small segment (or niche) in the market to focus on. Ideally, these niches should be high-margin, even if the volumes are low. Market nichers need to understand and deliver on customer needs to be successful. Doing this particularly well may enable them to block out competitors who lack the market knowledge to compete or who find the niche too small to support two companies.

The media world is full of examples of niches. Magazines are published for small groups such as caravan owners or model train enthusiasts. TV channels provide online casinos and poker.

The risk for market nichers is if the niche moves into decline or disappears completely. In these circumstances, the company will need to move niches or may go out of business.

4.6 Segmentation

To choose a path, you need to understand how the market is structured. This means understanding segmentation.

The differences between consumers form the basis for segmentation. The concept is that buyers can be grouped in terms of their behaviour and perceptions. This needs to be on the basis of important differences in behaviour rather than things which are common and don't change the way people perceive and buy products and services.

4.7 Benefits of segmenting markets

Segmentation:

- helps identify gaps in the market;
- can help indicate segments that are still growing – even in mature or declining markets; and
- enables the product management team to match the product/service more closely to market needs.

If you don't segment markets, you run the risk that the competition will, potentially leaving your offering out of step with the market.

The simpler forms of segmentation have been around for many years and look at consumer characteristics.

4.8 Simple approaches to segmentation

Demographics

This is relatively simple statistical information on the population and groups within it. For example, it may include the distribution of the population by age, sex, marital status or home location.

This type of information is relatively easy to gather as the statistics offices in most countries provide detailed information of this type – normally based on the most recent census, combined with data from the tax authorities and other statistical sources.

Demographic data is particularly useful in selecting media for advertising.

Socio-economic

This type of information includes income, education, social class and occupation. Socio-economic information tries to infer buying behaviour from people's lifestyles.

A scale of socio-economic status was developed to segment TV audiences by the National Readership Survey. The scale rates people into different grades as follows:[14]

Table 4.9: Scale of socio-economic status

Class	Description	% of population (NRS 2010)
A	Upper class – senior management and professions such as lawyers and doctors. Earnings above £50,000 per annum	4
B	Middle class – middle management or administrators	22
C1	Lower middle class – supervisory or highly skilled	29
C2	Skilled working class – skilled manual workers such as mechanics and plumbers	21
D	Lower working class – semi-skilled and unskilled, manual workers	15
E	Pensioners, widows, casual workers. Earnings below £7,000 per annum	8

Note: rounding means the numbers above only add to 99 per cent.

The audience profile for a programme will divide the audience into groups based on age, sex and social grade. For some advertisers, they may prefer a programme with a high percentage of the audience in the A and B categories above, while others may be targeting the larger C1 and C2 grades.

Personality

Work has been done on correlating buying behaviour with personality type and then marketing to those types. For example, Excedrin is a headache medication in the US. It contains caffeine that accelerates the action of the other ingredients and segmentation experts Rosetta found that Excedrin users are 'aggressive medicating believers' who are aiming to 'nuke' their headache.

Excedrin gains 42 per cent of revenue from just 18 per cent of the population and Rosetta told them to focus purely on this 18 per cent with a clear and consistent message.[15]

Lifestyle

This is an alternative to the socio-economic approach and looks at the detailed hobbies and habits of individuals including activities, interaction and opinions.

A variety of different classifications exist. The National Readership Survey describes different groups in the UK in their Super Profiles classification using terms such as *affluent achievers*, *thriving greys* and *have-nots*. Other companies have produced similar categorisations with the population divided using this type of descriptive labelling.

However, there are also more quantitative approaches that combine a number of lifestyle and associated factors such as marital status, future plans (e.g. having a baby), holiday habits and education.

Lifestyle segmentation can be helpful in guiding creative content in advertising, but can be too general to be of value in all cases.

Benefit segmentation

This concept is based on the idea that geographic and demographic segmentation are not good ways to segment the market. Market researcher Dik Twedt proposed the 'heavy half' theory that half of customers are responsible for 80 per cent of consumption.[16] People are then divided into segments by the benefits they are seeking and then each segment is considered in terms of the volume, demographics, brand perceptions, media consumption and lifestyle.

Examples of segments identified during benefit segmentation studies include:

- **Conservatives** – stick to large, successful companies;
- **Hedonists** – concerned with sensory benefits; and
- **Rational Man** – looking for economy, value and durability.

These studies have produced two important lessons:

1. It is easier to take advantage of existing market segments than try to create new ones.
2. No brand can appeal to all segments and so dominating a market may require multiple brands to be launched by the same company.

Targeting the 'heavy half' may seem sensible in theory. In practice, though, it may not always be the right solution, as you can assume that they are already buying the product/service from a competitor. In some cases, it may therefore be easier to sell to the 'other half' rather than try to convert your competitors' customers to your products/services.

4.8.1 Evaluating segments

A company can map out the products and services it delivers against the different customer groups defined through segmentation. In Figure 4.1, three products (P1, P2 and P3) are shown against three customer groups.

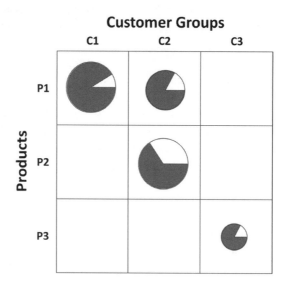

Figure 4.1: Market and Customer Group Matrix

The size of the market for the respective product within a particular customer group is shown as a circle where the size is proportional to the overall revenues in the market. The revenue share for the particular company is shown by the pie within the circle.

The company has a number of options about the products and markets it chooses to address.

Single-segment focus can work well but does create a risk for the company's long-term survival if customer needs change or the segment is attacked by another company. Rolls-Royce targets the ultra-luxury car segment. Porsche used to have a single-segment focus but moved to more affordable sports cars with the Boxster and then to the luxury SUV market with the Cayenne.

Product specialisation is where one product type serves multiple customer groups. An example would be a company such as Michelin. It only makes tyres, but it does so for cars, bikes, planes and motorbikes.

Market specialisation is when many different products are delivered to one market segment. For example, Rossignol delivers clothes, skis, snowboards, gloves, boots and helmets to winter sports enthusiasts.

Selective specialisation will allow a company to spread its risk across different segments but does mean it needs to understand more segments than one focusing on a single segment. Holding companies often end up using this approach to target particular segments through acquisition without having to cover the whole market.

Full coverage will obviously require a company of significant size to have the resources needed to deliver to each segment. Unilever and Coca-Cola are examples of companies that can cover every market segment relevant to them.

For each segment, the company will need to understand the details of revenues and forecast market share as well as the channel mix that will be used (as shown in Figure 4.2).

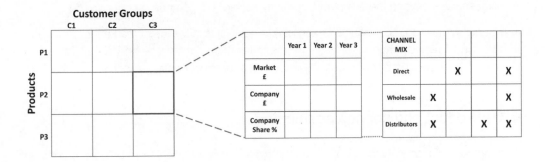

Figure 4.2: Detailed segment plans

4.9 Market estimation

To understand how the organisation is doing at present, or how it might do in the future, you need to understand the breakdown of the market into what the company can serve and what it is currently serving.

The market can be broken down into sections that define the parts of the market.

The **potential market** represents the total market that may be interested in the product or service.

The **available market** is the subset of the potential market that can actually make a purchase (e.g. they can afford to or have availability where they are). The difference between the two could be addressed with a lower-cost alternative but will represent latent demand (those wishing to make a purchase but unable to) until products/services appear at an affordable price.

The **served market** is the part of the market the company is actively targeting.

The **penetrated market** represents the part of the market that is buying from the organisation.

Figure 4.3 shows the ways the potential market reduces down to the actual market won by the company. The customers they do not serve in the potential market are referred to as the leaked market.

Potential Market			
Available Market			Latent Market
Served Market		Ignored Market	
Penetrated Market	Lost Market		
Customers Served	Customers Lost to Competitors	Customers Not Served	Products or Services Not Offered
WON MARKET		LEAKED MARKET	

Figure 4.3: Market leakage

To increase sales beyond the customers currently served, the company could consider:

- expanding the range of products or services to gain sales in the latent market;
- increasing sales coverage to gain sales in the 'customers not served'; and/or
- improving the products or services to win business that is currently going to competitors.

4.10 Product and service positioning

Once an organisation is thinking about committing to a market, it is vital to be able to compare different products/services within the market. Perceptual maps can be a very powerful way of doing this.

4.10.1 Perceptual maps

These maps are a commonly used way to visualise the different positions occupied by products in the market.

The strength of this approach is that it enables you to spot areas in the 'map' that are not currently occupied. This absence of competition may be for a logical reason but might also represent an opportunity.

Figure 4.4 shows makes of cars ranked against two attributes. The vertical axis positions the make between Luxury and Utility while the horizontal axis ranges from Conservative to Sporty.

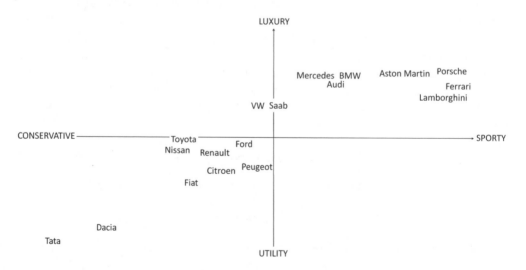

Figure 4.4: Perceptual map for the car industry

Creating maps like this combines qualitative as well as quantitative factors and so can sometimes be open to criticism and distortion.

To construct a simple perceptual map, the key benefits as perceived by the market are listed. The most important of these benefits are then paired to create the map space. As can be seen in Figure 4.4, the perceived benefits can normally be described on a continuum. For example, Sporty is used as the opposite end of the scale from Conservative. This may not be strictly accurate, but nonetheless the important thing about plotting the cars against this scale is to look at their relative position – even if the axes can sometimes be slightly contrived.

Finally, focus groups are used to discuss the attributes and rank the different products against the axes used on the map. As a product may have a number of benefits, there can also be more than one perceptual map to show the relationships between the products.

The idea of such a map is to provoke thinking and not for it to necessarily be an end in itself.

For example, Figure 4.4 shows that no major manufacturer is apparently in the Sporty/Utility quadrant. This might lead companies to consider if that is an area that could be exploited, but the map should perhaps prompt a number of thoughts:

- Some manufacturers appear to be missing. Which market is being examined and so which other marques should be added?
- There are smaller companies such as Caterham, Westfield and Lotus that could definitely be argued as serving the Sporty/Utility market. However, they are only doing this at volumes that are microscopic compared to the major car makers.
- The Mazda MX-5 is a mass-market car that does serve the Sporty/Utility area – offering low-cost thrills in a simple and financially appealing package.

The last point shows that the map may be at too high a level – focusing on the car brands rather than individual cars available in the target market.

The important thing to grasp is that perceptual maps are helpful in moving thinking forward and may need to be refined and iterated a number of times until they are truly meaningful.

A second use of perceptual mapping is to define customers' ideal positions in relation to the axes being considered. To be clear, these positions don't relate to measuring existing products but are expressions of the ideal combination of benefits expressed by potential customers.

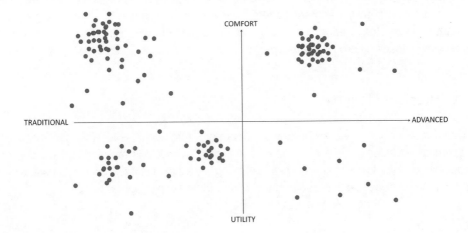

Figure 4.5: Clusters on a perceptual map

Figure 4.5 shows an example with responses from individual customers and illustrates the clustering that can occur in responses. Each of these clusters is a benefit combination that a company should consider if looking to serve this market.

A further variant on this type of map shows the ideal segments as a vector arrow where the slope of the graph indicates the relative importance of attributes shown on the vertical and horizontal axes.

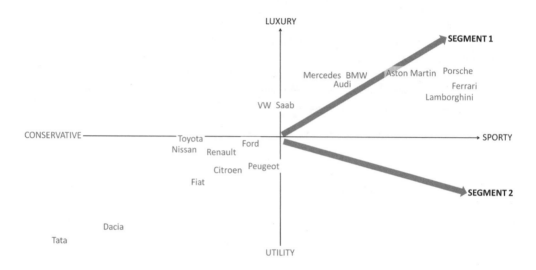

Figure 4.6: Perceptual map with target segments

In Figure 4.6, two example segments are shown as if they have been suggested by potential customers or the marketing team.

To illustrate this, Segment 1 shows a line that is approximately half way between the vertical (Luxury) and horizontal (Sporty) – a combination of high luxury and good sportiness (where Bentley might fit, perhaps). Segment 1 therefore views sportiness and luxury as being about as important as each other. Segment 2 ranks sportiness marginally above utility – very sporty but fairly simple (perhaps a Ford Mustang type).

4.11 Product lifecycle

Many of the concepts shown so far look at current or future positions for an organisation. They are essentially positions at a point in time. The product lifecycle is an important concept as it introduces the idea of products and services having a defined life. It is therefore a useful way to consider how products are adopted and the way that marketing supports this.

4.11.1 Introduction

During the cycle, there will be significant changes in the profitability and costs, and important choices will need to be made about whether to continue with, or withdraw, specific products/services.

Figure 4.7 shows the classic stages of the lifecycle.

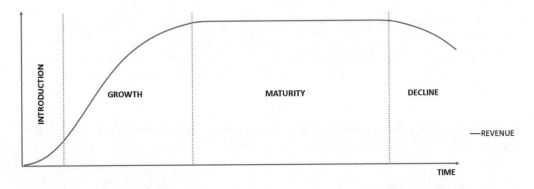

Figure 4.7: The product lifecycle

It is important to understand that the lifecycle represents the way that a market for a particular type of product or service develops. It isn't intended to show how a competitive product performs within the market. In other words, it is a model for the overall market itself. If a product arrives late into the market it may find itself arriving straight into the growth phase or even maturity.

The costs, profits, customers and competition evolve during the lifecycle – providing each stage with distinct characteristics and challenges.

Table 4.10: Stages of the lifecycle

Stage	Introduction	Growth	Maturity	Decline
Costs	High	Average	Low	Low
Profits	Negative	Improving	High	Declining
Leading customers	Innovators	Early adopters	Middle majority	Laggards
Competitors	Few	Increasing	Stable and beginning to decline	Declining

Costs are driven downwards through the lifecycle by a combination of economies of scale (allowing prices to be dropped as underlying costs reduce) and the effects of competition (forcing them down). By the maturity stage, the competition is driving companies out of the market. Those that remain can make reasonable profits provided the market is relatively stable in terms of necessary investments e.g. technology. Investments made at the maturity stage will only yield small-scale changes in market share.

It is worth looking at these phases in more detail, however, to understand the precise mechanics of what is happening at each step.

4.11.2 Introduction phase

A product or service has an initial Introduction phase when it starts to get traction in the market. This requires heavy marketing support to generate awareness of the product and possibly also educate the market. At the point of launch, the initial customers are likely to be Innovators who are keen to try new things.

Volumes are low at this point and products have had little chance to move down the cost reduction curve. In the absence of much benefit from economies of scale, prices are likely to be high for the product.

Advertising in this phase is aimed at creating awareness of the product's benefits rather than for competitive reasons versus other suppliers. The aim is to grow the overall market at this point and awareness, not customer preference, is the objective.

4.11.3 Growth phase

The Introduction phase gives way to faster growth where wider scale adoption takes place. The customers will change from innovators to early adopters and finally to the early majority – each group with their own unique characteristics.

Marketing initiatives and demand from the market will drive the product into new segments. At the same time, new competitors will be attracted by the growing market.

Economies of scale will provide cost reductions during this phase.

Promotion switches to developing awareness in the mass market as well as strengthening the brand perception.

4.11.4 Maturity phase

As the market proceeds towards maturity, the shape of the industry is stabilising.

Some weaker or less determined competitors will have been driven from the market in the transition from growth to maturity. This shakeout, as it is termed, sees companies leaving the market as they find the ongoing investment too great compared to the potential rewards. These departures may be complete exits or involve a buyout by a competitor looking to gain market share.

Costs are lower due to the ongoing progress down the cost reduction curve (accruing cost savings per unit as the volumes climb) and marketing costs tend to be lower as the potential returns for this type of investment are much lower than in the growth phase. The overall market size is relatively static and significantly increasing market share would require serious investment.

Marketing will now be focused on differentiation against similar offerings and driving promotion through the distribution network.

4.11.5 Decline phase

In the end, every market will start to decline. It might be a year, it might be 50 years, but the volume of sales will eventually drop off.

From this point, companies will reduce and possibly eliminate investment in marketing – allowing the product to decline naturally while maximising the profits during this phase.

The speed of the decline phase is important in thinking about pricing. If the decline is very rapid, pricing should be low to ensure full liquidation of existing stocks. However, the decline phase can last a long time and still provide profitability. In this case, any price reduction should be steadier.

Some products have reversed the price reduction completely once the decline has seriously reduced the availability of the product. For example, record players are now far more expensive than when they were a mass-market consumable. Similarly, the prices of other outdated technologies (like Telex machines) will also be higher than they were during maturity.

EXERCISE

This is a quick exercise to look at how your products sit within the lifecycle.

Draw out a product lifecycle and think about how you would position your own products/ services on that curve. This can be done for all product groups in a smaller organisation, or a selection if you want to examine the situation for just part of the business. There are a few important things to bear in mind as you do this:

- The products that are in the growth phase should be obvious but the economic climate may disguise whether a product is in the maturity phase or decline. If the economy is shrinking then a reduction in sales will not necessarily signal the market is in decline. This may just be a temporary contraction that will reverse when the market improves.
- Try to use the growth rate (or contraction) in the market rather than your own revenues to judge the phase for each product/service.

Once you have positioned the different products, you can add an estimate of the revenue for each product next to it and also whether it has low, medium or high market share. Absolute precision is not required at this point as this is a quick exercise to get an impression of how the different products fit.

Now sit back and look at the result. Is most of your income coming from products that have been in maturity for some time? Are you ready for decline if that starts for some of them? Is there enough revenue potential coming through from products in the growth phase?

Note: You could also do this exercise using the Hofer-Schendel Matrix discussed earlier. However, using the product lifecycle allows you to position products at the start or near the end of the growth phase. Also, showing products on the upslope of the growth phase nicely represents the uphill task a company faces to get to the maturity phase with decent market share.

4.11.6 Variations on the classic lifecycle

Not all products will follow the exact pattern set by the product lifecycle.

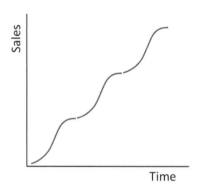

Figure 4.8: Scallop pattern lifecycle

Figure 4.8 shows a pattern created by continual reinvention of a product or service.

The s-curve shape as the initial version (or use) of a product approaches maturity doesn't flatten out as expected. A new use for the product creates a new s-curve that adds to the maturing sales of the first product version. This can continue a number of times as new uses and/or markets are found.

A classic example of this would be nylon, a material that found more and more uses over the years – from tights to luggage, clothing and even parachutes. More recently, light emitting diodes (LEDs) have moved from pure electronics into traffic lights, car lights, eye surgery, torches and bicycle lights.

The Cycle–Recycle version of the life shown in Figure 4.9 shows the impact of significant promotion that pushes sales higher than the normal and natural maturity point and means this peak is followed by an initial slump when the promotion ends. A second round of promotion pushes sales up but they slump again when this is complete – returning to their more normal level in the maturity phase.

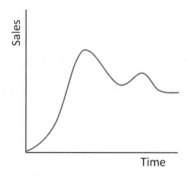

Figure 4.9: Cycle–recycle lifecycle

4.11.7 Profitability in the lifecycle

Let's consider the costs and profitability in the product lifecycle as shown in Figure 4.10.

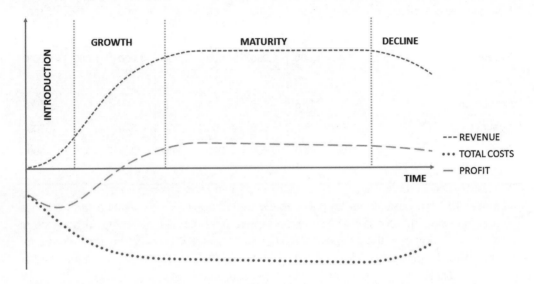

Figure 4.10: The product lifecycle – costs and profit

In the introduction phase, revenues are low (because volumes are low). Marketing costs are high relative to the revenues and development costs may also have been significant. In the maturity phase, the marketing costs will average out as a percentage of revenues. However, during the introduction phase, a fixed percentage of revenues would be too small to stimulate the market and launch the product effectively.

There may also be significant other launch costs to establish the operation that will then support and deliver the product.

Launch costs will be even higher compared to revenues if a complete new organisation is being built. The operating expenses for the company (or division) will also be significant compared to revenues as support services, customer support, admin, offices and warehouses all cost money, even while sales are very low.

For these reasons, the profit figure is typically negative during the introduction phase.

A cost problem in the introduction and growth phases is that the volumes being sold are constantly rising. In one respect, that seems a good thing, but it can create a cash flow issue.

Look at the example in Table 4.11. The sales volumes are static and so the volume manufactured remains static also. The situation means the operating profit is high at 50 per cent of sales (profit of 500 divided by the revenues of 1,000). Note the example ignores other costs apart from manufacturing (such as admin costs and marketing). It is only concerned with the profit on operations at this point.

Table 4.11: Sales volume and operating profit

Sales (this period)	100	100	100	100	100	100	100	100
Manufactured (this period)	100	100	100	100	100	100	100	100
Sales price per unit	10	10	10	10	10	10	10	10
Revenues	**1,000**	**1,000**	**1,000**	**1,000**	**1,000**	**1,000**	**1,000**	**1,000**
Cost per unit	5	5	5	5	5	5	5	5
Costs	500	500	500	500	500	500	500	500
Profit	**500**	**500**	**500**	**500**	**500**	**500**	**500**	**500**

Profit is both good and consistent as the volumes, cost and sales remain constant.

In Table 4.12, the costs and sales price are the same as before. However, the sales volumes are rising steadily. The company has to manufacture (and hence incur costs) in advance of sales. So, for example, in the first period, the company sells 100 units but incurs the costs for manufacturing the products it will sell in the fourth period (195 units). In any period, the number manufactured is equal to the number sold three periods later.

Table 4.12: Rising sales volumes

Sales (this period)	100	125	156	195	244	305	381	477
Manufactured (this period)	195	244	305	381	477	596	745	931
Sales price per unit	10	10	10	10	10	10	10	10
Revenues	**1,000**	**1,250**	**1,563**	**1,953**	**2,441**	**3,052**	**3,815**	**4,768**
Cost per unit	5	5	5	5	5	5	5	5
Costs	977	1221	1526	1907	2384	2980	3725	4657
Profit	**23**	**29**	**37**	**46**	**57**	**72**	**89**	**112**

The effect on operating profits can be seen very clearly with the company constantly having to manufacture more units than it sells in any period. This suppresses the operating profits significantly. Once the impact of other expenses is taken into account, the company may be making a loss, even though it is selling well in the growing market.

When the product reaches maturity, sales and manufacturing/production will be closer to one another and so profitability will improve. This is roughly the situation for the company in the first example and shows how attractive the maturity phase can be, as production volumes are very similar to sales. However the second example shows how costly it can be in cash flow terms to live through the growth phase on the way to maturity.

Figure 4.11 includes the cumulative cash flow over time. This is a simple measure that adds up the sum of all the profit figures over time (ignoring tax, depreciation, amortisation and interest charges).

The diagram is based around a given set of assumptions for a particular product lifecycle. The underlying assumptions will change from market to market and so this is an illustration rather than the definitive situation in all cases. The profit typically reduces during the maturity phase, reflecting increasing costs for retention and discounts over time. That will not be true in all markets and some may see an improvement in profits as the underlying costs continue to reduce while prices are maintained.

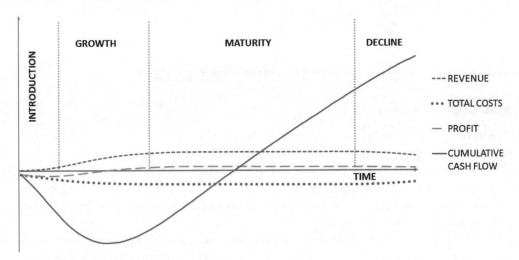

Figure 4.11: Cash flow in product lifecycle

One fact that will be consistent for nearly all markets is the significant time it takes to recover the early investment in the product/service.

Let's move forward by linking the competitive situation to elements of the product lifecycle.

4.12 The BCG Matrix (or Boston Box)

The 'Boston Box', developed by the Boston Consulting Group, is a two-by-two matrix that considers the competitive situation at different points in the life of a product or service.[17] The model (Figure 4.12) is a very clear piece of thinking that recognises that there are important choices to be made about products – depending on their relative strength in the market and the phase of the lifecycle.

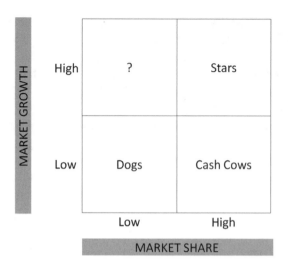

Figure 4.12: The Boston Box

The horizontal axis shows the relative market share and so considers the position of the company compared to the biggest competitor in the particular market. That means that the line dividing low and high relative market share is at one. In other words, on that line the market share of the company is the same size as the biggest competitor (a one-to-one ratio). If the company is the market leader, the relative market share number will be above one and it will be below one when the company is not the leader.

The model assumes that overall share of the market will influence the economies of scale that can drive cost savings. Higher market shares should therefore provide greater economies of scale and hence be related to lower operating costs. The market share axis will therefore also suggest profitability, while the position on the growth axis will influence the cash required/generated.

It's not immediately clear how this relates to the product lifecycle, but if you consider the market growth axis, low market growth occurs when you are into the maturity phase. High growth will be during the growth phase of the lifecycle.

The market share axis simply reflects how well the product is doing compared to the market.

Let's look at each position in the matrix in more detail.

4.12.1 High growth – low market share – question marks

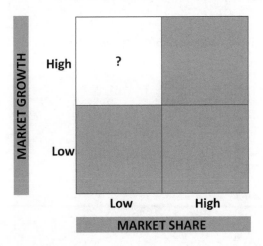

Figure 4.13: Boston Box – high growth – low market share

High growth implies the product is in the growth phase of the lifecycle. The problem is the low market share. There is plenty of potential in the market before it gets to maturity, but serious investment would be needed to capture market share. That investment is above and beyond the cash flow you need to put into any product as it rides up the growth curve.

This is the reason that a product in that part of the matrix is a question mark. It might become successful and gain serious market share, but it will be at a cost. If it doesn't grow market share, you're left with a product that will be taking resources and management attention from products that may potentially be far more profitable. It will essentially become a dog (see 4.12.3).

4.12.2 High growth – high market share – stars

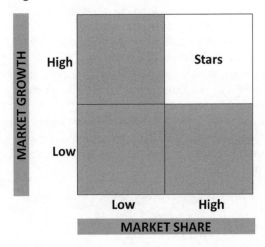

Figure 4.14: Boston Box – high growth – high market share

Stars differ from question marks in that they have high market share. This means they are in a good position to maintain this position into maturity – when things get profitable.

4.12.3 Low growth – low market share – dogs

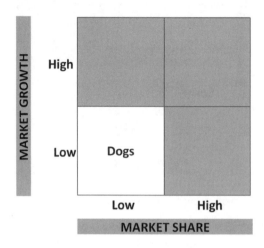

Figure 4.15: Boston Box – low growth – low market share

At the opposite extreme from stars are dogs. These have reached the low growth period of maturity but only have low market share. The product may be profitable but the low share means the actual volumes may not be enough to justify the time that is needed to manage them.

 SNAPSHOT

Saab hit bankruptcy after a takeover when even low projected sales of 55,000 were not reached in 2010 (under 32,000 vehicles were produced) and in 2011 sales were closer to 20,000.[18] However, they have many of the same overheads (e.g. factories, distribution, development) as companies with far larger sales volumes.

The new owners projected 120,000 cars as the breakeven point for the company and industry sources suggest closer to 200,000 is needed in the long term to cover the R&D costs to develop new models.[19]

The figure for sales was close to 125,000 in 2008[20] under General Motor's ownership, so this illustrates how badly things went wrong for the company in the following years.

Saab shows the danger of being a dog. In this case, low share in a low growth market equals no future.

4.12.4 Low growth – high market share – cash cows

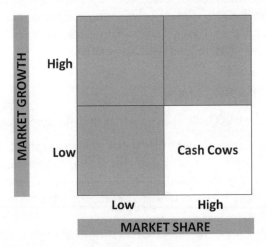

Figure 4.16: Boston Box – low growth – high market share

As discussed previously, the maturity phase offers the chance to make profits as sales and production of the product/service are at about the same level.

The strength of a cash cow is that it not only should be making a profit but, having high market share, should have the volumes that allow it to make more profit than most other competitors. This is because the company with the cash cow should be able to take advantage of economies of scale to have lowered costs more than other products in the market. The phrase 'cash cow' is apt as these products should be excellent money-making machines for the company until their sales eventually decline.

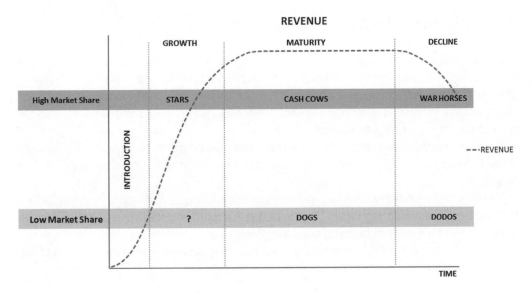

Figure 4.17: BCG classifications in the product lifecycle

Figure 4.17 shows the BCG Matrix classifications within the product lifecycle. In the decline phase, there are two additional classes called war horses and dodos. The war horse maintains high market share in the declining market. It should be providing positive cash flow – hence the name implying a solid performer. The second category is the dodo. This has low market share in the declining market and is likely to have negative cash flow.

4.12.5 Limitations of the BCG Matrix

Although a useful tool, the BCG Matrix has a number of limitations:

1. It is hard to judge the attractiveness of different SBUs or product sets. For example, one SBU's position may appear marginally better than another but the second could be 100 times the size. Adding the size of the market and market share can alleviate this.
2. The model does not take into account the overall, long-run profitability of a business unit's position.
3. It assumes that market share will have a direct relationship with costs. Although this should be true, companies that have failed to actively pursue cost-saving opportunities based on the volume of sales may have significant market share while the profit margin is lower than it should be (or is even negative). For example, a company may be producing goods in a higher-cost country than the competition or be refusing to invest in efficient but costly production machines as it prepares itself to be floated on the Stock Exchange.
4. The model cannot consider other 'unfair advantages' or challenges that may influence cash flow.

So far, we have considered products and services during their lifecycle. We now turn our attention to the way that customers adopt a product by looking at their behaviour and motivations.

4.13 The product diffusion curve

The diffusion curve models the adoption of technology-based products or services over time. It is interesting as it categorises people depending on how early they accept and buy the product after introduction. This is seen as a diffusion process where the growth in product sales is a function of word of mouth and other communication mechanisms which promote familiarity with the product and others who have bought it.

Previously we've seen customer groups categorised in a number of ways, but the product diffusion curve is a step beyond this as it shows an order in which different groups buy a product or service.

The diffusion curve categorises early purchase as being made by 'innovators' whereas the last to buy are categorised as 'laggards'. The reason this is important is that the psychology and the requirements of the different buying groups are different.

Figure 4.18 shows the different groups according to their position against the adoption curve.

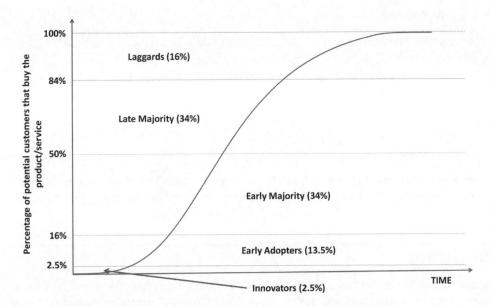

Figure 4.18: The product diffusion curve

The percentages of potential buyers in each category were calculated in Everett Rogers' work in 1983.[21] A lot of research has been carried out to deepen the understanding of the different categories and to tailor the marketing communications to each group. For example, early adopters are believed to have undergone more years of education than those adopting the product later on in the curve.

4.13.1 Innovators

These people are interested in having the newest products. They are prepared to deal with something that has not yet been perfected and which doesn't necessarily come in a nice box with perfectly printed instructions because it represents the 'leading edge'.

In the software world, these are the people who try 'beta' software – they want the latest functionality and accept the odd software crash.

4.13.2 Early adopters

Early adopters are not as prepared as Innovators to put up with problems in products and they prefer to have good documentation. However, they are the earliest buyers of a product once it has achieved what they perceive as a reasonable level of reliability and stability. That certainly means that software has left beta, for example.

The experience of the innovators may actually help the early adopters with their buying decision and act as a reference.

4.13.3 Early majority

More conservative than early adopters, the early majority waits until a product has been out for a little while and, in their minds, has had the flaws ironed out by the early adopters.

In *Crossing the Chasm*,[22] Geoffrey A. Moore referred to the early adopters as visionaries and the early majority as pragmatists. These descriptions rather nicely sum up the difference between the two.

4.13.4 Late majority

The late majority are similar to the early majority except they are even more risk-averse. There is a herd mentality at work. The late majority wait until a critical mass of friends, family and colleagues have bought a product and reported favourably on it before they take the plunge.

4.13.5 Laggards

These people are the last to buy a product or service and can be characterised as being very risk-averse and completely immune to the urge to have the latest, greatest thing. In fact, they may only buy a product or service when there is absolutely no alternative.

The most important lesson about the different categories is that you cannot use the same marketing approach across all of them. The innovators that start adoption of the product want something new and are far less concerned about reliability, usability and documentation. The laggards are almost diametrically opposite to them.

4.13.6 Is it still relevant?

Although the diffusion curve has value in helping you to understand the way that adoption takes place, it can be very difficult to identify who will be the innovators and early adopters for a particular product.

STOP AND THINK

What was your last purchase of a product over £100?

What influenced you to buy it? What information did you gather first and how? How is this different to what you would have done 10 years ago?

Do you think there has been an impact on the diffusion curve in the age of the internet and social media? Do we move up the adoption curve faster these days because of Twitter, Facebook and the like?

In spite of the above challenges, the curve still provides an excellent tool for understanding behaviour but may be less useful when trying to predict particular actions and/or the timings of transitions from one group to the next.

4.13.7 How fast will diffusion occur?

The rate of diffusion of the product will reflect the adopter group's perception of:

- the comparative competitive advantage of the product;
- complexity – more complicated and sophisticated products may take longer to diffuse as the market will take more time to understand and appreciate them. This is particularly true when you are trying to educate the market about a product;
- trialability. Are there samples? Can the product be bought on sale or return? Is there a 'freeware' type version (software)?;
- legal forces supporting/forcing take-up of a product;
- marketing messages; and
- information from their own network.

The messages and the marketing delivery of them changes from group to group. For example, the innovators and early adopters are more likely to rely on interpersonal channels (e.g. word of mouth) while later groups in the diffusion process can be more easily addressed by mass media.

Step by step, each group acts as a reference for the next group.

4.13.8 Diffusion of continuous and discontinuous innovations

The curve shows the take-up as a smooth trajectory with each group next to one another. It implies a simple process where sales move with no challenge or interruption. In fact, the transition from one group to the next can be very difficult.

Continuous innovations are where there are relatively frequent but minor changes. Although the change may be significant when looked at over a long period, the series of small steps make it easier to accept within the market. For example, the software on your PC or Mac has continuously innovated as Microsoft moved through Office 98, 2000, 2003, 2007 and 2010. Although the introduction of the ribbon control bar at the top of the screen created some confusion in the 2007 version, the software generally works in the same way with a few additional functions each time.

Discontinuous innovations are more challenging for the market to accept, as they represent more significant learning curves and mean that people have to adapt themselves. The Segway, iPod, iTunes, online banking and mobile phone are all examples of discontinuous innovations.

Discontinuous innovations are more difficult to progress successfully through the diffusion curve.

Geoffrey Moore described the specific challenges of moving through the diffusion curve with high-tech products that are discontinuous innovations. He suggested that the transition from the early adopters to the early majority is particularly difficult – likening it to a chasm that requires careful attention to cross successfully.[21]

Many companies/technologies have not succeeded in the transition to the early majority. For every product that crossed the chasm (for example, smartphones and digital video recorders such as TiVo), there have been many more failures such as Sony's Betamax video recorder and Philips' laser discs.

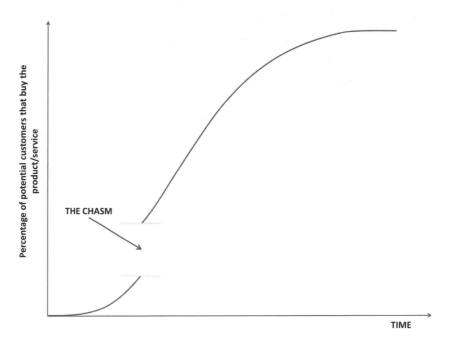

Figure 4.19: The 'chasm' between early adopters and the early majority

The keys to crossing the chasm are similar to the strategies needed for an army to take on a superior force:

- Find a beachhead and target this carefully.
- Use the beachhead to secure positions in the rest of the market.

Next, consider repackaging the product. The early majority may need a simpler or easier-to-use version than the more enthusiastic early adopters. The early majority may simply not accept the product without change.

This approach uses the limited resources wisely and in a concentrated fashion to enter a segment within the early majority, creating a reference for the rest of this group.

Having looked at the way different buyer groups adopt a product, we can consider the moving parts of the overall marketing approach.

4.14 The marketing mix – the 4Ps

One of the most familiar concepts in marketing is known as the Marketing Mix or the 4Ps. They signify four attributes of marketing: product, price, promotion and place. The concept of the 4Ps is to categorise all aspects of the marketing approach of service.

The original four have now been expanded to seven with the addition of process, people and physical evidence – factors relating to service delivery. This is known as the Extended Product Mix.

4.14.1 Product

This is the definition of the product or service. It may involve a wide variety of attributes including:

- performance;
- specifications;
- how the product will be used;
- where the product will be used;
- the physical dimensions;
- weight;
- colour;
- materials;
- name;
- brand;
- features and benefits; and
- positioning relative to competition.

The changes in manufacturing technology over time mean we are living in the era of mass customisation – where huge quantities of product can be made while maintaining high degrees of flexibility in the process. This has enabled companies to proliferate products in some markets.

CASE STUDY

The impact of platforms in the car industry

The impact of changes in manufacturing techniques in the automotive industry has had a profound effect on the number of models and variants available.

For example, in the 1990s you could buy only a handful of different types of Mercedes-Benz.

Model	Description
A-Class	Small MPV (multipurpose vehicle)
C-Class	Mid-size family car
CLK-Class	Small coupé and cabriolet
E-Class	Executive saloon
S-Class	Luxury saloon
SL-Class	Luxury two-door sports car

In the following decade, the ability to change platforms flexibly enabled Mercedes to create new niches or compete in small segments created by other manufacturers. Their line-up in the 2000s had grown from 6 to 16 discrete families from the A-class to the SLS sports car.

To give an idea about the flexibility in manufacturing systems now, the following VW group cars are all based on the same PQ35/46 platform.

CASE STUDY continued

VW car type	Models
Audi	A3 Mk2, TT Mk2, Q3
Volkswagen	Golf Mk5 and Mk6, Jetta Mk5 and Mk6, Eos, Scirocco Mk3, Touran, Golf Plus, Tiguan, New Beetle Mk2, Passat (extended platform), CC (extended platform)
Seat	Leon Mk2, Toledo Mk3, Altea,
Skoda	Octavia Mk2, Yeti

This platform sharing enables the manufacturers to spread R&D costs across a wide number of models and therefore minimise the development cost element in the overall production cost of each car. With the investment in these platforms reaching towards US$1 billion, it is clear why manufacturers try to use these platforms for multiple cars and even share them with other companies.

4.14.2 Price

This factor relates to the price and payment options available to buy the product or service, including:

- credit cards;
- cash;
- bulk discounts;
- buy one, get one free;
- cash in advance;
- instalments;
- deferred payments;
- price points in the market;
- discount structure to original equipment manufacturers, distributors, wholesale and retail;
- competitive pricing and discount structures;
- price comparisons to related products and alternative solutions;
- price sensitivity in the market; and
- price elasticity – the way that the volume of sales will be affected by changes in price.

4.14.3 Promotion

Promotion is how the marketing messages are delivered to the different target markets and segments.

CASE STUDY

Promotion through product placement

With TiVo and other personal video recorders becoming so commonplace, advertisers have been forced to look for other mechanisms to publicise their products and services. Product placement has been around for many years, but recently the pressure on advertising revenues during traditional commercial breaks has led to ITV in the UK being allowed to charge for product placement in programmes for the first time. In the US the practice is far more widespread and Nielsen reported more than 577 segments of *American Idol* that included product placement during 2011.[23]

To give an idea of the extent of this practice in cinema, the Ford Motor Company is rumoured to have paid US$35 million to place a variety of products from the group in the James Bond film *Die Another Day*.[24] Offsetting production costs of more than US$140 million, this investment by Ford is significant in its own right and also to the film's economics for the producers.

The film *Thunderbirds* had such obvious placement by Ford that even the director commented on it on the DVD audio. It sometimes appeared more like a brochure than a film.

Product placement is not limited to the promotion of a current product. In the film *I, Robot*, Will Smith's character drives a futuristic Audi in what is essentially a brand-building exercise.

Promotion methods can include

- TV;
- radio;
- cinema;
- billboards;
- newspapers;
- magazines;
- journals;
- direct mail;
- joint promotion (e.g. tie in deals with other products);
- websites;
- affiliate schemes;
- online advertising;
- social media (Twitter, Facebook, YouTube, etc.);
- packaging (e.g. tie-ins to films, sports events); and
- sponsorship of teams and/or events.

The pattern of sales may change over the course of the year for some products. For example, toys have a significant sales peak over Christmas. This will affect the timing and type of promotion required, with toy shops and manufacturers spending more money in Q3 and particularly Q4 to hit their target audience at the right moment.

SNAPSHOT

At the 2010 World Cup in South Africa, a group of women wearing orange mini dresses were removed from the stadium and detained. The official beer of the tournament was Budweiser but organisers accused the women of being hired to publicise another beer – Bavaria.

In Germany, four years previously, the same company had had fans at a match wearing orange lederhosen with the Bavaria branding at a game. In 2010 there was no branding present but the result was identical. The company received huge amounts of publicity across press and TV for almost zero investment.[25]

4.14.4 Place

This represents the different channels through which the particular service is sold and delivered. This can include:

● online;
● newspapers and magazines;
● wholesale;
● retail stores/department stores, specialist schools;
● direct mail; and
● sales force.

In the past, this discussion would have stopped here but now we have the three new elements in the extended version of the Marketing Mix.

4.14.5 Process

Another important part of how and sometimes why we buy a particular product or service is the process for making that purchase.

The number of pages that have to be navigated, the number of click-throughs, and the positioning and clarity of buttons will all have an impact on the ease of use of the website, and this in turn will have a direct impact on the number of sales.

An organisation that sells or promotes via the internet should look very hard at the statistics for their website, and track visitors from the home page through to the point at which they leave. Not everybody will reach the page where they can make a purchase. Some will stop because they are not interested in the product. However, you want 100 per cent of people who wish to make a purchase to be able to do so in a simple, clear and quick manner.

SNAPSHOT

Amazon has refined the buying process on its site through the addition of 1-click ordering. This streamlines the purchase with one button completing a transaction using the stored payment card details and default delivery address. The value of this as a competitive advantage led Amazon to patent this process and they have licensed this to Apple for their store.[26]

Competitors have responded with incredulity to the patent being granted and pressed successfully for it to be narrowed in the US. The European Patent Office rejected the patent as being 'too obvious'.[27] All parties recognised that streamlining the buying process was very important, creating the anger around the patent issue.

4.14.6 People

This additional P was added in recognition that customer service, expertise, helpfulness, atmosphere and responsiveness can all be important parts of the decision-making process in purchasing a product and/or recommending it to another person.

The human element is clearly important. If you are dealing with someone in a shop, does that person understand the product choices and can they provide the right level of help?

This personal element in the mix may be enhanced or weakened by technology. Do customers talk to a person or a voicemail system first and how do they feel about this? When they talk to somebody, are their details available to the person dealing with them via a Customer Relationship Management (CRM) system or similar?

STOP AND THINK

McDonald's have restaurants around the world but the way that staff are trained to handle customers means the experience from one branch to the next is very similar. You could probably write down the whole conversation you have while placing an order in McDonald's because, apart from the actual order, the elements don't change.

So think about your organisation for a moment and the different people that are customer facing. Do they have a consistent approach and standard or is there a high degree of variation? Which approach is actually better for your situation? What impression are your people giving to customers and could/should this be improved?

4.14.7 Physical evidence

The final part of the extended marketing mix is physical evidence. For the most part, service delivery involves lots of intangibles, but the physical evidence part is all around us.

When you buy from an Apple store, you enter a very carefully designed environment where even the design for the stairs was patented by the late Steve Jobs. The stores are clean, attractive and, in design terms, mirror Apple's products and packaging. The physical evidence is the store and the environment.

You wouldn't buy food in a dirty restaurant or use a limousine service with cars that are visibly falling apart. You would worry if your dentist had no teeth or a commercial pilot arrived to fly you somewhere looking like they had just slept rough for a week.

Physical evidence is important to customers!

4.15 Advertising

Although part of promotion within the Marketing Mix, it's worth taking a moment to consider the significant and ongoing changes in advertising. The importance of product placement has been noted already but there are a few other important trends to note.

The effectiveness of advertising on television is starting to be seriously questioned, with advertisers less happy to pay for placing adverts if users are fast forwarding over them using digital video recorders. Belief in advertising is also falling with just 14 per cent of people trusting advertisements compared to 90 per cent who trust peer reviews.[28]

At the same time, providers such as Netflix are using the internet to challenge the business model of traditional broadcasters (and hence threaten their advertising revenue). They go around the usual issues of building infrastructure (e.g. satellites or cable infrastructures) and simply use someone else's broadband architecture while not paying for it. They are referred to as Over The Top (OTT) players for this reason.

This effect is not only challenging for the broadcasters but creates a huge problem for telecoms operators as their 'pipe' is being filled and, although they have to continually invest to increase the throughput of their network, they don't get revenues from Netflix or other OTT providers.

Partly as a result of these trends, the BBC reported that in the first half of 2009, Britain became the first major economy where spend for online marketing exceeded spend for TV advertising.[29]

SNAPSHOT

VW's advert for the new Passat was shown in the traditionally powerful half-time slot during the Super Bowl in the US. Viewing figures were 111 million by the end of the game[30] but the video has been downloaded almost 53 million times on YouTube alone (as of April 2012). Assuming each download was viewed by more than one person, you can see the similar influence of the two media (except VW paid millions to air their advert on TV and nothing to put it on YouTube with a broadly similar number of viewers). Of course, viewers on the internet could be from around the world and might not be in the target demographic for VW, whereas the Super Bowl viewer demographic is well understood. But 53 million views for no cost is still incredible.

Magnaglobal, a market forecasting company, expect internet advertising worldwide to be around US$118 billion in 2016 against US$243 billion for TV. It's not caught up yet, but it's in the same ball park.[31]

This general trend of content consumption migrating to the internet is being slowed slightly by the habit of 'double screening' during popular programmes – in particular sports and reality television. One screen is the programme on TV and the other is the computer with the person reviewing and/or contributing to discussions on sites such as Twitter and Facebook. This won't hold back the rise of online content, but it's interesting nonetheless.

STOP AND THINK

Have you noticed that when you search online, there are advertisements for things you have searched for previously? Companies such as the BBC used cookies, your IP address and internet service provider to provide advertisements based on these factors (note that recent legislation means that websites will now need your consent to store cookies on your computer). However, behavioural advertising goes a step further and uses your browsing history to generate new advertisements that are embedded in sites you visit – even though the site may have nothing to do with the advertisement placed there for you.

What do you think of this approach?

4.16 The value proposition

Let's look a little deeper at the relationship between a product and the price it is pitched at.

A simple thing is to look at the way your offer and price compare to the market level. For example, you can offer more features/performance for less money. That would be 'more for less'. Table 4.13 shows a number of variations and examples to illustrate the concept.

Table 4.13: The value proposition approach

Approach	Description	Examples
Less for less	The low end, stripped out product to hit a lower price point	Supermarket 'value' own-brand products Tata Nano budget car
Less for the same	Removing features while trying to maintain prices	This can be seen in products that are engineered down to a price. Cadburys reduced the size of their 99p Dairy Milk bar from 140 to 120g but maintained the same price.[32]
Less for more	Strip out features potentially to increase some aspect of performance or deliver an elegant product	Some stripped-out sports cars have less equipment but charge a premium for the 'lightness' e.g. Lamborghini Gallardo Superleggera. However, marketing guru Philip Kotler suggests this strategy will fail for most products as customers feel cheated.[33]

Approach	Description	Examples
More for less	Often seen with bundling of products or services	Buy one, get one free (BOGOF) type offers. Expedia offers a further discount when customers combine (bundle) flights with hotels and car hire
More for the same	Maintain the market price but compete better (hopefully) with additional features/performance	Telecoms companies do this by offering increases in broadband speed over time, while maintaining the same monthly price. For example, Virgin Media in the UK is rolling out 100 Megabits to many of its current 50 Megabits customers but at the same price point
More for more	The basis of most rational pricing. You pay more to get more. However, there are also the extremes for luxury items that deliver some more but cost much more	Bentley, Rolls-Royce, designer goods

CASE STUDY

Razor and blade model

A number of technologies are based on an unusual business model. Instead of searching for a good profit on the basic product, the profit is targeted in the sale of accessories. This approach is sometimes called a razor and blade model, after the approach taken by companies like Gillette. They have historically subsidised the sale of the razor to make their margin on the blades. For example, the plain Fusion razor (handle with one blade unit) had an RRP of £7.49 (late 2011) but four more blades would be £9.69!

PS3/Xbox/Wii games consoles

These consoles are sold at relatively modest prices. This is partly because of the high volumes (e.g. Xbox sales stood at 65.8 million to the end of 2011)[34] but also because Sony, Microsoft and Nintendo are operating a different business model to mainstream electronics companies. Selling a laptop or a TV requires the manufacturer to make an immediate profit. With the games consoles, however, the real money is made on the games; Xbox games sales are around nine per console[34] on average and at retail prices up to £50 each. Each game attracts a licence fee for the console manufacturer.

The games themselves are getting more and more expensive to develop with the advent of photo-realistic cut scenes between gameplay and a constant drive to higher and higher resolutions. At $100 million, *Grand Theft Auto 4* was considered the most expensive game ever developed at the end of 2011.[35] However, estimates suggest the game has sold 15 million units worldwide to 2011 at a typical wholesale price of £20. That's not a bad return for just one game!

4.17 Pricing and sales volumes

Pricing is absolutely key. While this may seem obvious, it is often done badly and almost as if it's separate from the Marketing Mix. In fact, price and performance are the main drivers of the product's perceived value to customers.

Pricing is also the fastest way to change the competitive position of the product. It is clearly easier to implement a price change than to alter the fundamental characteristics and/or features of a product.

The influence that price can have will change according to the target market and the particular segment being served. A product that is positioned to be high quality and up market will be better able to support a high price than a product in a highly competitive commodity market.

Price can be closely linked to the organisation's strategy in that it can:

- communicate the value of the product to potential customers;
- act as a weapon against competitors; and
- strongly influence the company's ability to deliver against its financial objectives.

Price is about what people are prepared to pay (or are used to paying), and it's worth remembering this may be very different from the list price quoted in brochures or on the web.

SNAPSHOT

Philips, a major European electronics company, had an agreement with an American company in the same industry. The former had some interesting distributed intelligence technology for industrial computer components while the latter had a broader product range. The cooperation between the two should have increased the European company's competitiveness in the market enormously, although both companies would sell the components in Europe.

The pricing for the products sourced from the American company were announced to the Philips team as being identical to the American's prices. That should mean neither company had an advantage over the other in the market. However, it became clear that the list prices would be identical. No company in that industry ever bought at list price. Wholesalers and Original Equipment Manufacturers (OEMs) would have their own discount levels. However, the US company would normally offer an OEM '20 and 20' (20 per cent off list and then another 20 per cent off that price), whereas the Philips only gave OEMs 15 per cent discount.

A deal that seemed identical on paper was in fact very different in terms of street prices. Needless to say, the Philips sales team were not very happy at this price disadvantage compared to their 'partners'.

4.17.1 Willingness to pay

In parallel with understanding the costs related to a particular strategy, the pricing approach must also consider the willingness to pay.

The first simple rule is that if a product is priced at, say, £15, then introducing an identical product at a higher price is going to be a challenge. The bigger the difference, the more difficult it will be to sell. There are plenty of product configurations that might allow pricing above market level, but unless the company has a significant and real advantage, you cannot expect the market to pay much more.

However, individuals will have different prices at which they are willing to purchase a product or service. One way to consider this is to create a 'willingness to pay' curve as shown in Figure 4.20. This can be created through market research where respondents are asked if they will pay progressively higher amounts for a product or service. At a certain point, the 'yes' becomes a 'no'. As a check, the same exercise is done with another group asked the same question, but starting at a high price point and progressively lowering it until their 'no' becomes a 'yes'.

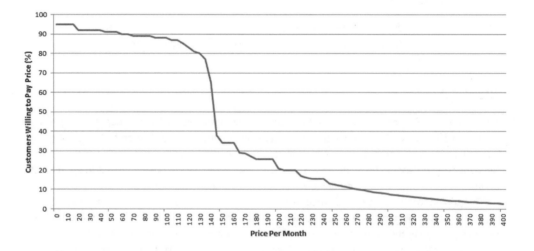

Figure 4.20: Example of a 'willingness to pay' curve – monthly subscription product

As shown in Figure 4.20, it is rarely the case that 100 per cent of people will state they would take a product, even if it is free. However, the curve shows the percentage of people that would pay a particular price (or lower). As the proposed price increases, the percentage of people willing to pay will reduce.

In Figure 4.20, 80 per cent of respondents said they would pay £130 per month. However, only 34 per cent said they would pay £150.

The challenge is that this type of survey is not always completely consistent with behaviour and a reality check may be needed.

In the real world, the best predictor of future behaviour is what has happened in the past. If there is no historical information on market prices, surveys may be the best information that you can obtain. However, it's only when people have to put their hand in their pockets that you can see whether they will really pay for something and how much. So if you are running a trial for a new product, ask people to pay for it. You can ask them to pay what they think it is worth or an amount close to your estimated sales price. However, by asking them to pay, the feedback you get will be more critical and not influenced by the fact that something is free.

4.17.2 Price elasticity

If the price for a product goes down by x per cent, then what happens to sales?

The principle of Price Elasticity of Demand for a product (PED) looks at this effect and tries to quantify it. In simple terms, you can look at the coefficient of price elasticity (E_D) as being the change in volume divided by the change in price that provoked the volume change. However, this elasticity coefficient is not consistent at different points on the demand curve. In other words, when 70 per cent of people are buying a product at a relatively low cost, the difference in demand for an x per cent change in price will be different from when 10 per cent of people are buying the product at a very high price.

Where E_D is -1, the changes in quantity and price are the same, and so revenues will remain constant.

Where E_D is 0, the changes in price do not impact the quantities sold and so increasing the price increases the revenues.

4.18 Planning pricing

The way you decide on pricing should be consistent with the overall objectives of the company.

There are several potential pricing objectives. The following are methods for defining pricing for a product or service against a certain benchmark (e.g. cost to manufacture, competition's price points).

Table 4.14: Pricing strategies

Pricing strategy	Definition	Comments
Cost plus	Add a margin on top of the cost to produce the product or service	This makes it easy to achieve the financial return targeted, but only if the volume estimates turn out to be correct. However, pricing using this approach almost implies a lack of thought about the market and the impact of pricing. In other words, in most cases, this would just be a lazy way of thinking about pricing. You might be committing the cardinal business sin of 'leaving money on the table' by undercharging what the market will bear.

Pricing strategy	Definition	Comments
Value-based pricing	Price on what the product is worth to the customer	This is a more sophisticated approach than cost-based pricing and requires an understanding of the benefits of the product to the customer. For example, if a product saves a customer a certain amount of money, then that saving probably represents the most the customer would pay for the product (assuming it is non-essential otherwise). In fact, they would probably only be willing to pay a percentage of the cost of the product (and hence of the saving). A more complex argument appears when the benefits are less clear. If we are buying a washing machine, we may understand that a budget brand will not last as long as a premium brand. That additional life is a benefit but not one we can easily quantify without additional information. The premium one may also wash clothes a little better or have some extra features. The value to the customer of the incremental benefits of the premium product will help the company charge the premium price.
Premium pricing	High price for uniqueness about the service	Charge what you can because you can.
Competitive pricing	Price to compete	The overall profit is a function of margin per product and the probability of selling at that margin. The higher you price the product, the less likely you are to make the sales volume and so this approach needs careful consideration (see examples below): 100% certainty of selling at 0 profit delivers 0 profit. 50% probability of selling at a total profit of 20,000 will provide an 'expected value' of 10,000 (50% of 20,000). 20% probability of selling at a total profit of 40,000 will provide an 'expected value' of 8,000 (20% of 40,000).

However, sometimes there is a need or desire to price a product without reference to the benchmarks that drive pricing in the table above. The options in Table 4.15 show different options that come into play if 'anything goes' on pricing.

Table 4.15: Business models

Business model	Approach	Description
Survival	Price low	If cash is very low, a company may choose to go with very low prices to be absolutely sure of sales (and hence cash flow) to keep them afloat a little longer. This mode may also occur when there is significant competition or severe overcapacity.
Maximising profit (current)/economy pricing	Marketing and operations costs are kept at a minimum	This can be a very short-term view and assumes you understand the cost-base precisely as you are maximising the total profit (current), not profit per item. These two are not equivalent as the total profit on a few items at a high price is likely to be less than many items at a lower price.
Maximising revenue	Using price elasticity	To achieve this objective, you need to understand the way customers respond to price (see 4.17.2). As your prices change, the volume of sales will also change and maximising this function is not simple.
Penetration pricing/ maximising growth	Prices set artificially low to gain market share	As an example of this strategy, in the early phases of the product lifecycle, a lower price may drive market share which will deliver profitability in the long term (assuming the product maintains high market share into the maturity phase). One potential side effect of penetration pricing is that this might trigger a price war.
Gouging/ skimming	Gaining maximum profit while the market bears it	This approach is more frequently seen where there is a sole supplier or a serious shortage of any realistic alternative. Airlines may offer the first seats on a flight cheaply but gradually the price will rise as the flight fills, until you could argue some airlines use skim pricing for the last few seats.

4.19 Identifying opportunities for products/services

There are plenty of ways to think creatively around development of new products and services, or enhancement of existing ones. There is a wide variety of approaches to this difficult task.

4.19.1 Assumption smashing

For this approach, you list each assumption about a product or service. Then you examine each assumption to try to come up with new ideas that might really challenge the status quo of the product. For example, the current assumption might be that a warranty is required. So you might brainstorm and think about what would happen if there was no warranty, if it was provided by someone else, if the duration was changed or it was delivered in a different way (e.g. on-site visit rather than posting the product to the manufacturer).

4.19.2 Attribute modification

Another technique you may come across involves changing each attribute of the product/service in turn. What if this was bigger? What if it was smaller? What if it wasn't there at all? It is essentially a more focused version of assumption smashing that concentrates on the product itself.

This allows you to think of radical variations to the basic product and perhaps come up with a winning new idea.

For example, the team at Nestlé looked at the classic Kit Kat and, in thinking about making it bigger, came across the idea for the Kit Kat Chunky. This has the proportions of a single finger from a normal Kit Kat, but is bigger. What if the chocolate wasn't milk? You arrive at the Kit Kat Dark. What if the filling was different? You create the Kit Kat Orange and Kit Kat Mint.

4.19.3 Using the value curve to position new products/services

This technique is particularly interesting and is worth looking at in some detail.

In their book *Blue Ocean Strategy,*[36] W. Chan Kim and Renee Mauborgne introduced a very useful way of comparing products to the competition. The approach is particularly interesting as it provides a visual way of representing different products. This enables you to see other potential combinations of the underlying characteristics and consider whether they might work in the market.

The first step to creating a curve is to consider the most important characteristics for the market. What do customers value? What is important to them? What factors do they consider in order to decide on a purchase?

Once a list of these attributes has been created, criteria are used to rate the different products in the market against a given scale (e.g. 0–100 per cent).

The important things about the scale are that it:

● relates to the sector of the market you are dealing with; and
● provides sufficient space between products that have different characteristics.

To illustrate these points, consider you are looking at the mountain bike market for teenagers.

The price range for these may lie in the £80–£400 range. There are bikes that cost several thousand pounds but they are not really in the same market. A scale on a value curve for these bikes should perhaps have a range between £0–£500. If you have too large a range to represent from 0–100 per cent (e.g. £0–£5,000) then the difference between a £100 and a £150 bike would be negligible on the scale, whereas it is a significant difference in the actual market being considered.

Figure 4.21 shows how a comparison of different mountain bikes in the market might look. The product named Jules is a premium product with a strong brand, superior components and a higher specification than the others. However, it is hand built and so the price is high.

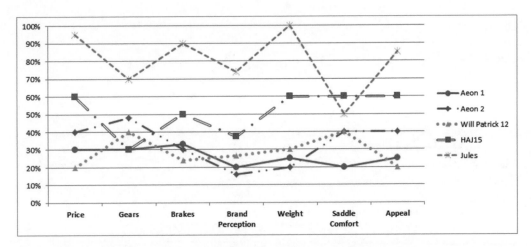

Figure 4.21: Example value curve for mountain bikes

The diagram shows a question that sometimes arises in setting up the value curves. A higher purchase price is represented as a larger percentage. However, lower weight (which is better) is also shown by a higher percentage.

In practice, it doesn't matter if there are logical inconsistencies as long as you understand what each category represents and whether higher or lower is better for each category.

The process now is to consider what can be changed about the current value curve. The suggested changes could fit into one or more categories as follows:

Table 4.16: Categories of change

Change	Question to ask
Eliminate	What aspects can be removed?
Add	What new factors can be added to the product/service?
Reduce	What can be reduced below the typical industry level?
Increase	What can be increased above the typical industry level?
Maintain	What can be left alone?

In the example of the mountain bikes, one set of possible changes reduces price while boosting the number of gears and the brake technology.

In Figure 4.22, the value curve for the potential new product is shown against the existing bikes in the market. The 'Rough Dog' does not match the specification of the premium Jules product but has superior gears, brakes and weight to the other bikes while matching them on saddle comfort. The design is seen as appealing in market tests, but the price is below the other main competitors in the market.

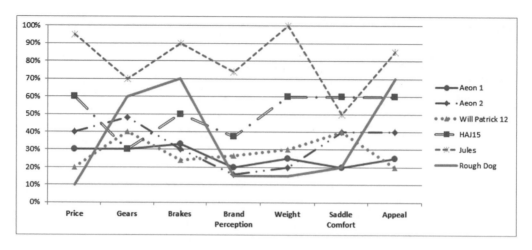

Figure 4.22: Example value curve with new product

The value curve in Figure 4.23 shows how Smart found some 'clear blue water' for their innovative Smart car. The two-seater didn't have the space for passengers in the back or luggage capacity of the typical family car. It had no pretensions of sportiness but provided a good driving environment and economy from a car ideally suited to city driving and parking – being able to park nose into the pavement as it is so short.

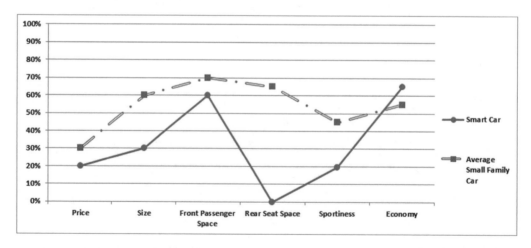

Figure 4.23: Value curve for Smart car vs. average family car

4.20 Customer retention and loyalty

4.20.1 Introduction

There's not a lot of point acquiring customers if you let them slip through your fingers. Conventional wisdom suggests it costs ten times as much to acquire a new customer than to keep an existing one. That is why customer retention is so important. The ability for unhappy customers to damage your reputation makes looking after your existing customers vital.

CASE STUDY

Loyalty and betrayal at Innocent Drinks

Three Cambridge graduates from St John's College, Cambridge worked in London but harboured a secret ambition to start their own company. They spent a period perfecting their smoothie recipes, spent £500 on fruit and set up at a music festival. They put two bins marked YES and NO in place, with a sign asking festival goers if they should quit their jobs and start a smoothie business. All but three bottles went into the YES bin.[37]

They set up and grew their Innocent Drinks business with help from a brilliant brand identity based around the concept of pure and healthy drinks. The whole company identity seemed to match the Innocent name, with a friendly and approachable brand image compared to 'mega-corporations' in the drinks industry. The company set up a foundation to donate 10 per cent of profits to charity from 1994 onwards and traded on their ethical approach with, for example, 100 per cent recyclable containers.

The name, ethical approach and branding all generated a particular image for the company and it traded strongly on this over the years. However, trying to be the small ethical player is not easy and the company's image has suffered as a result of some decisions they have made.

Innocent attracted criticism for trialling products in McDonald's, a company not noted for its healthy food range.[38] However, fiercer criticism was to come with the sale of a minority of the business for £30 million to the Coca-Cola Company. The *Independent* article on the investment was titled, 'Slaughter of the Innocent'.[37] The 'independent and ethical' company had 'sold out' to big business and generated extraordinary anger among customers at the perceived mismatch between Innocent and Coca-Cola, the ultimate multi-national.

Their strong identification with being an ethical company became a stick to beat them with when they started to do the deals needed to grow their business – tarnishing their previously perfect brand.

Generating revenues from customers requires that you acquire as many as possible for the business (and that can be serviced correctly by the organisation), keep them (retention) and increase the amount that you are selling to them.

However, the concept of customer retention is badly understood. It's not just about keeping your existing customers. It is also about:

- referrals to friends and colleagues;
- satisfaction;
- selling other products from the company (cross-selling);
- selling higher-value products or more of the same (up-selling); and
- generating trust.

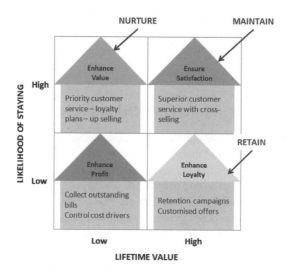

Figure 4.24: The customer cycle

When you annoy or upset your customers, they can damage your brand and reputation – and much more so now than in the past. Classic marketing thinking was that a happy customer would tell three people and an unhappy customer would tell 10. Times have changed beyond all recognition in the era of social media. There were 425 million users of Facebook on mobile reported by the company in December 2011.[39] That means you have nearly half a billion people capable of addressing feedback on a product or service instantly and to a large group of people.

CASE STUDY

Social media and unhappy customers

Dave Carroll is a musician who was flying with United Airlines in 2008. He alleged that baggage handlers broke the neck of his $3,500 guitar by throwing it and that this was also witnessed by other passengers. United rejected the claim and after a long process trying to get compensation, Dave posted up a YouTube song that became a sensation. 'United breaks guitars' has had 11.8 million hits (as of April 2012).[40] Each viewer is not exactly going to get a positive impression about United Airlines or their standards of customer service.

The Sunday Times reported that four days after the video was posted on YouTube, Delta's share price was down 10 per cent, representing a loss of around £120 million.[41]

Dave is now helping organisations think about their strategies for dealing with customers,[42] sharing his experiences and writing a book that should be required reading for companies that care about their reputation in the digital age.[43]

4.20.2 The value of a customer

Customer retention and loyalty is a balance of two different costs:

Cost of loss   Lost revenues
                      Damage to reputation – leading to loss of future business from people
                      that would otherwise become customers
                      VS.

Cost to retain   Incentives
                      Rebates
                      Discounts
                      Gifts

Too many retention programmes simply throw incentives at customers to ensure retention. They pay more than is needed to keep the customer's business for the future.

It is important to understand the cost of loss and cost of retention so that the right compromise can be reached between the two. In particular, the company needs to understand the value of the customer to the business in the future and also the likelihood of them leaving.

The first part of this is to understand the lifetime value of the customer.

4.20.3 Calculating Lifetime Value (CLV) or Lifetime Value (LTV)

The concept of customer lifetime value or lifetime value (CLV/LTV) is the current value of the future revenues less the costs to retain the customer.

In the future, a customer will provide a stream of revenues to the business. However, the business may also have to pay costs to retain the customer (e.g. discounts and upgrades).

4.20.4 Predicting customers changing products or service (churn)

In some businesses, there may be indicators that a client is about to churn. For example:

- reduced service usage;
- slower recharge cycle (e.g. you top up your credit on a phone, utility, travel card (Oyster) or payment card less often);
- stopping using the service (e.g. you don't show up to the gym any more);
- failure to take up new offers/services.

All of these can be measured by a company and acted upon, as long as the criteria for raising an alarm are understood and the internal systems can support this.

CASE STUDY

An airline improves punctuality but fails to delight some of its best customers

SAS understood that their business customers were the most important to them in terms of profit. It therefore made sense to ask them what was important in their experience of flying. The number one response was punctuality.

SAS was near the bottom of the league table for punctuality (14th out of 17 operators) and was losing nearly £12 million a year. It seemed to make sense to try to improve punctuality as this was important for their key customers[44] and Carlzon's ambition was to become 'the businessman's airline'.[45] Punctuality became one key area among a suite of operational improvements targeting a return to profitability. However, SAS didn't cheat and adopt the trick of overstating journey times to make punctuality easier to achieve.

A meeting was held with the employees in a large hangar and every one of the 12,000 employees in the company underwent two days of special training.[45] Employees were given watches with a small aircraft on the second hand as a reminder of the attention needed on timekeeping.

Now, punctuality relies on a lot of different factors but only some of these are under the control of the airline. It was decided that the measure for punctuality would be closing the doors on the aircraft as once this was done, the ability to arrive on schedule was in the hands of other people such as air traffic control.

So SAS gave more autonomy to staff members, who would be measured on the percentage of on-time door closings. Sounds sensible so far?

The results

In the short term, the financial results improved with the company moving to profit of £35 million in 1982.[44]

However, one unfortunate side effect was actually to annoy the most profitable passengers – the ones sitting up the front end in business class. Previously they could phone ahead if they were delayed and doors would remain open until the last minute to give them the best chance of making the flight. Under the new regime, the aircraft doors shut bang on time and so there was no longer a chance of making a flight if you were late (or even if you were on the jet way in sight of the door).

SAS were surprised to find that a successful change programme carefully designed to increase customer satisfaction had actually had the opposite effect!

In the longer run, SAS started to struggle once again as other airlines transformed their own businesses and competed more effectively. SAS carried 27.2 million passengers in 2011,[46] roughly half the passengers carried by easyJet.

4.20.5 Managing trigger events

The initial event that can 'trigger' churn is not necessarily the problem. Often, how customer services deal with the issue becomes the problem when they:

- 'don't listen';
- 'don't care'; or
- 'don't do anything'.

SNAPSHOT

Walmart had taken orders for a limited edition version of the video game *Forza 4*. When they realised they could not deliver due to a supply issue, they had a choice. They could just let the customers down or could manage the situation as best they could.

They actually wrote an apology to each person who had ordered the game, explaining the situation, how to get a refund but also sending out a free copy of the standard edition of *Forza 4* (worth around £40) and giving access to a download for a limited edition car to use in the game.

The situation they found themselves in was tricky but they did the best they could and probably left most customers feeling very well treated in the circumstances.[47]

4.20.6 Targeting the retention strategy

The key to a good retention strategy is to sort customers against their future value to the company and their likelihood of remaining as a customer. Figure 4.25 shows how companies can categorise customers and therefore target the retention strategy.

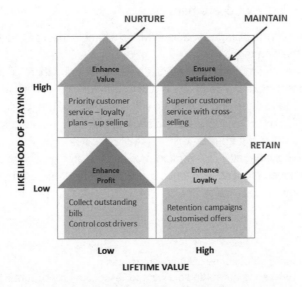

Figure 4.25: Lifetime value against likelihood of remaining a customer (source: Satyam)

Figure 4.26 shows how you prioritise different customers depending on their future value and probability of leaving. The darker squares represent higher priorities. Logically the highest priority for action is the group of customers with the highest lifetime value alongside the highest probability of leaving.

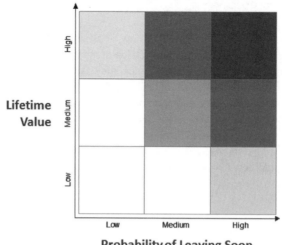

Figure 4.26: Prioritising customers to retain

4.20.7 Understanding your customers

There are several steps in the dialogue you have with customers that can maximise your chances of retaining them in the long term.

The first is to ensure that the 'voice of the customer' is heard. If there is no dialogue or communications are not recorded, the company is acting blind. It will not have any radar about how its products are perceived, used and compared with competitors' offerings.

If feedback from customers is captured, the second step is to respond to this and integrate changes into all parts of the enterprise.

The third part is to consider every interaction between the organisation and the clients. These 'touch points' may happen thousands of times every day for the company but they are individual and important to clients.

SNAPSHOT

Giving customers money off coupons can't go wrong, can it?

As I travel a lot, I wanted to buy a Kindle. I went to Tesco and duly bought a Kindle and a case. The receipt I was given after the purchase included a coupon for money off a Kindle accessory. I asked and the coupon was for buying the Kindle. So I asked if I could have the money off the case. I couldn't because they were put through as a single purchase. If I had bought them separately I would have benefited from the discount on the case.

Now, I didn't expect the discount/coupon but I'd now got it and my satisfaction at the purchase had moved to frustration.

I went to customer services to see if they could help – mostly out of curiosity at this strange approach. They confirmed that if I returned the case and then re-bought it, I would get the discount.

By giving me a discount, Tesco wanted to make me happy and buy more. However, they managed to change a perfectly happy customer into a slightly confused and mildly annoyed one.

4.20.8 Driving customer preference

By creating customer preference for a brand, shop or service, the implication should almost always be improved business performance (and longer retention).

A key example of understanding and influencing customer preference is in the rise of highly tailored loyalty programmes that are based on acquiring and using very deep knowledge about individual customers and what they like and need.

Let's consider one way this information can be captured from the retail sector.

When you start to use a supermarket loyalty card, the first stage is to capture information about you. In particular this may be about your family, with details about whether you have children and how old they are. This information is requested to help target you with offers.

Once the card is registered, your purchasing behaviour is recorded. This will include what you buy and when, and will be analysed to look for changes in behaviour that are seasonal or are based on other changes in circumstance.

This enables the retailer to gather very detailed information about what you like and don't like, and to offer you vouchers and deals that are relevant to you.

The detailed analysis of the data from the population of loyalty card holders enables the supermarket to carry out promotions and measure the impact. This can be done by targeting customers who are likely to be interested in a particular product and providing them with a voucher or some kind of promotional material. The performance of the promotion can be tested against a control group of buyers who did not receive any of the special offers.

The large numbers of customers in these schemes means the results are statistically significant and there is plenty of scope to target particular groups and measure the impact.

The buying patterns built up over time enable the supermarkets to create a picture of individuals and families with their:

- buying power of individuals;
- preferences;
- susceptibility to offers;
- redemption rates; and
- responses to different types of deals.

It enables the supermarkets to influence:

- brand loyalty;
- sales increases;
- changes to shopping behaviour; and
- increased visits.

The bottom line is that they can deliver solid evidence on the effectiveness of investments in marketing.

CASE STUDY

Using customer data

An interesting article in Forbes[48] describes how Andrew Pole, a statistician for American retailer Target, has been hard at work reviewing the data they hold for their customers. He correlated all the data for ladies that Target knew had given birth. This enabled them to identify products that women buy in the period leading up to the birth – including lotions and supplements.

Pole eventually found 25 indicator products that, when considered together, enabled Target not only to make a prediction on pregnancy, but also to estimate the due date to a good level of accuracy.

Using the data has proved sensitive, as boldly telling someone you know they are pregnant can smack of Big Brother. However, Target now provides offers within bundles to disguise their knowledge while nonetheless offering carefully selected products in line with the relative stage of the pregnancy.

In the UK, Dunn Humby is credited with playing a major role in the success of Tesco. They are the analytical power behind the Clubcard with the Tesco Chairman quoted as saying, 'What scares me is you know more about my customers after three months than I know after 30 years!'

The company is now majority owned by Tesco and has grown to more than 1,000 people globally with a desire to build turnover to £650 million per annum.

Using Dunn Humby's knowledge about the customers, Tesco achieved a 24 per cent redemption rate for a targeted mailing campaign for a pet food brand. It contributed to an 8 per cent sales uplift for the brand overall and a 1.2 per cent increase in market share.

4.20.9 Keeping it simple

The internet has allowed customers to compare competing offers far more easily than used to be the case. Some companies (often the ones that are dominating the market) tend to keep their offers complicated to make comparing offers more difficult. New entrants competing on price will want to see the opposite as they may rely on the ability of the consumer to understand the savings possible by choosing their product/service.

There is a trade-off between complexity and customer satisfaction (and hence retention) as shown in Figure 4.27.

The more products you have, the more chances there are for errors to take place. Each initial call to customer services will be longer as agents take time to explain all the different options and then the chances of issues later will increase from both mistakes in ordering/fulfilment and customers unhappy with their choice. During the lifetime of the customer, they will have more options to choose from and hence are likely to change their product/service – leading to more calls.

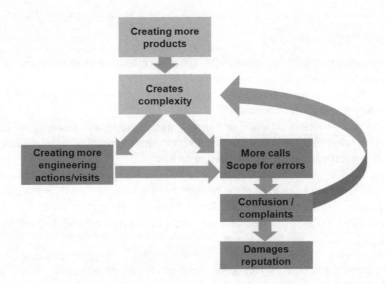

Figure 4.27: The impact of product/service complexity

4.20.10 Real-world tactics

Customers who only buy a single product have a higher tendency to churn than customers who buy multiple services. A competitor might try to tempt a buyer with one product/service but if the customer is already taking a bundle, then they are less likely to change, as only one part of the bundle is being targeted.

A few other lessons include:

- cross-sell and up-sell avoids churn;
- identify tipping points for subscriber segments and work with a communication programme;
- best in class customer service is important if you can deliver it;
- offer new products, pilot test new products;
- extend contracts/relationships with (free) benefits, etc.;
- reward loyal customers;
- invite customers to events based on loyalty (music, for example); and
- invite customers to focus groups.

CASE STUDY

BA's new terminal – failure to launch (properly)

It's rare that a company has a day when they can rightly show off to the world. The opening of the dedicated £4.3 billion British Airways terminal at Heathrow (T5) should have been a great day for the company to re-establish some of its reputation as a premier airline. The terminal itself is modern, comfortable and generally well thought out. It's a nice place to be. However, the

CASE STUDY continued

company managed to destroy any positive PR on the launch day, when the baggage handling systems failed to cope with the day one luggage.

Staff couldn't find car parks and so were late. Baggage was mishandled on the 12,000 bag-per-hour handling system and it jammed.[49]

This should not have been an issue, as you can simulate this type of situation. You can have dry runs on the handling system. You can test, test and retest to make sure that it doesn't fall over on your biggest day. Somehow BA failed to do this.

Then, the situation was compounded by the handling of the incident. The sight of a senior member of BA staff running away from the press must have provoked laughter and amazement in equal measure. The Operations Director, Gareth Kirkwood, refused to answer questions and the PR Head Richard Goodfellow resorted to putting a locked door between him and frustrated journalists.[50]

The terminal has settled down now and is a nice place to be. The only strange and lingering oddity for passengers is when they arrive at Heathrow and their plane is parked nearer to Terminal 4. They are then bussed to Terminal 5 as there are sometimes not enough gates to handle all the outbound and inbound aircraft. For a premium terminal operated by a premium airline, this is a mystifying state of affairs. You can't imagine Emirates making the same type of mistake.

As is frequently the case with keeping customers happy, the issue is not the issue – how you handle it is!

Summary

Marketing aims to satisfy the needs of a customer with a product or service and all things the customer experiences in it being purchased, delivered, used and supported.

However, to position a product or service successfully, a company needs to understand the potential for the market and the competition they will or are likely to face. Delivering to a market takes investment, and surviving through the product lifecycle until profits can be accrued during the maturity phase is difficult.

Individual products need to be designed carefully to match the needs of the market in all regards from the design through to the channels, promotion and pricing.

An organisation should also consider the current portfolio of products before launching a new one. This is to ensure that finite financial and managerial resources, particularly time, are used wisely.

What's next?

Now that we've looked at the environment around an organisation and the development of its strategies, products, services and marketing approaches, the next stage is to consider how to understand the financial side of an organisation.

Notes

1. *Jack: Straight from the Gut* by Jack Welch, Headline Publishing, London, 2003.
2. 'Marketing Myopia' by Theodore Levitt, *Harvard Business Review*, 1960.
3. *Competitive Advantage* by Michael E. Porter, the Free Press, New York, 1985.
4. *The Discipline of Market Leaders: Choose Your Customers, Narrow Your Focus, Dominate Your Market*, Michael Treacy and Fred Wiersema, Perseus Books, New York, 1996.
5. J D Power Survey 2011, *What Car?*
6. 'Ryanair to repay illegal subsidy', BBC News, 28 October 2004.
7. *Airport Competition: The European Experience*, Peter Forsyth and David Gillen, Ashgate Publishing Limited, Farnham, 2009.
8. 'Heathrow landing fees', www.thisismoney.com, 25 January 2011.
9. 'Ryanair in the dock', www.centreforaviation.com, 21 February 2011.
10. 'Go team to fly solo as BA sells airline', Benjamin Wootliff, *Daily Telegraph*, 15 June 2001.
11. 'BA to sell Go airline as profits surge', BBC News, 6 November 2000.
12. 'EasyJet to buy Go for $525 million', CNN.com, 16 May 2002.
13. 'KLM sells Buzz to Ryanair', KLM press release, 31 January 2003.
14. 'Social Grade – Definitions', National Readership Survey: www.nrs.co.uk/lifestyle.
15. 'Rosetta's Rise: No 1?', Barbara Figge Fox in US 1 newspaper. Reprinted at www.princetoninfo.com.
16. 'How Important to Marketing Strategy is the Heavy User?', Dik Warren Twedt, 1964, *Journal of Marketing*, 28, 71–72.
17. www.bcg.com/about_bcg/history/history_1968.aspx.
18. 'Saab vs Volvo: a tale of two Swedes', Greg Fountain, *Car Magazine*, 6 February 2012.
19. 'Saab's demise seems inevitable', Jord Madslien, BBC News, 8 September 2011.
20. 'GM Announces 2008 Global Sales of 8.35 Million Vehicles', GM press release, 21 January 2009.
21. *Diffusion of Innovations*, Everett M. Rogers, the Free Press, New York, 1983.
22. *Crossing the Chasm: Marketing and Selling High-Tech Products to Mainstream Customers* by Geoffrey A. Moore, HarperBusiness, New York, 1999.
23. 'Top 10 Primetime Programs with Product Placement Activity', blog.nielsen.com, 20 December 2011.
24. *Branded Entertainment: Product Placement & Brand Strategy in the Entertainment Industry*, Jean-Marc Lehu, Kogan Page, London, 2007.
25. 'World Cup 2010: Police arrest women in Dutch orange dresses', *Daily Telegraph*, 16 June 2010.
26. 'Apple Licenses Amazon.com 1-Click Patent and Trademark', Apple press release, 18 September 2000.
27. European Patent Office, Case T 1244/07, Publication 1134680, 27 January 2011.
28. 'Social Media Revolution 3 Video – Long Version', Erik Qualman, socialnomics.net.
29. 'Online advertising overtakes TV', BBC News, 30 September 2009.
30. 'Super Bowl Sets Record Viewing Figures of 111M', Glen Levy, Time.com, 8 February 2011.
31. '2011 Advertising Forecast', Magnaglobal: www.neoadvertising.com.
32. 'Cadbury downsizes Dairy Milk bars and other products', Madii Lown, BBC News, 2 February 2011.
33. *Kotler on Marketing: How to Create, Win, and Dominate Markets*, Philip Kotler, Simon and Schuster, New York, 1999.
34. 'Earnings Release Q2 FY12', investor information at Microsoft.com,
35. Interview with Rockstar's Leslie Benzies, *The Sunday Times*, 27 April 2008.
36. *Blue Ocean Strategy*, W. Chan Kim and Renee Mauborgne, Harvard Business School Press, Boston, 2005.

37. 'Slaughter of the Innocent? Or is Coke the real deal?', Richard Northedge, *Independent*, 12 April 2009.

38. 'Innocent sells £30m stake to Coca Cola', Jonathan Sibun, *Telegraph* online, 6 April 2009.

39. http://newsroom.fb.com/content/default.aspx?NewsAreaId=22.

40. www.youtube.com/watch?v=5YGc4zOqozo.

41. 'Revenge is best served cold – on YouTube: How a broken guitar became a smash hit', Chris Ayres, *The Sunday Times*, 22 July 2009.

42. www.davecarrollmusic.com.

43. *United Breaks Guitars: The power of one voice in the age of social media*, Dave Carroll, Hay House, London, 2012.

44. www.womenetics.com/Workplace/business-success-hinges-on-an-empowered-staff.

45. www.tmiaust.com.au/track_record/case_studies/scandinavian_airlines.htm.

46. 'SAS Annual Report 2011' at www.sasgroup.net.

47. http://jalopnik.com/5849616/walmart-ships-free-forza-4-copies-after-whiffing-limited-edition.

48. 'How Target Figured Out A Teen Girl Was Pregnant Before Her Father Did', Kashmir Hill, Forbes.com, 16 February 2012.

49. 'Two British Airways directors "sacked" over the Terminal 5 fiasco', Dan Newling, *Daily Mail*, 16 April 2008.

50. www.guardian.co.uk/media/2008/apr/07/marketingandpr.

5
Finance

5.1 Introduction

Finance touches almost every other area of activity in an organisation and a good command of the topic is important for managers.

This chapter will address some of the key techniques and types of information that a non-specialist needs to understand about finance and accounting techniques within one chapter. Resources for learning more about the topic are listed at the end of the book.

A further point worth making is that finance is a highly technical subject with many specialist terms. As most readers of this book will not be finance professionals, we will try to explain concepts in a way that is simple to understand and assumes no formal training in accounting. However, the chapter also makes reference to the different terms you may encounter to bridge between commonly understood terms and those used by professionals.

This chapter looks at the some of the key planning, decision-making and monitoring activities that are seen in an organisation, including:

- understanding and assessing company accounts;
- basic tools that are used in business cases, e.g. payback, internal rate of return (IRR), and net present value (NPV);
- tools to assess investment decisions;
- methods for valuing a project/business; and
- types of funding available to a business.

Understanding the processes for monitoring, assessment and decision making related to financial aspects of a business enables you to participate in many areas of management including:

- forecasting future performance;
- creation of budgets;
- full business planning;
- pricing decisions;
- modelling the impact of strategic scenarios;
- managing the performance of organisations, business units, departments or groups;
- identifying variance of actual performance against budget;
- defining remedial action to get back on track;
- calculating the value of different investment options;

- creation of financial scenarios related to different strategic options; and
- due diligence of potential acquisitions or merger partners – verifying the investment is worth making.

To begin, we will look at the type of information you will find in your own organisation's accounts as well as those of your current and potential business customers (if applicable).

A better appreciation of these elements can help in the management of your own organisation, but may also help you to identify some of the challenges facing companies with which you are currently working (or with which you wish to do business). Understanding your customers better, and getting closer to them, is particularly important for service organisations in today's competitive markets where companies are often trying to reduce the number of suppliers to them.

5.2   Understanding company accounts

For a manager moving to the higher levels in an organisation, it is very useful to have a good working understanding of financial reporting. This may be something you use to understand what is happening in your own company or to look at third parties for various reasons, for example:

- a potential acquisition target;
- a competitor you wish to benchmark; or
- a company you wish to sell services to.

There are a couple of fundamental principles to remember for a non-finance professional looking at company accounts.

First, it is not typically the role of those outside the finance function to understand the subtleties of accounting practices and finance in perfect detail. It is tremendously helpful if they have a good working knowledge of the subject, but we will assume for the moment that they do not.

As we've discussed earlier, a manager needs to use their finite time effectively – identifying the things that need their attention and leaving or delegating the rest. The next sections aim to help familiarise non-finance professionals with the parts of a set of accounts and help them to identify relevant questions to ask.

Second, financial reports provide a snapshot of the financial position of a company at a single point in time. If different parts of a report were prepared at different times, it would be much harder to draw conclusions from the figures as, for example, the costs recorded might not correspond to the products that make up the revenue figure.

A snapshot of the financial position at a given time can reveal important information about the health of an organisation. For example, figures may show a company does not have the resources it needs to continue trading or, conversely, that it is in good shape financially. However, reports showing a snapshot in time cannot reveal everything about the organisation. To gain a fuller picture, you also need to consider the relationship between results in the organisation from one period to the next. This might involve comparing monthly sales figures, quarterly results or the audited company accounts that appear annually. In all cases, the comparison of the figures provides important information about changes and trends within the organisation.

SNAPSHOT

BMW Group sold 1.46 million cars in 2010. In isolation it's hard to understand if that is a good result or not. The previous year they sold only 1.29 million and so by considering the year-on-year change, the 13 per cent increase seems impressive. However, the figure for 2008 was 1.44 million cars. Having more information on the sales trend, we can see the impact of the economic downturn on BMW's sales.[1] From 2007, sales went down before they began to grow again in 2010 and 2011 saw annual growth of 14 per cent.

Any year's figures in isolation only show part of the picture. Even figures showing two years do not provide the full picture in the case of the BMW example. In general, looking at figures over several years is more useful in identifying trends in company accounts.

In the BMW case, the reasons behind the dip in sales are reasonably clear. However, in other cases, you need to remember that the numbers will let you identify a trend but the explanation will require further discussion inside the organisation.

The first step needed is to understand the mechanics of different financial reports.

5.3 Income statement or profit and loss (P&L)

The income statement is also known as a profit and loss (P&L) account. The statement can look very complex when seen in company accounts but is based on some very simple principles. Figure 5.1 shows the logic used in creating the statement.

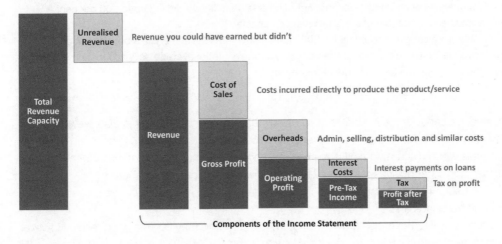

Figure 5.1: Income statement from revenue to profit

An organisation sells products or services, which deliver revenue. From the revenue, you take away the cost of sales. These are costs associated directly with producing the goods or service rather than say distribution costs or administration costs for HR. The result is the gross profit figure.

From the gross profit, you next remove the costs for overheads in the business. These are the costs that are not directly involved in producing the product/service and are typically related to administration, selling and distribution. This delivers an operating profit figure. Interest costs on any loans are removed from the operating profit to give the pre-tax income and finally the tax is removed from this to show the profit after tax.

The principle is as simple as that. However, before going through the income statement categories in more detail, the diagram also illustrates an interesting figure called the total revenue capacity.

5.3.1 Total revenue capacity

Total revenue capacity (TRC) is not part of an income statement but can be a useful measure for a management team to consider. It represents the total amount of revenue the company could generate at the limit of capacity. The revenue figure is therefore the TRC less the unrealised capacity.

SNAPSHOT

Partners in law firms work at around 40–50 per cent of their billable time, as they are managing clients and generating business during the remainder. However, the layer underneath them in the firm operates at around 91–92 per cent of billable time. If they moved up to 100 per cent, you would have a measure of the total revenue capacity.

Similarly, if a car plant could make 1,000 cars a day normally, that gives a benchmark on the total revenue it could generate for the company. However, if the average daily production is only 950, the company will forego some of the revenue.

Total revenue capacity may be difficult to calculate in some industries. It is also likely to be an estimate in some cases rather than a precisely calculated figure. However, in spite of these limitations, it is worth discussing as it is relevant and potentially important in manufacturing, service industries and other businesses where total capacity or sales can be measured.

TRC is useful in these businesses to provide a baseline, and therefore context, against which the current revenue can be judged.

For example, if turnover has grown from £5m to £10m, this may seem a good result. However the estimate of TRC puts the turnover into context. If the TRC is £10.5m, the turnover figure is far better than if the total capacity figure is £50m. In the first case, the organisation is running close to the limit and so may be considering expanding capacity. In the second case, the organisation is operating far below capacity and may well be unprofitable as it is paying for a significant part of its capacity that is not generating revenue.

5.3.2 Revenue

So, returning to the items you will see in the income statement, revenue is traditionally the first line. It may also be referred to as sales or net sales.

5.3.3 Cost of sales

These costs refer to items that are either consumed to create products or services, or purchased to be resold. This includes the relevant production costs in addition to the raw materials (if applicable).

For example, a pen company will need to buy plastics and ink to make the pens, and will use power in running the production line. These costs are directly related to the production of the pen. Distribution costs to shops or salaries for the sales force are not included in cost of sales, as they do not relate to the manufacture of the pens.

A couple of simple characteristics about these costs can help you to understand which should be included at this stage. Cost of sales:

- tend to increase as production or output increases; and
- would probably disappear if there was no production.

If you made no pens, you would not need to buy plastic. The more pens you make, the more plastic you need to buy. Similarly, the longer you run the production line, the more electricity you will use. If you closed down production, there will be no power consumed by the line.

People that are directly involved in this production of the products/services should also be charged to cost of sales. It can sometimes be difficult to allocate people, but again the simple principle should be that if production of the product/service were stopped, the people who would stop working are those who are included in cost of sales.

Depreciation

The machinery and equipment used in a manufacturing business will not last forever. In cash terms, they are paid for and then have limited life spans. However, charging all of the initial costs of these assets to the business at once would be excessive, as these assets are used up over what could be decades.

The answer is to use depreciation, where the cost of an asset (over its lifetime) can be apportioned on an annual basis (in the income statement and other places). In other words, if an asset that cost £2 million to buy is used up after 10 years and there is no residual value, an annual charge of £200,000 (£2 million divided by 10) would be a fair representation of what it cost for the business to use the asset during a year.

As an asset may still have a value at the end of its life, we can consider this too. The net cost during a period is taken as the initial cost of the asset less the remaining or residual cost at the end of its life – divided into the lifetime of use. In other words, you are calculating the drop in value across the life of the asset and applying this in some way to each year of life.

There are a variety of mechanisms for allocating this cost, but the simplest is called straight line depreciation. An equal share of the net cost of the asset is shared equally across the asset life.

For many assets, this is as simple as the purchase price of the asset divided into the expected lifetime. So if an asset loses £200,000 over a 10-year life, the annual depreciation would be £20,000 and would be termed a depreciation expense. Note, in this example, we're not considering the purchase price, just the drop over the period.

In some industries, the asset life that has to be used is defined by a regulator and so companies have to depreciate similar types of asset over the same period and in the same way. This is one way of ensuring consistency and supporting like-for-like comparisons to be made between companies.

The concept of depreciation is easier to understand if we think about a production environment. However, it will also apply to some assets in a service-based business.

The depreciation expense figure for assets related to *production* of the product/service is included in the cost of sales.

Amortisation

Amortisation is similar in principle to depreciation but applies to intangible assets such as patents and licences. For example, licences to operate a service may have a fixed life span and so would have zero value at the end of that period.

The amortisation figure for assets related to *production* of the product/service is included in the cost of sales.

5.3.4 Gross profit

The gross profit is the revenue less the cost of sales:

Gross profit = Revenue – Cost of sales

The gross profit is expressed as an amount of money but it is even more informative to consider the gross profit as a percentage of the revenue:

$$\text{Gross profit margin or Gross margin (\%)} = \frac{\text{Revenue} - \text{Cost of sales}}{\text{Revenue}} \times 100$$

The reason to calculate this figure is that it provides an initial view on the profitability of creating the products or services. The gross margin can help in pricing decisions as well as benchmarking operations against competitors or other parts of the same business.

5.3.5 Overheads

The overheads are the ones that don't change as you ramp production up or down. They are the costs for the headquarters, support staff, rentals, advertising, for example.

The gross profit you make from the business has to more than cover these overheads to make a profit.

5.3.6 Operating profit or Earnings Before Interest and Taxation (EBIT)

The operating profit is the money generated through operations and is calculated as the gross profit less the overheads.

Overall you can think of it as follows.

Operating profit (EBIT) = Revenue – Cost of sales – Overheads

The costs for interest payments and taxes are the only expenses not yet considered at this point – hence the name 'Earnings Before Interest and Taxation'.

Again, for comparison purposes, it is really helpful to consider this as a percentage.

$$\text{Operating profit margin (\%)} = \frac{\text{Revenue} - \text{Cost of sales} - \text{Central costs}}{\text{Revenue}} \times 100$$

This margin figure can provide another important benchmark to compare a company against its competitors.

5.3.7 Interest and tax expenses

At this stage, interest costs are removed to provide a profit-before-tax figure that is then used to calculate the tax that can be charged.

The final figure is therefore the profit after tax (also known as the net income).

5.3.8 The income statement in figures

The table of figures in Table 5.1 is the same structure as in Figure 5.1 in the way that it breaks down from the revenue to the final profit after tax figure. This is the typical layout for an income statement, but the level of detail in each section can increase – giving the impression of great complexity. In fact, income statements retain this simple format, even when you're looking at the accounts for the largest corporations. The level of detail may change but the structure remains the same.

Table 5.1: The income statement in figures

	£000s		Notes
Revenues	27,000		
Cost of sales	9,504		Direct costs such as raw materials
Gross profit	**17,496**	*64.8%*	
Overheads	10,530		Central costs, admin, general expenses, etc.
Operating profit (EBIT)	**6,966**	*25.8%*	
Interest	2,000		Interest payments on loans to the company
Pre-tax income	**4,966**		
Tax	1,043		Tax on profits
Profit after tax	**3,923**		Net income

Remember that it is tricky to deduce too much from one of these statements on its own. You can see if the company has made a profit or loss, but consider the following:

- How does that relate to other companies in the same market?
- How does it relate to last year?

Let's look at example income statements with more detail included and spanning two years.

	This year		Last year	
	£000s		£000s	
Revenues	27,000	100.0%	23,000	100.0%
Cost of sales	9,504	35.2%	5,704	24.8%
Gross profit	**17,496**	64.8%	**17,296**	75.2%
Administration	2,160	8.0%	1,610	7.0%
Finance department	810	3.0%	805	3.5%
Legal department	270	1.0%	276	1.2%
Marketing	2,160	8.0%	2,100	9.1%
Advertising	1,350	5.0%	1,350	5.9%
Rent	2,700	10.0%	2,530	11.0%
Power	810	3.0%	702	3.1%
Insurance	270	1.0%	276	1.2%
Operating profit (EBIT)	**6,966**	25.8%	**7,647**	33.2%
Interest	2,000		2,000	
Pre-tax income	**4,966**		**5,647**	
Tax	1,043		1,186	
Profit after tax	**3,923**		**4,461**	

Figure 5.2: Example income statement

Side by side, we can look at the results to help work out which questions to ask.

The percentage values show the individual items as a percentage of the revenue. This can be a helpful measurement to see how particular expenses have evolved compared to revenue. However, the version below shows the changes in each item from one year to the next, which is equally helpful in identifying which questions to ask.

	This year		Last year
	£000s	Change	£000s
Revenues	27,000	17.4%	23,000
Cost of sales	9,504	66.6%	5,704
Gross profit	**17,496**	1.2%	**17,296**
Administration	2,160	34.2%	1,610
Finance department	810	0.6%	805
Legal department	270	–2.2%	276
Marketing	2,160	2.9%	2,100
Advertising	1,350	0.0%	1,350
Rent	2,700	6.7%	2,530
Power	810	15.4%	702
Insurance	270	–2.2%	276
Operating profit (EBIT)	**6,966**	–14.2%	**8,119**
Interest	2,000		2,000
Pre-tax income	**4,966**	–18.8%	**6,119**
Tax	1,043		1,285
Profit after tax	**3,923**	–18.8%	**4,834**

Figure 5.3: Example profit and loss statement (percentage change shown year on year)

STOP AND THINK

Look at Figures 5.2 and 5.3, and think about which questions you would ask if this was your business. Take a moment to decide before reading on.

OK, there are a few figures that stand out. Revenues are up by 17.4 per cent. However, the operating profit has fallen by 14.2 per cent. So you need to look at the costs to see what's caused these changes.

Starting with the cost of sales figure, you can see this has jumped from 24.8 per cent of revenues to 35.2 per cent. Given that the cost of sales relate to production of the products/services, you would expect them to change roughly in line with revenues. You therefore need to investigate why this increase has occurred. As a result of this increase, the gross profit is down from 75.2 per cent to 64.8 per cent.

However, you can also see significant changes in the overheads. Administration is up 34.2 per cent, power has risen by 15.4 per cent and rent is up by 6.7 per cent. The other overheads have changed by only a small amount but these three are significant and you need to ask why they have also changed.

You can look at the separate impacts that the changes in cost of sales and overheads have had on the final profit. Revenues went up by £4 million but the cost of sales rose by £3.8 million. Overheads only went up by £0.91 million (the difference in the total overheads in the two years). Although the change in overheads may be an issue, the big change in cost of sales is unusual and is also the major driver in the reduction in profits.

It is worth saying again that the figures themselves don't provide the answers to these questions. You might form some ideas about why things have changed (for better or worse), but a manager's job is to ask the questions to establish facts and respond as necessary.

5.4 Balance sheet or statement of financial position (SoFP)

The term balance sheet is very familiar but a new term for this report is statement of financial position. It is important to note both terms as major companies such as BT and Coca-Cola are presently using balance sheet in their accounts, but statement of financial position is likely to become more common.

5.4.1 What is a balance sheet?

The balance sheet provides a statement of the assets, liabilities and shareholders' funds for a company at a certain point in time. This is different from the income statement and statement of cash flows (see section 5.8) that cover a particular period.

Balance sheets are most often seen as part of a set of company accounts.

5.4.2 Limitations of financial reports

There are a number of issues with income statements and balance sheets that should be understood when you consider them.

- The first and potentially most serious is that they are always out of date to some extent. They represent information from the months before the issuing of the company accounts and so could be a year out of date if read just before the next set of accounts is published.
- Partnerships or companies within a group may not publish separate accounts. The information for the latter may be captured within the accounts of the holding company, or group company they belong to, and so therefore will be masked by information for other parts of the business.

- Consolidation within the business, sales of assets, and purchase of new assets may mean it is difficult to do a meaningful comparison of the accounts with previous years and/or other companies.
- The nature of the way the organisation operates may make it difficult to compare information with other companies and even use typical measures of financial health. For example, Dell's business model (described later in this chapter) means that it pays suppliers 44 days after they have received payment from customers. This is the reverse of many businesses that need to pay suppliers before they receive payment from customers at a later date.
- The differences in how organisations operate mean the results of standard benchmarks (e.g. ratios of figures in the reports) will vary hugely from one industry to the next.

There are also issues that are specific to balance sheets.

- Different valuation methods for assets can be used and so figures need to be accompanied by a description of the method employed in the accounts to ensure you understand what they mean. Errors or deliberate misrepresentation within a particular valuation methodology should be minimised through the ongoing improvement in accounting standards.
- 'Window dressing' may occur where a company acts to improve the look of the financials just before the end of the accounting year. This could, for example, involve paying off some debt from cash to improve the ratio of short term assets the company has compared to liabilities, knowing that the organisation will almost certainly need to take new loans immediately after the end of the period. The actions make the figures look better temporarily but don't reflect the real situation in the business.

SNAPSHOT

The 2010 report looking into the collapse of Lehman Brothers suggested that there was 'balance sheet manipulation' and efforts to hide £36 billion of debts in the business.[2] The real level of debt in the business was hidden from the firm's board, according to the examiner who was appointed to look into the collapse. For the two quarters before the collapse, a set of accounting tactics were used to remove the £36 billion from the firm's balance sheet.[3] The advisers, auditors and lawyers around the organisation are all well-known companies but the Lehman Brothers story shows that the real situation can be very different from the figures reported by a business.

Enron and Bernie Madoff's massive Ponzi fraud both show that even the most visible of companies can behave in ways that get around the relevant accounting standards and regulations. However, there is steady work to improve regulation and minimise the potential for errors and misrepresentation in accounts.

5.4.3 The role of Generally Accepted Accounting Principles (GAAP)

It is important to mention at this point the regulation of accounting practices and how these ensure financial reports are a fair reflection of the true situation in a business.

GAAPs cover the set of rules, regulations and conventions that operate in a particular country (e.g. US GAAP refers to practices in the United States). The aim is to ensure that financial reports are accurate and consistent from one company to the next. This should allow comparisons to be made between different companies on the basis that the accounts have been prepared in the same way.

In the UK, the Accounting Standards Board publishes Financial Reporting Standards that fall into the legal definition of accounting standards.[4]

Internationally, the International Accounting Standards Boards (IASB) works to develop International Accounting Standards with adoption in the European Union and in countries such as Hong Kong and Australia.[5]

Although there is a constant drive to improve standards, the previous examples show that caution should always be exercised before acting solely on the basis of the accounts.

5.5 The anatomy of a balance sheet

The balance sheet in Figure 5.4 shows the general categories and layout that are typically used, although sometimes the assets are shown on the left and liabilities on the right.

The letters to the right are labels to show how certain results are calculated.

5.5.1 Fixed assets

Fixed assets are also increasingly known as non-current assets. Virgin Media and Coca-Cola are using the original term while companies such as BT are using the new one. For simplicity we will use the more familiar term, fixed assets, in this chapter.

Fixed assets are the assets of the company that are not expected to be consumed or converted to cash in the next year. They are long-term assets used in their existing form within the business. Their purpose is to help generate revenue.

Examples of fixed assets might include property, plant and equipment. The notes to the accounts would provide more detail of the breakdown within these categories.

Patents, trademarks and goodwill have a long-term value to a business but are referred to as fixed intangible assets to highlight the fact they are not physical assets.

Goodwill is unusual in that it stems from non-financial concepts like brand and reputation. However, a simple definition is that goodwill is equal to the difference between the net assets of a company and the price that is actually paid by a purchaser. It is a premium above and beyond the simple financial value of the business to show the worth of the name and trading relationships of the business.

BALANCE SHEET (ALL FIGURES IN £000's)

ASSETS	2010	2011	
Fixed Assets			
Fixed assets	1,565	1,812	
Total Fixed Assets	1,565	1,812	a
Current Assets			
Inventories	875	954	
Trade receivables	1,652	2,155	
Cash and Cash Equivalents	30	22	j
Total Current Assets	2,527	3,109	b
TOTAL ASSETS	4,092	4,921	c = a+b
LIABILITIES			
Current Liabilities			
Trade payables	651	602	
Bank overdraft	650	1,100	
Trade loans			
Total Current Liabilities	1,301	1,702	d
Long-term Liabilities			
Loans	932	1,203	
Total Long-term Liabilities	932	1,203	e
TOTAL LIABILITIES	2,233	2,905	d + e
SHAREHOLDERS' EQUITY			
Share Capital	150	150	f
Retained earnings	1,709	1,866	g = c - d - e - f
Total Shareholders' Equity	1,859	2,016	h = f + g
TOTAL LIABILITIES & EQUITY	4,092	4,921	i = d + e + h
Information			
Net Current Assets	*1,652*	*2,155*	
Net Assets	*1,859*	*2,016*	
Current Ratio (Current Assets/Current Liabilities)	*194%*	*183%*	b/d
Quick Ratio ((C.A. less Inventories) /C.L.)	*127%*	*127%*	(b-j)/d

Figure 5.4: Example balance sheet information

Imagine for a second that Kellogg's stopped all activities, sold their factories and all other assets, and did nothing for a year. Their accounts would show no revenue, no costs, no assets and no liabilities – essentially they would show that the business has no 'value'. However, if you wanted to start a new business making breakfast cereals, being able to use the Kellogg's brand would be of great value as the brand is known worldwide and associated with quality and goodness.

If you looked at the balance sheet for the hypothetical case where the company is dormant, you could theoretically pick up the Kellogg's name for almost nothing (as there is no purely financial value in this strange example). However, in the real world, you would actually have to pay tens if not hundreds of millions of pounds for that name. That money you're paying in that case is for the goodwill.

5.5.2 Current assets

Current assets are the assets that are continually being used and then replenished by the company – effectively they are likely to be converted to cash within the next year.

There are a number of different categories for such assets and it is important to understand the differences and some of the potential pitfalls in valuations of these assets.

Inventories

Inventories refer to stocks and WIP (work in progress) in the organisation. Different companies may use different terms in their balance sheets.

In a production environment, inventories relate to the parts sat on shelves ready to be used in the manufacturing process as well as completed goods ready for sale. In other environments this might be books at a warehouse, CDs on their way to stores or component parts ready for assembly.

The WIP will include uncompleted items that are being made for stock or that are being made for order. In a professional services company, WIP will include work that has been carried out for clients but that is unpaid at the time the balance sheet is prepared.

The problem with this category is that you cannot be sure that these goods, even if they are complete, will actually convert to cash at any point.

SNAPSHOT

A company such as Lexmark will have a carefully controlled level of stock to deliver to the forecasted number of customers in a controlled period. They can use past sales to predict future sales performance and their experience means their stock is all likely to be used in creating finished laptops and desktops within a short time. Their sales are high compared to the stock levels and so the average amount of time that stock remains on the shelf will be low.

In this situation, the value of their stock should be accurate and the risk that these components will not be used is very low.

Compare this to a building company. It will have a stock of materials to finish houses that are under way and start new ones. They will also have houses that are not completed (WIP) and some that are complete but not sold.

The value of these in a balance sheet created at one point could be radically different only a few months later. The economic crisis led very quickly to:

- a fall in house prices (affecting the price of their stock of completed homes); and
- a slowdown in the housing market (impacting the probability that completed or partially completed houses would sell in the short term).

If you looked at the balance sheet as the world entered the crisis, you would see a very false picture about the value of these assets.

To try to ensure that a company's accounts are a true reflection of the situation, the finance team in the company will try to find a fair valuation for both the stock and work in progress elements within the Inventories total.

To ensure the valuation is conservative, the finance team will value the assets at the lower of the cost paid for the items or the net realisable value (NRV). The NRV is simply what they believe the goods would fetch if sold. The concept of being conservative is to try to avoid an overoptimistic view being presented in the accounts. This should avoid an overvaluation of a business or misrepresentation of the actual situation causing management to act in the wrong way.

All you see on the balance sheet is a number and so you need to understand what is really behind the stated values.

Trade receivables

This figure represents the money that is owed to the company by third parties. If all the outstanding money is paid to the company, everything is fine. Unfortunately, like inventories, this is another area that can hide issues.

The assumption is that the money will come into the company at some point, but there is a risk that something may happen before the money is actually paid.

The balance sheet might show a multi-million pound debt that a company believed would be paid to them when the accounts were prepared. The day after, news may arrive that the company owing the money has gone into administration. However, nobody sends a message to the recipients of the company accounts to update them on this news.

Alternatively, when a company is under severe pressure, there may be a tendency to keep dubious debts on the books – even though there is a strong suspicion that they won't be paid. The debt will help the books look better and so some may be tempted to bend the truth.

The finance team are there to minimise the chance of this happening and to ensure that bad debts are written off rather than lingering on the books. However, they are only as good as the information they receive. The ideal is that the finance team work with the credit control team to obtain an objective view on the debt. However, in smaller organisations there may be no formal credit control function or it may not be as independent as necessary. In this case, if the salesperson dealing with the company in question insists the debt is good, it can be hard to argue otherwise.

STOP AND THINK

Why might a salesperson insist a debt is good or be pushing the credit team to say that it is? Pause a moment before reading on.

If the salesperson receives a bonus on the basis of the sale, this might be recovered from them in the case of non-payment by the client. It's therefore in the salesperson's interest to be optimistic about the chance of recovering the debt – even in the face of overwhelming evidence to the contrary.

Alternatively, they might want to avoid losing face or just be optimistic about everything.

Cash

Cash and/or equivalents which can be used to make purchases are what's sitting in your bank and is available to be spent. There should be no valuation issues about it unless the cash is in foreign currencies whose exchange rates may have changed since preparation of the accounts. The assumptions for any such valuation will be included in the notes to the accounts.

5.5.3 Total current assets

The total current assets figure represents the total of the inventories, trade receivables and cash.

Current asset type	Case A	Case B
Inventories	10,000,000	1,000,000
Trade receivables	9,000,000	1,000,000
Cash and cash equivalents	1,000,000	18,000,000
Total	**20,000,000**	**20,000,000**

Figure 5.5: Current assets – two examples

The cases in Figure 5.5 show the same total current assets but the way the figures are made up is very different. The most certain element (cash) is very low in Case A. The company has high outstanding debtors (trade receivables) and also is placing a high value on the stock and WIP. This is not necessarily unreasonable, but the low cash figure compared to the other two should perhaps ring alarm bells.

The situation in Case B is preferable as the accounts receivable and stock/WIP are low while cash is high. Case B is far less susceptible to problems arising by non-payment of the trade receivables or any overstatement of inventories.

5.5.4 Current liabilities

In the same way as the enterprise has amounts that will convert to cash in the short term, it will also have commitments to pay money out in the same time frame. These are the current liabilities.

Trade payables

This represents the creditors to whom the company owes money and that are scheduled for payment in the next 12 months.

Short-term debt

Short-term debt normally represents loans taken from individuals (perhaps directors) or from the bank.

Although some of these can be due for repayment over years, the amount that will be paid within 12 months falls into this category of short-term debt. In other words, this category will include short-term loan repayments and the relevant payments in the period on longer-term loans.

The payments on this type of debt are normally scheduled and so it is clear when and how much needs to be paid. However, if interest rates are volatile, this liability can vary significantly over a year.

5.5.5 Total current liabilities

This is the total of the short-term debt and trade payables.

5.5.6 Net current assets

The net current assets figure is equal to the current assets less the current liabilities. It is a very useful figure to think about the liquidity of the organisation.

On a personal basis, you might look at your finances, while also totalling up the bills you need to pay. If your bank balance plus the money you will receive at the end of the month is much more than the bills and loan repayments, you can be relatively relaxed. However, if your bills outweigh your cash and the upcoming pay cheque, you have a problem. The closer your personal current assets (cash plus pay cheque) are to your current liabilities (bills to pay), the more concerned you will be.

The situation is exactly the same in a company. If the net current assets is a small amount or negative, there are serious problems to resolve.

5.5.7 Long-term liabilities

To relate to the new term for fixed assets (non-current), long-term liabilities are now also increasingly known as non-current liabilities. The term used will depend on the territory where the accounts are prepared.

Long-term liabilities are the payments and other liabilities that will occur after one year from the preparation date of the accounts. As mentioned previously, the payments on a long-term loan that occur in the following 12 months would appear in the current liabilities, even though the debt itself is a long-term one.

5.5.8 Shareholders' equity/funds

This is the value of the shareholders' interest in the company on the balance sheet and is equal to the total assets less the total liabilities. It is made up of the share capital and any retained earnings.

Share capital
This is the amount of money that's been invested by shareholders as equity – in other words, for ownership of part of the company.

It is equal to the number of shares issued multiplied by the price paid when the share was issued – not the current value of the shares. Over the life of a company, shares will normally be issued at a premium to their face value and this premium is shown as part of the reserves in the share premium account.

Retained earnings

The retained earnings result from a company generating profits over time (hopefully) and equal the total assets minus total liabilities less the share capital. It reflects the increase in the value generated in the business above the money invested by shareholders.

5.6 Gearing

In order to invest more, and hopefully move faster in the market or consolidate a position, companies do not rely solely on the money received from shareholders. Businesses can also attract external funding as loans at interest rates and terms that will reflect the maturity and profitability of the business as well as the perceived risk.

The total capital employed is the money invested in the company by shareholders (as equity) and the loans the company has taken. It is the money owed to shareholders and to financial institutions.

Gearing shows how much of the company's funding is provided by external loans compared to the owners (the shareholders). It can be defined in a number of different ways, including:

- the percentage of the company's capital employed that comes from loans; or
- the ratio of the loan to the investment in equity.

Early on in the life of a company, interest rates will be relatively high on loans (compared to more mature companies) and the amount a company can borrow will be limited. Later on, if revenues and profits are higher, the business should be able to borrow money on more favourable terms.

5.6.1 The impact of gearing

Let's consider an example to illustrate the practical differences between a company having high and low gearing.

Imagine a company requires just over £1m to launch. In the scenario below, the majority of the funding comes from shareholders and so the firm has low gearing.

Table 5.2: Example of low gearing

Share capital	£1,000,000
Loan capital	£10,000
Total capital employed	**£1,010,000**

If a profit of £120,000 is made (before interest), the company has done well, but it's worth considering the impact of the level of debt.

The interest on the loan, at an interest rate of 10 per cent, would be £1,000, reducing the profit to £119,000.

If the shareholders removed the profit as a dividend now, it is an 11.9 per cent return on their money in the year.

Now consider a second scenario where the majority of funding comes from loans from a bank (and so the company has high gearing).

Table 5.3: Example of high gearing

Share capital	£10,000
Loan capital	£1,000,000
Total capital employed	**£1,010,000**

The interest charge to be paid in this case would be much higher at £100,000 (10 per cent of £1m). The profit after the interest is paid will be only £20,000.

However, if the shareholders took the profit out, it would represent a 200 per cent return on their investment in this case.

You can see from the two scenarios that the effect of being highly geared is to reduce potential profits but provide a better return on shareholders' money.

A danger of high levels of gearing is that small increases in the interest rates could eradicate the profit completely. Above 12 per cent and the company would actually be making a loss after interest payments were made (in the second scenario).

There is therefore some optimal level of gearing for a company that appropriately balances risk to the company and return for the investors.

5.7 Key measures and ratios

Different measures and ratios indicate the health of the organisation relating to liquidity (the ability to pay its bills as they fall due), financial strength and performance.

The balance sheet in Figure 5.6 shows a number of interesting figures and ratios below the main financial information. This information shows the evolution within the business over time in a more detailed format. It is worth noting that you are likely to see many variations of how a balance sheet is laid out. The general structure remains the same but there may be more entries in each category and some of the terms may vary slightly. However, the underlying principles do not change.

5.7.1 Net assets

This is simply the assets of the company less the liabilities.

Previously we discussed the net current assets as one way to consider the health of a business. Net assets is less helpful.

BALANCE SHEET (ALL FIGURES IN £000's)

ASSETS	2008	2009	2010	2011	
Fixed Assets					
Long-term investments	546	573	602	602	
Land	8,528	8,954	8,891	9,011	
Buildings (net of depreciation)	11,739	12,326	12,578	13,004	
Plant & equipment (net)	7,904	8,299	8,704	8,901	
Furniture & fixtures (net)	793	833	854	877	
Total Fixed Assets	29,510	30,986	31,629	32,395	a
Current Assets					
Inventories	2,301	2,502	2,601	2,750	j
Net accounts receivable	4,771	5,012	5,111	5,325	
Cash and cash equivalents	702	750	752	815	
Prepayments	26	26	26	26	
Total Current Assets	7,800	8,290	8,490	8,916	b
TOTAL ASSETS	37,310	39,276	40,119	41,311	c = a+b
LIABILITIES					
Current Liabilities					
Trade payables	3,189	3,256	3,316	3,524	
Short-term loans	324	333	343	356	
Current portion of long-term loans	182	187	189	192	
Accruals & other payables	178	178	178	178	
Total Current Liabilities	3,873	3,954	4,026	4,250	d
Long-term Liabilities					
Mortgage	11,234	11,589	12,514	12,978	
Other long-term liabilities	5,578	5,612	5,663	5,874	
Total Long-term Liabilities	16,812	17,201	18,177	18,852	e
TOTAL LIABILITIES	20,685	21,155	22,203	23,102	d + e
SHAREHOLDERS' EQUITY					
Share Capital	4,000	4,000	4,000	4,000	f
Retained earnings	12,625	14,121	13,916	14,209	g = c - d - e - f
Total Shareholders' Equity	16,625	18,121	17,916	18,209	h = f + g
TOTAL LIABILITIES & EQUITY	37,310	39,276	40,119	41,311	i = d + e + h
Information					
Net Current Assets	*3,927*	*4,336*	*4,464*	*4,666*	
Net Assets	*16,625*	*18,121*	*17,916*	*18,209*	
Current Ratio (Current Assets/Current Liabilities)	*201%*	*210%*	*211%*	*210%*	b/d
Quick Ratio ((C.A. less Inventories) /C.L.)	*142%*	*146%*	*146%*	*145%*	(b-j)/d

Figure 5.6: Example balance sheet

The net assets are identical in Cases A and B in Figure 5.7, but they are very different situations.

In Case A, the net current assets would be -£9,000,000, whereas in Case B the figure is +£10,000,000. So you see how even an apparently good net assets figure does not reveal the complete picture.

	Case A (£000s)	Case B (£000s)
Fixed assets	12,000	1,000
Current assets	1,000	12,000
Total assets	**13,000**	**13,000**
Current liabilities	10,000	1,000
Long-term liabilities	1,000	10,000
Total liabilities	**11,000**	**11,000**
NET ASSETS	**2,000**	**2,000**

Figure 5.7: Example of abridged balance sheets

5.7.2 Net current assets (working capital)

To understand the importance of the net current assets figure, it is useful to first understand the cash cycle in a business. This can be thought of as flow through the operations of a business from:

- cash, to…
- fund purchases of raw materials that create trade payables, which…
- need salaries and other production costs to then deliver…
- work in progress and then finished goods, which…
- are sold creating trade receivables, which…
- are then paid to create cash.

As an organisation moves through repeated cash cycles, the hope is that profits from trading will be created and swell the reserves of cash.

A common analogy is that the cash in the business is like blood pumping through a body. If there is a constriction at any point, or even a reduction, the different organs of the business may quickly be in trouble.

The net current assets figure is what you are owed (or own) less what you owe in the short term. It is calculated as the current assets less the current liabilities. In Figure 5.6, this figure has increased year on year so the company's ability to pay its liabilities in the short term appears to have consistently improved.

However, net current assets is not a perfect measure as it doesn't show if the actual figure is a significant buffer for the business or not. The current ratio shown next is perhaps a better measure.

5.7.3 Current ratio

The current ratio is, as shown in Figure 5.6, the ratio of the current assets over the current liabilities.

The current ratio and net current assets show the ability for a company to pay its short-term liabilities as they fall due. It is a very important measurement for the management of an organisation. Failure to cease trading can render a director personally liable for shareholders' losses if 'that person knew or ought to have concluded that there was no reasonable prospect that the company would avoid going into insolvent liquidation'.[6]

Action can be taken against the formally appointed directors as well as those acting as if they are directors (so-called shadow directors).

Now that you understand why this ratio is important, let's look at the balance sheet from Figure 5.6 again.

The target for the current ratio is to be above 1 as a minimum and clearly you want to be well above this value for comfort. The current ratios for the company in the example balance sheet are consistently above 2 and so the impression is that there is not a concern over liquidity in the company.

Although a useful financial measure, the current ratio does not differentiate between the different types of current asset. High levels of cash coupled to small amounts of inventory is a more liquid situation than where cash is short but there is plenty of inventory. A company could therefore have a good current ratio and still be struggling with a shortage of cash.

Also, the type of inventory may be very different from one company to the next, depending on the line of business. A stock of gold in a jewellery company is far easier to convert to cash than a partially completed yacht. This ratio would not distinguish between the two.

5.7.4 Quick ratio (also known as the acid test ratio)

The solution to the issue about the mix of assets hidden within the current ratio is to remove the inventories from the current assets total. The quick ratio is therefore:

$$\frac{\text{Current assets} - \text{Inventories}}{\text{Current liabilities}}$$

In the example balance sheet, the quick ratio is around 1.4. A value of 1 is considered comfortable for this ratio and so again, the company in the example seems fine.

STOP AND THINK

It is interesting to consider the two ratios together. What can you deduce using these ratios? Think about this before reading on.

	Q1	Q2	Q3
Current ratio	2.05	2.02	2.01
Quick ratio	0.9	0.85	0.7

The current ratio is relatively stable but the quick ratio is falling. This might suggest cash is falling in the business. The current ratio would therefore have remained stable because inventories are building up at approximately the same rate as cash is falling (and assuming liabilities are not changing significantly).

As has been stated several times, the financials and related measurements are there to signal areas of concern. In this case, if cash is leaking from the business and stocks are growing, it may be that sales have stalled. This would lead to cash falling while inventories of unsold stock build up.

This would be a good time to glance at the income statement to see if revenues are indeed falling and it would definitely be time to find out more about what's going on.

5.7.5 Interest cover

We discussed the potential issues of a company being highly geared and the ability to pay interest if rates change. Interest cover is a simple measure to see how well a company has its interest payments covered.

Interest cover is the ratio of the interest payments divided into the operating profit (EBIT) figure in the income statement. A comfortable figure is harder to define when interest rates are low. From 1–2 per cent levels, rates could quadruple or worse. If rates are already higher, they will definitely not multiply up in the same way. A figure of five for interest cover may be a reasonable target for comfort when interest rates are in the 4–8 per cent bracket.

5.7.6 Debt to equity ratios

This ratio is calculated as:

$$\frac{\text{Long-term liabilities} + \text{Current liabilities}}{\text{Equity}}$$

This ratio adds in the current liabilities to the gearing calculation explained previously but the observations are fundamentally similar as for gearing. The trick is to select the right balance between external funding and funds invested by shareholders.

5.7.7 Sales margin

Sales margin is calculated by dividing the operating profit (EBIT) into the revenues.

This measure comes from the income statement and considers performance relative to the costs in the business to deliver the products/services.

This is a useful measurement to benchmark across competitors or similar countries abroad.

In the statement in Figure 5.2, the sales margin has fallen from 35 per cent to 25 per cent. This is clearly another indication that costs are somewhat out of control and that further investigation is vital.

5.7.8 Sales to total assets ratio

This is measured as the revenues divided by the total of the fixed and current assets. It is also called the asset utilisation ratio and is linked to how well the organisation uses its assets to create revenues.

There is no one right answer for this figure as the nature of the asset base changes from one business to the next. Wal-Mart's sales to total assets were 2.356 in Jan 2012[7] while Boeing's was reported as 0.96 in March 2012 – very different businesses with very different ratios. Using benchmarks would only be informative if used across the same industry sector.

5.7.9 Return on total assets

This ratio is the result of multiplying the sales to assets ratio by the sales margin or can be calculated directly as operating profit (EBIT) divided by the total assets figure.

This measure is useful to consider how well the company is generating profit from the assets at its disposal.

STOP AND THINK

Look at the balance sheet in Figure 5.8 and think about what questions you would ask in this case.

BALANCE SHEET (ALL FIGURES IN £000's)

ASSETS		2010	2011	
Fixed Assets				
	Fixed assets	1,565	1,812	
Total Fixed Assets		1,565	1,812	a
Current Assets				
	Inventories	875	954	
	Trade receivables	1,652	2,155	
	Cash and Cash Equivalents	30	22	j
Total Current Assets		2,527	3,109	b
TOTAL ASSETS		4,092	4,921	c = a+b
LIABILITIES				
Current Liabilities				
	Trade payables	651	602	
	Bank overdraft	650	1,100	
	Trade loans			
Total Current Liabilities		1,301	1,702	d

STOP AND THINK continued

Long-term Liabilities

Loans	932	1,203		
Total Long-term Liabilities	932	1,203	e	

TOTAL LIABILITIES	2,233	2,905	d + e

SHAREHOLDERS' EQUITY

Share Capital	150	150	f
Retained earnings	1,709	1,866	g = c - d - e - f
Total Shareholders' Equity	1,859	2,016	h = f + g
TOTAL LIABILITIES & EQUITY	4,092	4,921	i = d + e + h

Information

Net Current Assets	1,652	2,155	
Net Assets	1,859	2,016	
Current Ratio (Current Assets/Current Liabilities)	194%	183%	b/d
Quick Ratio ((C.A. less Inventories) /C.L.)	127%	127%	(b-j)/d

Figure 5.8: Example balance sheet 2

Take some time to think about this before you read on.

It is possible to make a few immediate observations.

The current assets figure has increased sharply. This is not necessarily a good thing, as it is the trade receivables that has increased while cash remains very low and has decreased to 2011. This needs to be investigated as allowing the amount of debts to grow so rapidly is not good practice.

I would want to look at the breakdown of trade receivables to show how:

- the average debt per client has changed;
- if any of the clients owes a significant part of the total receivables (e.g. one client owing more than 20 per cent); and
- the debtor days for each receivable (i.e. what is the number of days since the invoice was raised).

The level of cash in the business should be a major concern. Even though the quick ratio figures appear OK, the business is heavily reliant on the liquidity of the inventories.

Short-term debt and the loans under long-term liabilities have also increased. It appears these changes have funded the investment in fixed assets as well as the increases in inventories and trade receivables.

5.8   Cash flow

5.8.1   The statement of cash flows

The statement of cash flows can help identify how cash flows through the business and how it has been used. In simple terms, the following gives you an idea of how and why cash changes.

The cash account will increase when:

- a liability increases (e.g. the company takes out a loan);
- shareholder's equity increases (they have injected more money); or
- an asset (excluding cash) decreases.

The cash account will decrease when:

- a liability decreases (e.g. you are owed less money);
- shareholder's equity decreases (e.g. they have taken money out of the company as a dividend); or
- an asset (excluding cash) increases (e.g. you have purchased an asset and so the cash reduces).

The statement of cash flows includes four sections to help identify the sources for the change in cash.

5.8.2   Cash related to operating activities

This starts with the profit after tax (net income) figure from the income statement. Items are then added or subtracted from this until the final change in cash is shown at the end of the calculation.

This net income figure does not equate to a change in cash in the business because of changes in the current assets and current liabilities (and the other impacts discussed shortly). Some items may have increased during the period considered in the accounts while others will have decreased.

The statement of cash flows starts by looking at the overall changes in each of the current assets and current liabilities categories.

The depreciation expense is also added back in this section of the statement. Let's take a second to examine why. Remember that we are tracking the movement of cash in the business.

The profit after tax figure is the figure we begin with in the assessment of cash flows shown in this statement. The income statement that produces that profit after tax figure starts with the revenues and then deducts costs, including the cost of sales. This includes an expense for depreciation of assets relating to producing the goods or services in the organisation. The final profit figure derived in the income statement is therefore after the depreciation expense has been charged – reducing the overall profit.

So for an asset with a five-year life and an initial cost of £5 million, a charge of £1 million would be made as a cost of sale item for every year of the five-year life of the asset. The depreciation charge is not equal to the cash that flows out of the business; it is an allocation of the initial cost of the asset over its life.

Let's look at the differences here in the following table.

Table 5.4: Depreciation expenses

	Year 1	Year 2	Year 3	Year 4	Year 5
Cash	£5,000,000				
Depreciation expense	£1,000,000	£1,000,000	£1,000,000	£1,000,000	£1,000,000

To understand the cash flows, you want to see the cost for the asset in the year it was purchased at the full amount (as this is what happened from a cash perspective). In the statement of cash flows this will happen as the cash figure will change by this amount in the year of purchase.

However, if you look at Year 3, for example, you see the depreciation expense of £1,000,000 that will have been removed from revenues in the income statement – even though it is not a movement in cash in the business. This is why it is has to be added back at this stage when you are looking at cash flows.

Cash related to investing activities
This category looks at changes of long-term assets in the balance sheet. This is impacted by the sale or purchase of long-term assets such as buildings or equipment.

Cash related to financing activities
This section considers changes in the long-term liabilities and shareholders' equity.

Supplemental Information
This section explains other significant items such as payment of interest and tax, as well as any share exchange with another company.

An example of a statement of cash flows is shown in Table 5.5.

Table 5.5: Example of a statement of cash flows

Statement of cash flows		
(£000s)		
Period ending	30 December 2011	
Profit after tax (net income)	21,538	
Operating activities: cash flows provided by or used in…		
Depreciation and amortisation	12,534	
Decrease (increase) in trade receivables	40,758	
Increase (decrease) in liabilities	420,997	

Decrease (increase) in inventories	3,621	
Increase (decrease) in other operating activities	−301,245	
Net cash flow from operating activities	198,203	**a**
Investing activities: cash flows provided by or used in...		
Capital expenditures	−705,113	
Investments	−13,020	
Other cash flows from investing activities	0	
Net cash flows from investing activities	−718,133	**b**
Financing activities: cash flows provided by or used in...		
Dividends paid	34,557	
Sale (repurchase) of shares	−12,055	
Increase (decrease) in debt	402,310	
Other cash flows from financing activities	350,001	
Net cash flows from financing activities	**774,813**	**c**
Net increase (decrease) in cash/cash equivalents	**254,883**	**a+b+c**

5.8.3 Changing the rules of cash flow

A few companies have changed the way that their cash flow works in order to improve their businesses.

SNAPSHOT

Dell has a remarkable business model. Having struggled and nearly crashed due to the cash flow drain for a fast-growing business in 1993 (following growth of 126 per cent in 1992),[8] the way Dell works was overhauled. Now, when you order a Dell laptop, it will be made from components off the shelf and your credit card will be charged immediately. It will be put together, tested, shipped and delivered to you in a few days, and you're a happy customer. However, the suppliers for the components in the Dell hardware are only paid 44 days after Dell receives payment from customers. Usually a company lays out money buying items for stock, puts the finished product together, delivers it to stores and finally waits for someone to buy the product before the money comes in.

Dell gets the money in from customers first and pays suppliers later in their 'negative cash conversion cycle' – meaning Dell's cash requirements are limited, even if their sales explode upwards.[9]

5.9 Key investment assessment

There are a number of measures that are used in finance to look at the set of cash flows (money out and money in) that would be generated by a particular investment or project. We will begin by describing some of these measures.

5.9.1 Payback

This is a very simple measure. Let's consider an easy example. This year, the company will invest £10,000 in the project. From then on, the net difference between the money out (for further capex and for opex) and money in (revenues) provides a cash flow result in each year as shown below.

Table 5.6: Payback example

	Year						
	0	**1**	**2**	**3**	**4**	**5**	**7**
Cash flows	−10,000	2,000	2,500	2,500	3,000	3,000	3,500

Payback calculates how long it is before the initial investment is matched by the cash flow in.

To calculate the payback, you can simply work out the cumulative cash flow from the start of the project to each particular year, as shown below.

Table 5.7: Working out the cumulative cash flow

	Year						
	0	**1**	**2**	**3**	**4**	**5**	**7**
Cash flows	−10,000	2,000	2,500	2,500	3,000	3,000	3,500
Cumulative total	−10,000	−8,000	−5,500	−3,000	0	3,000	6,500

The cumulative total remains negative until Year 4, when the total positive cash flows equal the total cash out (as can also be seen in Figure 5.9). The payback is therefore four years in this example.

If the cash flow goes negative in some years, the approach does not change. You still look for the first year (or month if doing a more detailed analysis) that the cumulative positive cash flows are greater than the cumulative total of negative cash flows.

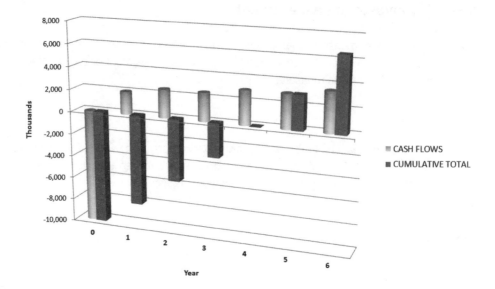

Figure 5.9: Annual cash flow and cumulative cash flow total (£)

5.9.2 Usage and weaknesses of payback

Payback is a very simple measure and is sometimes used as a quick check on a project, but it suffers from significant problems.

If, in the example above, there was a large cash outflow in Year 5, the payback measure would ignore it as payback occurred by the end of Year 4. So the calculation is correct but the issue is that the payback method ignores all the cash flows once payback has been achieved.

Secondly, payback does not consider the cost of money (i.e. the interest rate on a loan needed to invest in the opportunity). If a company invests £100 million in a project that does not pay that back for 20 years, that is not as good an investment as if they put the money into a bank and received interest on it or another type of return.

The exception is if interest rates are very low. In this case, positive cash flows after the payback has occurred may make it an attractive investment. However, you would then be betting on interest rates remaining low for 20 years and the cyclical nature of the economy makes that unlikely.

There is also an inherent weakness with this approach for big capital projects, as companies that think in these terms often put very short timescales on targets for payback and capital projects are frequently only going to pay back in 8–15 years minimum. Sometimes you find a way to change the rules of the project and achieve a return faster, but companies often work with payback targets of a few years, meaning a significant infrastructure project would be almost impossible to approve.

Though payback as an approach is interesting, we will move on to more accepted methods of looking at cash flows.

5.9.3 Discounted cash flow

To get around one of the weaknesses of payback, we can reflect the cost of money by modifying the cash flows. First, let's explain the idea of a discount rate.

Think of a choice between of being given £100 now or £110 in one years' time. Which should you take?

In one year's time, if you invested £100 in a project and it gave you a 10 per cent return, you would have £110. A discounted cash flow works in reverse by calculating the equivalent value to you today of receiving an amount sometime in the future. If the return you could expect on an investment made today is x per cent (the discount rate), you can calculate the equivalent of a future sum at today's value.

In one year's time, £110 is the same as £110/(1 + x%) today. If x is 10 per cent, we are simply reversing the sum above. In a year's time, £110 at 10 per cent discount rate is the same as £100 today.

The discount rate (also sometimes known as a discount factor) is chosen to include two aspects:

- A risk-free return element. If the money was placed in low risk bonds, it would deliver a guaranteed return (or as near as possible in these tricky times).
- A risk premium. No project is ever guaranteed to succeed. A utility project (e.g. a water company) may be quite low risk because of a monopoly position. The risk premium may only be a couple of per cent. A different type of project will almost certainly be a riskier proposition than a stable utility business and so the risk premium is consequently higher.

The above example showed an amount in one year's time. If we invested money for two years, the percentage increase in value would be (1 + x%) x (1 + x%).

If we (conveniently) calculate the current value of £121 received in two years and we again use a discount rate of 10 per cent, the current value would be calculated as:

$$\frac{£121}{((1+10\%) \times (1+10\%))} = £100$$

So if the potential growth in the value of investing £100 (including a risk premium) is 10 per cent per annum, the £100 is equivalent to receiving £121 in two years.

The generic formula that can be applied to calculate the value today of cash received in year (n) is simply:

Cash flow in Year n /(1 + x%)^n

The current year should be n = 0 for the current year for the formula to work correctly.

The formula enables us to calculate today's value for the cash flow in any year. So, to create the discounted cash flow, we take the actual cash flows we had before and apply the formula to the net cash flow (positive or negative) in each year.

Table 5.8: Applying the formula to the net cash flow in each year

Discount rate	10%						
				Year			
	0	1	2	3	4	5	6
Cash flows	−10,000	2,000	2,500	2,500	3,000	3,000	3,500
Calculation	$-10,000/(1+10\%)^0$	$2,000/(1+10\%)^1$	$2,500/(1+10\%)^2$	$2,500/(1+10\%)^3$	$3,000/(1+10\%)^4$	$3,000/(1+10\%)^5$	$3,500/(1+10\%)^6$
Discounted cash flow (DCF)	−10,000	1,818	2,066	1,878	2,049	1,863	1,976
Cumulative DCF	−10,000	−8,182	−6,116	−4,237	−2,188	−326	1,650

Notes: The DCF line shows the values adjusted with the given discount rate (10 per cent). This model also assumes that there are no cash flows after Year 6.

The reason for actually going through the calculations is that it is very easy to make a mistake using a spreadsheet to do this calculation and, if you don't understand the underlying principles, you won't necessarily spot any errors. Also, finance professionals have discount tables available that provide the discount factors for different interest rates and periods; you probably won't!

As with payback, we can look at the cumulative total of the DCFs. In the table above, the cumulative total only goes positive in Year 6 (as opposed to Year 4 using straight payback).

This discounted payback is superior to the straight payback method as it reflects the returns that could be obtained 'risk free' and also a risk premium – the extra that makes it worthwhile doing the project in the face of the fact it may fail to deliver the desired results.

The higher the risk perceived for the money, the higher the discount percentage. The larger the discount rate, the more it will reduce the present value of future cash flows and the further into the future it will be before payback occurs.

Although this is a better approach than payback, the discounted payback method still ignores cash flows after the end of the payback period.

The discounted cash flows themselves are the basis for another calculation that is very commonly used and is more useful – net present value or NPV.

5.9.4 Net present value (NPV)

The NPV of a series of cash flows is a single number calculated using a given discount rate on a set of cash flows. It is simply the addition of all the discounted cash flows for a project. From the example above, it is very easy to create the NPV as a final step.

Table 5.9: Net present value

Discount rate	10%						
	Year						
	0	**1**	**2**	**3**	**4**	**5**	**6**
Cash flows	−10,000	2,000	2,500	2,500	3,000	3,000	3,500
Discounted cash flow (DCF)	−10,000	1,818	2,066	1,878	2,049	1,863	1,976
NPV	1,650						

The NPV is the sum of the DCF figures in each year above and is £1,650 in this case.

The simple approach with the calculated NPV is that if it is greater than zero, the project may be worth executing. If it is less than zero, the project is probably not worth executing, unless there are other strategic reasons to press on regardless of the financial result.

This does assume that money to invest is not in short supply and there are no alternative projects. If other projects are candidates for investment, the NPV of each should be compared and consideration made of which individual or combination of projects would provide the best return.

However, if we stick to the concept of one project, the NPV provides a good reference value for different scenarios. Investors and bankers are likely to ask for sensitivity analyses that reflect what may happen in the business e.g. subscriber take-up 10 per cent lower than expected. The NPV of these new scenarios compared to the original will then show if this change in prospects for the business has a serious impact or not.

5.9.5 Internal rate of return (IRR)

In looking at the NPV of a project, a discount rate is required. The internal rate of return (IRR) is almost a reverse of the NPV process. It is the discount rate that would be applied to create an NPV of zero.

As stated previously, if the NPV is positive then in simple terms, the project is worth considering and, if the NPV is negative, the project should be dropped. On one side of zero there is one decision (ignoring all other factors) and the other side of zero, the decision will be the reverse. That means the point where the NPV is zero is an important point.

In addition, if you can earn a particular return from an investment, this can be compared to the IRR of a project. A high-risk project with an IRR of only 6 per cent does not seem very attractive compared to putting money into a very safe investment elsewhere with a return of 5.5 per cent!

Investors and companies normally have a target IRR figure that a project must exceed to receive funding. This 'hurdle rate', as it is known, will reflect a premium on risk-free returns that could be made.

Weighted average cost of capital (WACC) is a calculated discount rate used in some companies (as opposed to just selecting a figure) to be the hurdle rate for investment. WACC is calculated from a risk-free rate for capital in the country (e.g. a bond rate) with a risk premium applied.

Table 5.10: Three different cash flows and their respective IRRs

	Year						
	0	1	2	3	4	5	6
Cash flows	−10,000	2,000	2,500	2,500	3,000	3,000	3,500
IRR	15%						
Cash flows	−10,000	2,500	2,500	3,000	3,500	3,500	3,500
IRR	19%						
Cash flows	−10,000	3,000	3,500	3,500	5,000	5,000	5,000
IRR	30%						

One thing to be careful of with the IRR is that, if the cumulative cash flows start negative, then go positive at one point before going negative again, there will actually be two values for the IRR. For example, the following cash flows have an IRR of both 4 per cent and 19 per cent.

Table 5.11: Cash flows with IRRs of 4 per cent and 19 per cent

	Year						
	0	1	2	3	4	5	6
Cash flows	−10,000	5,000	6,000	6,500	7,000	−7,500	−7,500

SNAPSHOT

Telecom Egypt has a ratio of 1 employee to 450 subscribers but Riksnet, a telecoms start-up bootstrapped by my colleague, has a ratio of 1 employee to 2,500 subscribers (while delivering a full range of services and ranking number 4 in the world for service value).

Do not be afraid to do better than a benchmark, but be aware that company boards (and in particular analysts and bankers) will want to know very clearly why you are going to do better than a company for whom they have a benchmark.[10]

5.9.6 Free cash flow (FCF)

Free cash flow (FCF) is an important measure as it shows the ability for the company to fund its future and is relatively resistant to being manipulated for accounting purposes.

Among many definitions of FCF, perhaps the simplest starting point is that it is the cash generated by the business once it has paid for ongoing operations and growth.

The following shows how to derive the FCF. Don't worry if you don't understand every step – that's why companies employ finance people. However, it is useful to understand the use of FCF which we will discuss later.

		Year 1	Year 2	Year 3	Year 4	Year 5
EBITDA	A	17.3	206.6	382.0	476.2	477.0
Change in working capital	B	59.1	-5.7	-9.6	-19.7	-38.5
Taxes Cash out	C	-12.8	-12.6	-37.7	-42.5	-34.4
Cash flow from Operations	**D = A + B + C**	**63.6**	**188.3**	**334.7**	**414.0**	**404.1**
CAPEX	E	-499.8	-598.5	-656.0	-571.1	-262.4
Intangible Assets	F					
Financial Expenses	G	0.0	-15.0	-42.8	-43.1	-56.3
Capex & Financial Expenses	**H = E + F + G**	**-499.8**	**-613.5**	**-698.8**	**-614.2**	**-318.7**
Free Cash Flow	**= D + H**	**-436.2**	**-425.2**	**-364.1**	**-200.2**	**85.4**

Figure 5.10: Example of free cash flow over time

The second column has reference letters to indicate the simple mathematics being used.

Free cash flow (FCF) starts with the Earnings Before Interest, Tax, Depreciation and Amortisation (EBITDA) figure for a given year. To get this figure you can simply add back the depreciation and amortisation to the EBIT figure from the income statement. You then add the impact of:

- changes in working capital derived from
  - changes in accounts receivables (year on year) plus
  - changes in VAT (Value Added Tax) receivables (year on year) less
  - changes in current liabilities; and
- taxes (cash out)

The company needs to build its operations so you need to consider the capital expenditure (capex) needed to build a call centre, shops, a factory or whatever.

To fund this capex, there are likely to be financial expenses to pay and these are also considered (see the example above). These expenses will mainly be interest payments with some costs to obtain the finance included.

At the end of the calculation in the example, the FCF figure starts off very negative – reflecting the fact that the business is not generating much cash (EBITDA is very low), but investing large amounts on capex. Over the years, the FCF figure becomes less negative (as revenues and hence EBITDA increase) and the capex falls significantly (in Year 5).

5.9.7 Beyond the theory – how these calculations can go wrong

Let's look at an example to illustrate how these simple mechanical exercises to calculate the return on an investment can provide the wrong solution. The theory is fine but in practice they can go wrong and here's why. This is based on real issues within a Caribbean company trying to calculate project returns to justify investments to their board.

A company is considering investing in a power supply that costs £4,000,000 and will last six years. Each year the power supply will produce £900,000 in cost reductions. However the sensors in the power supply will wear out after three years and have to be replaced at a cost of £1,000,000.

Therefore the cash flow for the third year will be -£100,000.

What is the NPV at a discount rate of 20 per cent?

When I look at the answer I get the following.

Time	Cash flow	Discount factor @ 20%	Present value of cash flow
0	4,000,000	1.000	−4,000,000
1	900,000	0.833	749,700
2	900,000	0.694	624,600
3	−100,000	0.579	−57,900
4	900,000	0.482	433,800
5	900,000	0.402	361,800
6	900,000	0.335	301,500
		NPV	£1,586,500

Figure 5.11: NPV calculation example

However, other people look at the same basic information and get the following variations (and nobody is necessarily right without further information).

Instead of an NPV of -£1.58 million, the NPV is now -£1.7 million as the cost in 'Year 3' defined in the description is actually taken in the third year of operation of the power supply (i.e. Year 2 in the example above, rather than after three years as assumed in the first calculation).

In other words, it assumes that the initial payment is made in the first year (shown as 0 above) and the clock until the next payment starts immediately so in the third year, the payment is made. In the calculation in Figure 5.11, the initial purchase was made and then you assumed that the company would wait until three years after that to make the payment for the new sensors.

Which is right? Well, until we ask someone to look hard at the contract, it's impossible to know. Both are mathematically correct but one is factually incorrect.

Let's think about when this power supply is purchased.

If you bought it on 1 January, there will be a year's benefit from using it in that same year (Year 0). The clock has started and you've used up a year of the power supply's useful life in that first year of purchase. The sensor purchase could be after three years of use but is still potentially ambiguous and needs to be checked.

However, now let's imagine the power supply was bought on 31 December. In that case, the first year of real usage will be in the year after purchase. That means there will be six years of use after the year of purchase (as in Figure 5.11).

It's impossible to know which calculation would be correct without further information.

5.10 The importance of timing

Let's take the final point about timing a little further.

The relationship between investment (meaning cash flow in this case), income and time is very important, as the following will illustrate.

The two profiles that follow show the investment (cash outflows) and income (cash inflows) for a particular case over time. The total cost and income are equivalent in both cases but the timing of the major investment costs differ. In the 'late cost' case shown in Figure 5.12, the significant costs ramp up to the fourth year. In the 'early cost' case in Figure 5.13, the largest cost occurs in Year 1 and costs ramp down from there.

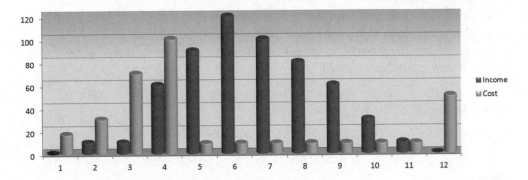

Figure 5.12: Cash inflows and outflows profile – late cost case

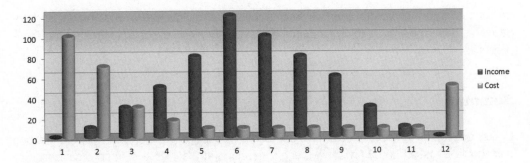

Figure 5.13: Cost and income profile – early cost case

Although the two cases appear similar, the net cash flow by year is shown for the two in Figure 5.14. This is the difference between the total cash inflow and outflow for each year.

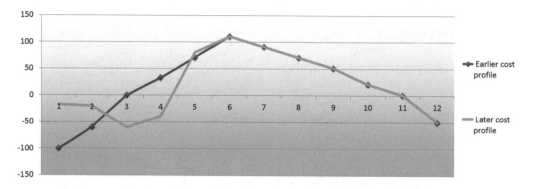

Figure 5.14: Net cash profile (income – cost) for early and late cost cases

You can see the impact on the net cash profile in the two cases. The early cost case starts more negatively but steadily improves as the annual costs reduce. The late cost case begins only slightly negative and worsens. Year 4 improves slightly as even though the costs are at a maximum, income has risen steadily and offsets the costs better than in Year 3.

The results are very different between the two cases, even though they involve the same amount of cost and look quite similar.

Table 5.12: Impact on the net present value

Case	Net present value (£ millions)
Costs taken early	7.6
Costs taken later	44.8

So negotiating on the cost of the investments made may yield lower savings than timing the payments over time. Paying for investments later has a dramatic effect on returns for the same project.

Summary

Understanding the way businesses measure themselves financially is a challenge, but it is one that should be taken up by anyone wishing to manage at a senior level in an organisation or create their own business. This understanding provides the ability to plan, implement and then monitor performance, and to see past the spot and investigate issues beyond the raw figures themselves.

Accounting standards provide us with relatively standardised formats for financial reports and we can use the:

- income statement to look at the operating costs and overheads in the business and the impact these have on revenue in delivering profit;
- statement of cash flows to understand the ways that cash is being used in the business; and
- balance sheet to see the way the assets and liabilities in the business have changed and how these have been funded.

What's next?

Having introduced the basics of finance in this chapter, the next will look at some of the investment decisions that need to be made in producing portfolios of interesting products and services. This will introduce wider concerns than simple financial measures – including considering technical and market risk, time to market and the level of competitiveness of any new product/service.

Notes

1. *BMW Annual Report 2011*, www.bmwgroup.com.
2. 'British law firm 'conspired' to hide $50bn debts of Wall St giant', Lucy Farndon, *Daily Mail*, 13 March 2010.
3. http://dealbook.nytimes.com/2010/03/11/lehman-directors-did-not-breach-duties-examiner-finds.
4. www.frc.org.uk/asb/about.
5. ifrs.org.
6. The Insolvency Act 1986: www.legislation.gov.uk/ukpga/1986/45/section/214.
7. http://ycharts.com/companies/WMT/asset_utilization.
8. www.hbs.edu/research/pdf/10-063.pdf.
9. Dell Quarterly Analyst Conference Call, reported at http://hardware.seekingalpha.com/article/18116-dell-too-cheap-to-pass-up.
10. Tarek Tantawi, former CFO and CEO of Telecom Egypt, Mikael Sandberg, Ventura Team LLP.

6

Product development, portfolio management and launch

This chapter looks at some of the concepts you need to consider in selecting, developing and launching products.

6.1 Product development

To ensure a stream of good products or services, a company will need to start with a larger number of concepts and then cull these over time. The hope is that only the good products survive through to launch and only the bad ones are stopped. However, things are rarely quite this simple.

Figure 6.1 shows two different lifecycles for projects through to launch.

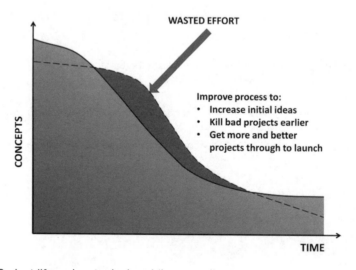

Figure 6.1: Project lifecycle – typical and 'improved' curve

The dotted line shows a less effective portfolio. Fewer projects are started and fewer are finished than in the other portfolio. However, in between, too many of the projects proceed until near the end of development where they are killed. All the resources and time spent on the projects that don't reach launch are wasted.

The objective is to start more projects (have more ideas) but to recognise those that won't succeed earlier and kill them quickly to save on resources and wasted management time. At the same time, you want more 'good' products successfully reaching launch at the end of the process. The second 'improved' curve (with the solid line) in Figure 6.1 shows how this approach saves effort overall while launching more products. Remember, using limited resources effectively is vital if your organisation is to succeed in the longer term.

The more work that is done on development, the more you learn about potential problems and the more of these can be fixed. The 'product risk' – the risk that the product will not deliver to the defined specification – decreases as you invest more time and effort in perfecting the product, as shown in Figure 6.2.

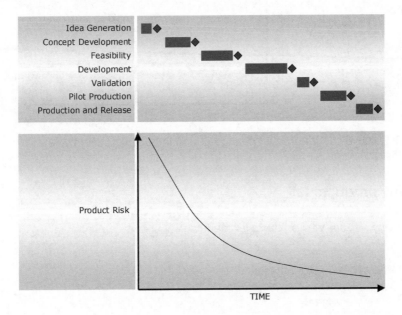

Figure 6.2: Product risk during the development cycle

It is important to note that the cost, time and resource usage increases dramatically during the product development lifecycle. An idea is simple to come up with and change while it is in your head. However, by the time you try to stop or change something that is close to production (or worse, that is already being produced), the costs have risen significantly, as shown in Figure 6.3.

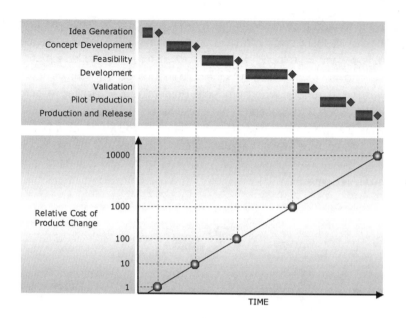

Figure 6.3: Relative cost of product change during the development cycle

6.2 Why products fail

There are many reasons why products fail, as Table 6.1 shows.

Table 6.1: Reasons why products fail

Problem	Example
Bad positioning	Microsoft's Zune was an attempt at an iPod but struggled with less attractive design features and the inability to access the leviathan that is Apple's iTunes store.
Early problems	3G services in some parts of the world (e.g. Saudi Arabia) suffered incredibly slow download speeds at busy times. Allowing too many users to access the service created significant issues but interestingly, the absence of any viable alternative meant the subscribers kept increasing. The networks caught up eventually – providing a reasonable quality service across wide areas under-served by traditional telecoms.
Delays	The sophisticated Boeing 787 Dreamliner has suffered three years of delays against its original schedule. However, the cut-throat nature of the aviation business has surely allowed Airbus to capitalise on these delays with increased sales of their more conservative designs.

Problem	Example
Poor quality	Mercedes-Benz had a long-held reputation for quality, producing bulletproof cars that went on to stratospheric mileages. However, by 2004 the ML model was ranked flat last in a car ratings survey for Top Gear.[1] This created issues for the company which subsequently made moves to restore its damaged reputation. The NSU Ro80 didn't have as much luck. The revolutionary rotary engine had serious design issues and owners passing each other were known to signal each other indicating how many engines they had been through. The company was eventually sold to VW in 1969.[2]
Failure to manufacture enough examples	The JICC plant in Sweden was aiming to build ceramic, inkjet print heads for companies such as Amstrad. The print heads were aiming to defeat bubble jet print technology on speed and cost.[3] However, the manufacturing process was so complex that at one point their output of working print heads was only 0.5 per cent of those started. The innovative technology was shown on the BBC but proved too complex for them to industrialise and manufacture in volume. The result was the closure of the business.
Over-promising	The indomitable Apple found a way to fail with the Apple Newton. Despite US$100 million being spent on development, the device's handwriting recognition never really performed as expected and went on to be ridiculed in an episode of *The Simpsons*. Steve Jobs, although not in power at the company at the time, kept pushing the CEO to shut it down and this eventually occurred.[4]
Failure to hit sales targets	There are myriad stories of products that were supposed to dominate the mass-market and failed spectacularly. The Dyson washing machine was revolutionary but, at £1,000 each, was criticised by *Which?* magazine as being poor value for money and it was discontinued in 2005 after disappointing sales.[5]
Too late to market	If you have a toy to market, it's not December (Christmas) that is the key month but January, when the major toy fairs occur. If you're not ready to market the product to the channels in Q1, then you're not going to make Christmas.
Insufficient marketing support	Viva was one of the first beers for vegetarians. The company managed to persuade Tesco to trial the product, but a lack of awareness of the existence of a vegetarian beer meant potential customers were not looking for this product. Lack of funds for informing the market meant the trial was short lived.
Economic turmoil	The market for housing and apartments in Dubai had been fuelled by speculation for some time prior to the global economic crisis and prices were savaged as the downturn hit this fast-moving emirate.

Problem	Example
Cannibalising other products in your range	This occurs when a product is introduced that has similar performance to an existing product, but at a lower price. The new product 'eats' the old one – hence the term cannibalisation.
	Essentially, customers swap from one to another and the company will have lower revenues for a similar product while also having invested in the design and introduction of the new product.
	If there is no threat from competitors or potential to significantly increase sales beyond the current numbers, then this looks like a questionable move.
Failure to get traction	Sony's Betamax video recorder technology had superior picture quality to the VHS alternative. However, initially it could only record one hour per tape compared to two hours for VHS. It failed to get picked up by enough Original Equipment Manufacturers (OEMs) and VHS, with 85 per cent global market share in 1986, was able to push costs down further than Sony. VHS was also strengthened by deals with Hollywood studios that enabled them to offer films that Betamax could not. Eventually Sony had to accept defeat and started shipping VHS recorders.[6]
	The lesson of failure to control the content behind the Betamax technology led Sony to enter the media world. They bought Columbia, CBS Records and TriStar Pictures at the end of the 80s.[7]
Priced too high	The 3DO video game console hit an already competitive market with a street price of nearly £500. It failed badly against the Super Nintendo (SNES) and Sega Mega Drive, which both dominated the market at the time with far lower price points for the consoles.
Failure to achieve desired specification	The Jaguar XJ220 was promised as a V12, four-wheel drive supercar that attracted speculators and keen buyers alike. In a tricky economic climate, Jaguar's production version was rear-wheel drive and powered by a V6 (albeit a rather powerful one). Disappointed buyers tried to pull out of deals because the car wasn't what they had thought they were signing up for.[8]
No significant advantages	This is the classic 'me too' product that enters the market at a similar price, with a similar feature set and from a company that has no particular unique strengths. Succeeding with a pure 'me too' product like this is a very difficult trick to pull off.
	The standardisation of the processors, architecture and operating system mean that Windows laptops are often very similar to one another with only a low level of innovation. Many products are essentially 'me too' products with near identical specifications and consumer choice coming down to brand and price.

Problem	Example
Failure to keep up	From a towering market position in the mid-80s to bankruptcy 20 years later, Polaroid seemed to be stuck around the business model of 'instant pictures' and failed to gain enough traction in other areas to survive the birth of the digital era. Kodak has been navigating similar waters, as digital photography and photo sharing sites decimate sales in their traditional film and paper business.

STOP AND THINK

If anyone says to not worry about quality problems, 'because Apple overcame them', then it's worth remembering that probably only Apple's brand and huge cash reserves could have survived the different problems they have suffered (e.g. battery life on iPods, screen cracking on early Nanos, poor/no signal on the iPhone 4).

Can you think of any other company with serious issues that has been able to overcome them as easily?

There is no excuse for launching a bad product and 'hoping for the best'. That's not to say that every product should be a Rolls-Royce. Every product should be fit for purpose, and launching something that doesn't do what it is supposed to (and hoping you can fix it later) really isn't acceptable. Take the minimum time needed to get things right.

Decisions about which projects to pursue are not made in isolation; they draw on a finite set of resources such as:

● cash;
● management attention;
● expertise;
● time; and
● hardware resources.

The effect of each project therefore needs to be understood within the context of the total set of projects so that the management team can:

● deploy a limited budget most effectively;
● understand the effect of programme failures;
● reduce time to market; and
● manage risk within R&D.

CASE STUDY

The democratisation of technology: presentations move from professionals to the desktop

Twenty-five years ago, company presentations normally used a set of 35mm slides and a slide projector. Producing these slides was generally expensive and time consuming, and therefore they were not changed very frequently.

The availability of overhead projectors and acetates that could be passed through a photocopier allowed more flexibility but the next big change was when a company's reprographic (reproduction and graphics) department got their hands on Harvard Graphics (released in 1986). This software allowed a user to create pie charts and other graphical features for presentations.

The software did not remain the domain of the reprographic department for long though. Other software appeared, such as IBM Storyboard Plus, and inexorably the ability to create presentations moved to the desktops of staff within the organisation. Microsoft PowerPoint is now available to almost all as part of the Microsoft Office package.

What has happened is that the capability of making presentations was originally high cost, highly skilled and relatively rare (i.e. only a few people could do this).

Now the evolution in products means making a presentation is low cost with a relatively low skill level required and many professionals able to do this for themselves.

This is a pattern for products and services and it doesn't reverse. Let's look at another example.

From main frames to the desktop

Some people reading this book may have started work in companies that had large computers with data entered via punch cards. The programmers and data analysts had to book time to get access and then come back the day after for the results.

The first work computers for some would have been an Apple II and it was probably shared across a department. This computer could have up to 48 kbytes of data compared to today's desktops with 4 gigabytes (or more than 80,000 times as much memory). IBM then revolutionised the industry with the appearance of the IBM PC that is the forerunner of every laptop and desktop.

If we fast forward to today, many of us have computers at home as well as work, and the skills needed to use a computer are now the norm rather than the exception.

It's the same effect as for presentations. Something is a relatively rare, specialist skill that is expensive and gradually it becomes more widely available, less expensive and easier to use.

Leading by leapfrogging the competition

Many companies succeeded by exploiting this democratisation trend and making a bigger leap forward than the competition – reducing costs and/or simplifying the experience for users.

For example, Tata Motors in India announced the Nano in 2003. Costing just one lakh (100,000 rupees – equivalent to around £1,350), this car aims to provide four-door transport to the masses. Since its launch in July 2009, sales have not been as high as hoped. Ratan Tata, the head of the company, was hoping to democratise car transport in the subcontinent.[9]

6.3 Portfolio management

Portfolio management is the set of activities that identify and maintain the optimum balance of projects to support the current and future business strategy. It is difficult to get right as it requires constant rebalancing as new projects are launched and older ones finish or are stopped.

New ideas for products, services and innovations are generated and then an outline definition produced for ones that are considered of interest. This project definition is then considered in terms of attractiveness – firstly in isolation and then in terms of how it fits into the current portfolio. This fit is particularly important.

Let's look at the individual steps one by one.

6.3.1 Idea generation – the product development funnel

Figure 6.4 shows the overall process for developing new ideas. This view is based on Wheelwright and Clark's work.[10]

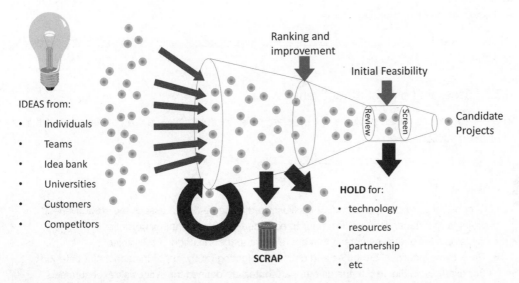

Figure 6.4: Ideas screening

The funnel demonstrates how candidate products can be identified from a variety of sources. However, not all of these will make it through to launch. To filter out the products, there are a variety of screens and different paths that the products can follow.

For example, at any point within the funnel, a product concept can be scrapped. Ideas can also be put on hold because the resources, technology or market are not present at that point to warrant continuing. For example, a project may need the use of a particular piece of plant or be waiting for team members to become available.

Those are relatively obvious reasons to put a project on hold. However, it may also be that the company is waiting for a new technology to appear or reach a particular price point, or for a market to develop for a product.

6.3.2 Project definition

This is discussed in more detail in Chapter 11, but a minimum amount of information is required to understand the scope and requirements to push a product development opportunity forward.

Initial feasibility studies may be required as ideas are generated to sort the potential projects early on, although there is a need to provide a greater level of detail as financial and time investments become greater during the cycle.

Candidate projects can initially be defined in terms of:

- goals and objectives;
- major milestones;
- time, cost and performance constraints;
- investment requirements;
- timescales;
- resources (human and material);
- risks; and
- links to other projects/programmes.

It may also be the case that the value of a particular project can only be realised if other projects take place.

6.3.3 Assessing project attractiveness

In order to choose which projects will proceed, it is helpful to have a way to assess them in a consistent fashion.

EXERCISE

Let's consider a simple approach first (as illustrated in Figure 6.5) to assess the attractiveness of projects as independent entities, prior to considering their fit within a portfolio:
- Develop a list of the key criteria that are relevant to the selection of the project.
- Rank these individual attributes and define a weighting for them within each major category. For example, in Figure 6.5, the different attributes are defined for utility, risk/exposure and time. The total for weightings in each category should total 100 per cent (in other words the groupings a–e, f–l and j–k should add up to 100 per cent).
- The relative weight of the three categories is also defined (utility, risk/exposure and time in the example) – again adding up to 100 per cent.
- Each project is then scored against each attribute within the categories.
- Multiplying the attribute score by the weighting percentage for the attribute provides a score.
- All of the scores for a category (e.g. Utility) are added up and multiplied by the category weighting.
- All the category weightings are added up to provide a total score.

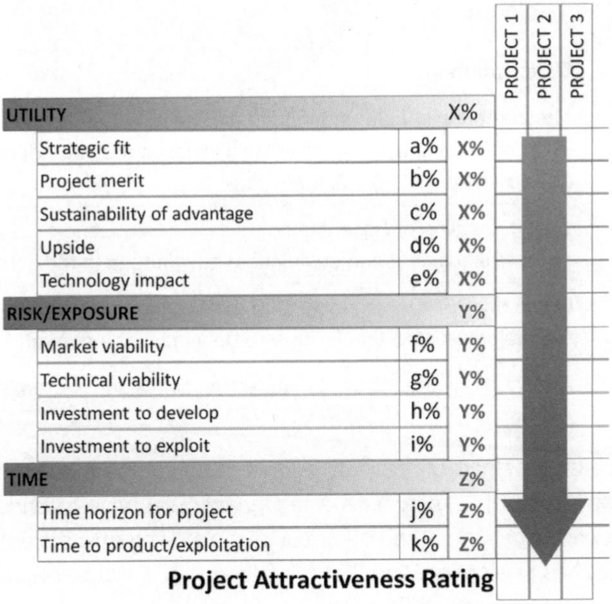

		PROJECT 1	PROJECT 2	PROJECT 3
UTILITY	X%			
Strategic fit	a%	X%		
Project merit	b%	X%		
Sustainability of advantage	c%	X%		
Upside	d%	X%		
Technology impact	e%	X%		
RISK/EXPOSURE	Y%			
Market viability	f%	Y%		
Technical viability	g%	Y%		
Investment to develop	h%	Y%		
Investment to exploit	i%	Y%		
TIME	Z%			
Time horizon for project	j%	Z%		
Time to product/exploitation	k%	Z%		

Project Attractiveness Rating

Figure 6.5: Ranking project attractiveness

Attractiveness ratings show the desirability of carrying out a project in isolation, but projects must be rationalised and portfolios selected:

- taking account of overlaps and common resource requirements between projects;
- with respect to the direction provided by the overall strategy and the technology strategy (if appropriate);
- as an iterative process refining the portfolio to find the optimum balance between available projects and the strategic direction.

A potential portfolio can be assessed in terms of the balance and timescales of delivered programmes. The example in Figure 6.6 below shows a series of projects viewed against the budget required to complete them. The right-hand diagram shows the projects looking at the time to completion.

The left-hand uses a very interesting categorisation (with some terms developed by consulting firm, Arthur D. Little) to consider the value of technologies (see also Table 6.2).

Technology may not be an important element of the products or services in a company, but these example portfolios illustrate how to consider the current and potential future mix of projects or products.

Table 6.2: Valuing technologies

Technology	Description
Enabling/base	The company should understand and be able to manage these technologies in order to compete in the market. However, they do not necessarily provide any source of differential advantage.
Differentiating/key	Unlike enabling or base technologies, differentiating or key ones provide one or more significant and sustainable advantages to the company.
Pacing	Some competitors are looking at this technology, which represents the next technological step that is likely to be used in the market.
Emerging	A technology that has not matured yet but which is promising for the future.

In Figure 6.6, the biggest part of the R&D budget is being spent in the enabling (base) category. As discussed above, that means it's a technology you have to understand and master to compete but it doesn't provide a source of sustainable differential advantage. The important pacing category only has one project and that is relatively small. Worse still, the time to complete the big emerging technology project (C) is more than five years. It is not certain that this technology will become critical to the market but in five years it may have appeared and be dominating – while the company is still waiting for project C to finish.

The overall impression is that the portfolio does not match the current and future requirements of the business. It is out of balance.

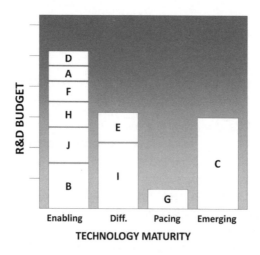 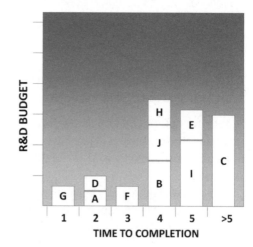

Figure 6.6: Example Portfolio A

The portfolio in Figure 6.7 is different. There is a more balanced set of projects across the different technology candidates. There are more projects in the pacing section compared to Portfolio A and fewer in the enabling category. On first glance, this mix of projects seems better, although the emerging area still has one very large, very long timescale project in it.

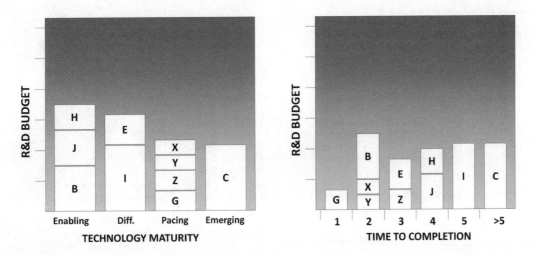

Figure 6.7: Example Portfolio B

Let's look at a different way of considering a portfolio by looking at Figure 6.8.

The idea of 'new to firm' means a technology or market (as appropriate) that the company is currently not familiar with but which does already exist. In the case of 'new to world', we are talking about either a new market or technology that nobody has experience of delivering at present.

The circles are proportional to the total spend in each project.

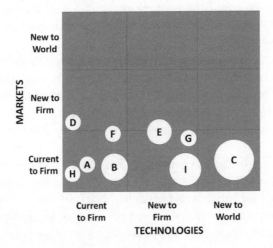

Figure 6.8: Portfolio C – technologies against markets

The portfolio above may be acceptable by some companies, while others would consider it too conservative.

Consider the two portfolios below.

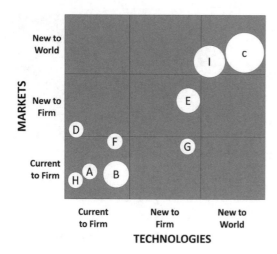 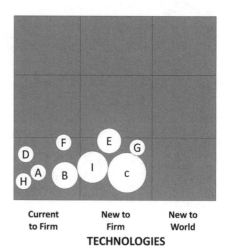

Figure 6.9: Adventurous and conservative portfolios

The portfolio on the left is clearly far more ambitious than the one on the right. Again, neither is necessarily correct. It absolutely depends on the market situation and the company's position and strategy.

On the left, the company is trying some new-to-world technologies in some new-to-world markets. That's compounding market risk with technology risk to an extreme. It will have worked for a few companies in the past, but it certainly requires caution. The visual nature of displaying the portfolios in this way enables you to form a rapid judgement about the balance of risk in both markets and technologies.

It appears obvious that the company's two biggest projects in terms of investment are in this dangerous box where both the market and technology are new. That should ring alarm bells.

The right-hand portfolio sticks doggedly to the firm's current markets but adds some technologies that are new to it, but not to the world. In other words, someone is already successfully using that technology so, although it is a risk to the company, it is not as extreme as if it was completely new.

The key learning point is that the contents of the current portfolio should inform decisions about what projects should be commenced. A company may want to reduce production costs for a component. That may have the highest priority but how many projects are enough? One, two, ten, twenty? If the decision-making process doesn't take account of the ongoing projects, all you risk doing is starting more and more projects on the highest priority issues.

Decision making should therefore allow for:

● projects to be held until the resources become available for them; and
● criteria to evolve so that the portfolio maintains the right balance between risk and return.

Looking more deeply, you can consider the portfolio against other variables – for example, the three diagrams in Figure 6.10.

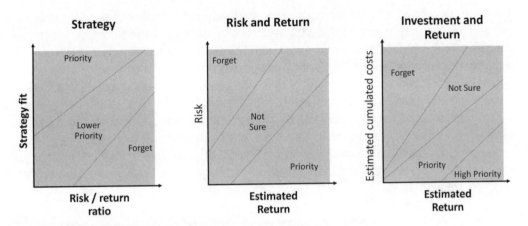

Figure 6.10: Various portfolio assessment approaches

The version in the middle is the classic risk-return diagram. Projects would be plotted on this with an option being the size of the circle relating to the investment in the project. The important thing is to understand that logically you are trying to achieve a high return with low risk.

That risk could usefully be considered as technology or market risk – i.e. the technology fails or the market doesn't appear as expected. Discrete versions of the portfolio diagram could be produced for each type of risk or the vertical axis could just represent a scoring for all relevant risks.

Projects that deliver good results and low risk should clearly be the priority. Ones that deliver high risk and low returns should probably be avoided wherever possible.

The left-hand diagram considers the strategic fit to the risk–return ratio. The higher the risk–return ratio, the less attractive the project will be. So for this view, the 'best' position is for a high fit to the strategy and a low risk–return ratio.

Finally the right-hand diagram in Figure 6.10 shows the total investment required to complete a project against the estimated return. Here, you would ideally like to choose projects that offer high returns for minimal investment.

As before, the art is to consider the portfolio of different projects and consider whether the balance matches the requirements for the company and its appetite for risk.

6.3.4 Stage-Gate processes

R.G. Cooper developed the definitive approach to selecting projects and then managing the Go/No Go decisions during the lifetime of those projects.[11]

The process is known as Stage Gate and breaks down into two parts:

1. **Stages** – Periods of activity to progress the project while also preparing the information and justifications necessary to pass to the next stage.
2. **Gates** – These are the decision points in the overall process. At these points, certain information is required and criteria must be met in order to allow the project to proceed.

The detail and amount of information required at each stage will normally increase the further you proceed through the process. Similarly, the seniority of those agreeing whether a project passes the gate will also increase. However, the idea is to create a process where individual power in the organisation cannot be used to ensure the passage of pet projects. For that reason, clear criteria should be established, scoping the level of time, money and resources that can be used in each stage and under what circumstances gates can be passed.

For example, it may be necessary to have an internal or external customer sign up to join the team at a particular point to ensure that the 'voice of the customer' will be heard.

A real-world Stage-Gate process is shown in Figure 6.11. It shows the progression from initial idea through to managing the product in the market (Stage 5) and finally even Stage 6 where products are terminated.

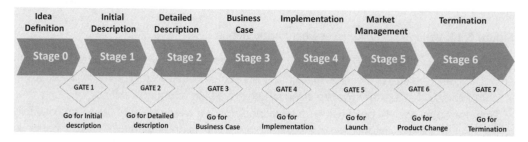

Figure 6.11: A Stage-Gate process

6.3.5 Differences between gates and milestones

Sometimes there is confusion about the relationship between Stage-Gate processes and project plans.

During the life of a project, the team will define milestones specific to the project and also pass gates that are imposed to allow review of the project at important stages in the project.

- Stage-Gate processes are generic for a specific type of project in a company (e.g. R&D).
- Project plans are unique with a dedicated team to execute the project objectives.

Within a portfolio of projects, each one will be following the Stage-Gate approach to gain permission to continue at each relevant decision point. However, each one will also have a unique project plan.

In other words, the project will need to pass the Gate decision points between the generic stages, but will have milestones, activities and tasks that are unique and specific to that particular project, as shown in Figure 6.12.

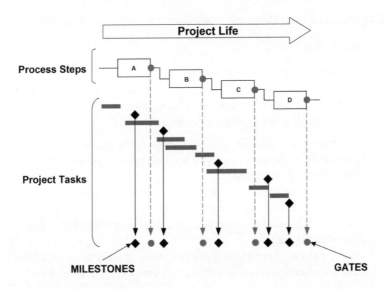

Figure 6.12: Milestones and Stage-Gate processes

The project can therefore be stopped if it:

- fails to pass the criteria at a particular gate; or
- cannot reach the state of achievement necessary to meet an upcoming milestone.

6.4 The complexity of launching products

After the problems of developing the right products (and doing it well), the launch of new products is another serious challenge for any organisation.

A product goes through a number of discrete phases and companies may need to manage from initial enquiry and purchase through to a customer stopping using the product or leaving a service. Launching a product successfully requires them to be ready for all of these stages.

Some of the challenges faced at each stage are shown in Table 6.3.

This list is just the tip of the iceberg. Remember these steps are for a buyer who wants to purchase the product. The full sales cycle would start long before these phases to get a potential buyer up to the purchase decision.

Table 6.3: Challenges at each stage for a product

Phase	Description
Buying	How does a customer purchase the product/service?
	If they ring a call centre, what is on the screen of the person taking the call? What information do they need and how is it captured?
	How do they link this through to delivery or installation?
Using	How does a system know if you are a valid user and have paid?
	How is access granted to a service and how is the user informed?
	How is a product delivered?
	What checks exist to show that users have been able to access the product (e.g. successful delivery, downloaded the product)?
	What help is given to help users with the product or service (manuals, online information, e-mails)?
	What checks are there to verify the user is not abusing the service?
	How is customer usage linked through to payment for any suppliers?
Contacting	How does the customer get in touch and what happens when they do?
	How are problems recorded and dealt with?
	How are changes made?
Activating	How are changes to the product confirmed and activated?
	How would the change take place?
Paying	How can customers pay?
	What agreements are necessary?
	What needs to be signed?
	What links to banking and credit systems are needed?
Leaving	How does a customer leave the service?
	Who do they call?
	What steps are taken to retain them?
	What information is available to retention staff?

STOP AND THINK

A very expensive consultant stood up at a conference to explain how his team's work in a major company had streamlined the 'Leaving' process to make it much easier and quicker. Think about that for a second. Do you want customers to find it really easy to leave? Obviously you don't want to frustrate them, but you do want to put some steps in place so that you can salvage the relationship and retain them if you possibly can.

Using the phases above, think about how your own organisation delivers at each point. Who is involved? What systems support the activities? What coordination is required across departments/divisions?

Unless you have a very simple business model, it should quickly become obvious how complex these phases are, and how they call on many different parts of the organisation.

Not every product or service will need this amount of planning before launch, but the level of disruption, as well as the investment necessary, is clearly significant.

Summary

Developing a good product or service is obviously important but it is rarely done in isolation. It requires consideration of the existing portfolio of products within the company as well as future developments.

Once the product has been defined, an organisation needs to do the work needed to ensure it is ready to launch it correctly. This requires careful coordination across all phases of the customer's lifecycle as well as across different parts of the organisation.

What's next?

The next chapter will look at the different potential structures and how these may help or hinder operations within the organisation. For example, it will define a project matrix type organisation that supports running portfolios of projects.

Notes

1. 'Top Gear Survey 2004', BBC Website, 10 November 2004.
2. 'A History of Audi – The 1960s': www.audi.co.uk/content/dam/audi/production/RestOfSite/FleetSales/03_2010/PDF/History/AudiHistory_60s_161009.pdf.
3. www.fundinguniverse.com/company-histories/Nukote-Holding-Inc-company-History.html.
4. *Steve Jobs*, Walter Isaacson, Little, Brown, New York, 2011.
5. 'Interview Dyson CEO Max Conze: "Our lifeblood is inventing. That is where we spend all of our money."', Kamal Ahmed, the *Telegraph*, 11 February 2012.
6. 'The format wars: of lasers and (creative) destruction', Anders Bylund, *Ars Technica*.
7. *The Star System: Hollywood's Production of Popular Identities*, Paul McDonald, Columbia University Press, Columbia, 2000.
8. *Jaguar XJ220 - The Inside Story* by Mike Moreton, Veloce, Dorset, 2010.
9. http://tatanano.inservices.tatamotors.com/tatamotors/home.htm.
10. *Revolutionizing Product Development*, by S.C. Wheelwright and K.B. Clark, the Free Press, New York, 1992.
11. *Winning at New Products, Creating Value Through Innovation*, R.G. Cooper, Basic Books, New York, 2011.

7
Organisational design

The way an organisation is structured has a major impact on its ability to deliver against its objectives and strategy.

Rigid, hierarchical organisations can deliver strategies where markets (and the work needed to deliver to them) are relatively stable. However, rapidly changing markets and products need more flexible structures.

The organisation may therefore need to be changed because it is badly matched to the current needs of the business, or to deliver against a new strategic direction.

7.1 Organisational structure

The two generic ways in which an organisation can be structured are:

- functional hierarchies (command and control); and
- matrix organisations.

Within each generic type, there are a number of variations aimed at aligning the organisation to the strategy and markets it is pursuing. We will consider both types in more detail to understand where they may fit best and also how roles and responsibilities differ between them.

7.2 Functional hierarchies

7.2.1 The logic of functional organisations

At the beginning of the life of an organisation, a sensible way to organise it is to group employees together by their function. This helps to:

- promote communication and coordination of a particular function's activities;
- allow members of the group to learn from one another; and
- optimise use of technical resources by centralising them within the functional group, rather than scattering them across market-focused groups, for example.

Another benefit is that the members of the department can be used flexibly to resource the pool of activities they need to carry out. Splitting them across the organisation will mean the smaller groups of similar resources will sometimes be under-capacity while other groups have spare capacity. Careful resource management across the organisation can minimise this effect but it is easier to use resources efficiently when they are managed in one group (and hopefully located together also).

7.2.2 The need for specialisation

While the organisation remains relatively small (say 10–50 people), this compartmentalisation does not hamper communication as people know one another and the area they cover in a building is unlikely to be very large. However, as the organisation grows, the ability to know everybody will be lost and the number of premises may increase. This will begin to build barriers to communication.

7.2.3 Anatomy of a functional organisation

The simplest version of a functional hierarchy is shown in Figure 7.1. This will help highlight key points about the management of groups operating in the organisation.

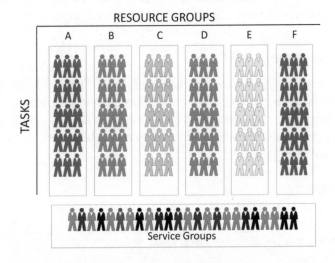

Figure 7.1: A 'command and control' functional hierarchy

The structure is broken down into different functional groups (labelled A to F in Figure 7.1) that look after specific areas of responsibility and are led by an individual. There may also be horizontal 'service groups' that deliver across the whole organisation (e.g. maintenance, HR, IT, legal).

This approach to managing an organisation is known as a functional hierarchy and may also be referred to as a command and control structure. The individual members of groups have their work directed by their line manager (the head of their functional unit). The ultimate example of this management style is in the military, where the ranks and relationships between the different units are completely clear and unambiguous.

Although this approach works well in the military and some organisations, it is not ideal in all situations.

This type of organisation works well where the work to be done is relatively consistent over time. The stability allows people to adopt specialised roles and for departments and groups to take care of specific parts of the business.

However, a pure functional hierarchy can be a challenge to operate where the organisation has to deal with varying types and volumes of work, as the strict separation of responsibilities makes it hard to resource what needs to be done.

Where the organisation is relatively new, or has a higher than normal percentage of inexperienced personnel, this hierarchical focus may extend to decisions being sent higher up the management structure than is strictly necessary. This is because employees and even managers do not have:

- confidence that making a decision will not result in negative consequences for them;
- sufficiently clear authority for decisions that they can make (in other words they do not have, or are not confident that they have, clear authority levels for making decisions); or
- processes to follow that provide them with criteria for decision making at any particular point.

The need to improve the fit between organisations and the markets they serve means that a number of variations of a functional hierarchy have appeared. In each case, they rely on departments led by an individual but each department is tailored to a particular direction.

7.2.4 Product structure

This approach creates an organisation that reflects the products being made, or services being delivered. Departments are centred on different products, but this structure only makes sense if the lifecycle of the products is relatively short. If the product life is longer, then there would be less need to be flexible and there might be a better focus for the business. Another structure might be more appropriate in that case.

Geographical structure
This structure suits an organisation that is seeking to minimise transportation costs or needs to be close to customers within the sale, delivery or service process. This may be a real need to be close to the markets or a perception of being local.

Market structure
An organisation can configure itself to align departments and processes with the most important market segments. This works best if the products or services are also aligned with the segment. This provides clarity about who is responsible for what product and minimises someone in one department needing to direct the work of people in a different department. In other words, this structure works particularly well if each market-focused department is relatively autonomous and self-contained.

The right structure on its own is not enough. Organisational effectiveness needs the correct structure with matching processes, capabilities, roles, responsibilities and systems wrapped around. The change programme attempted to resolve many of these shortcomings in this challenging situation.

7.3 Matrix organisations

Matrix organisations aim to address some of the weaknesses in functional hierarchies by delivering more flexibility.

7.3.1 Project-focused or project matrix organisations

At the other end of the organisational spectrum from functional hierarchies are project-focused organisations.

In this type of organisation, the head of a group acts as a resource manager rather than a line manager. The resource manager does not direct the day-to-day work of individuals in the group. Instead, their responsibility is to ensure the welfare of those underneath them on matters such as HR, payments and expenses. The resource manager helps people managing projects to find appropriate resources and the individuals in the resource manager's group are then seconded into one or more project teams.

Figure 7.2 illustrates different projects running with teams across the whole organisation (and even outside).

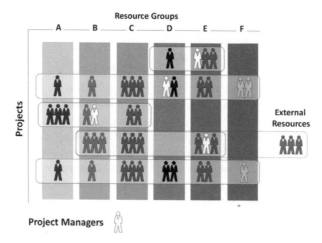

Figure 7.2: A project-focused organisation

As shown in the diagram, the project manager may come from a group rather than being a resource or line manager. On occasion, they may even come from outside the organisation. However, in every case, the project manager is responsible for the execution of the project and therefore directs the team members drawn from across the organisation. This is the key difference from a functional hierarchy.

In project-focused organisations, the resources follow the lead of the project manager(s) they are working for in defining what they do on a daily basis. In a functional hierarchy, they would be taking their lead from their line manager.

So to reiterate, the resource manager does not direct individuals' work and only gets involved to manage problems and at the end of the project when individuals' performance and contribution (within the project) are assessed for review and developmental purposes.

Project focus is excellent where the organisation constantly faces a changing portfolio of activities. The flexibility that can be achieved when this approach works well can radically outperform a 'command and control' organisation in these circumstances.

CASE STUDY

French R&D organisation

A division of Saint-Gobain operates an R&D facility that stretches across a 2km-long site. The facility develops both the new products and manufacturing processes for manufacturing glass wool insulation for houses and offices.

The product could be broken down into component parts and the organisation was split up along similar lines. Each component had its own discrete department and almost all of these were separated into different buildings.

CASE STUDY continued

The organisation was already a functional hierarchy but the physical separation of departments reinforced this. People didn't see colleagues in other departments' buildings very often (particularly if it was raining or cold) and most communication travelled up the departmental 'silo' to the group head who then passed it on their equivalent in another department to pass on to the correct person.

Research and development are very fluid activities where projects will frequently be starting, stalled, on hold, failing or completing successfully. However, the rigid structure and lack of communication in the organisation did not support this. Projects that should have operated across the organisation were either run within a single department or coordination was very limited.

A change programme was run to identify and then implement a more successful mode of operation for the facility and this was extended to include other R&D sites in the group.

The facility was converted to a matrix organisation with a support team providing common services across the site. This improved flexibility and ensured that all parts of the manufacturing process contributed to product development.

7.4 The process vector

The two approaches described above are extremes and normally an organisation will operate somewhere between the two.

The power of the line manager increases as the organisation moves towards a purely functional hierarchy and the power of the project manager increases as the organisation moves towards being project focused.

The position an organisation takes between a functional hierarchy and a project focus can be thought of as a vector. If the arrow is horizontal, it would show a project focus. Similarly, if it was fully vertical, it would indicate a functional hierarchy

The processes for decision making, review, resource allocation, metrics and rewards all need to be very clearly defined to avoid any kind of confusion or problems where the vector is more towards the horizontal.

Two intermediate positions between a project matrix and functional hierarchy can be defined.

7.4.1 Weak/functional matrix organisation

Project managers run projects across the organisation (but this is more about coordination) and the line/functional managers (at the top of each resource group) act to manage the project work in their area. This can be a complex structure to get right as the project manager does not have complete control to execute the project as they might wish.

7.4.2   Balanced/functional matrix organisation

In vector terms, this is the halfway position between a functional hierarchy and a project matrix approach. The power of the resource/line manager and project manager is roughly equivalent and this structure relies on cooperation and coordination.

Although a useful approach if operated well, this can introduce significant problems where resources feel they have two reporting lines and potentially two different targets and sets of priorities.

7.4.3   The challenge of matrix organisations

A common and very serious problem in 'matrix' organisations is where people feel they have two direct lines of control. In other words, the resource manager is acting like a line manager and is trying to direct the work of those in the resource group. They are potentially operating in conflict with what the resource's project managers want. In this situation, individuals feel as if they have two line managers rather than a project and a resource manager. This leads to lack of clarity about where authority lies and who should be listened to when there are resourcing conflicts.

Remember, the line management function manages rewards and sanctions for individuals in their group, and so may exercise too much control compared to a project manager.

Summary

Choosing the right structure is about finding the best compromise. There is no 'one size fits all' approach and the structure needs to reflect the way that the organisation delivers to the market (geography, products, markets, technologies) and the level of flexibility required in doing so.

Functional hierarchies benefit from concentrating specialist areas together but are poor when resources need to be shared flexibly. Matrix organisations can be extremely flexible but sometimes lead to conflict between the line/resource manager and project managers about who is managing the day-to-day work of individuals.

What's next?

We've looked at how organisations can be set up and configured. Now let's look at keeping things on course. Part C is about staying on track.

Part C
Staying on track

8
Understanding and managing people

No institution can possibly survive if it needs geniuses or supermen to manage it. It must be organized in such a way as to be able to get along under a leadership composed of average human beings.[1]

Peter Drucker

Managing people well is probably one of the toughest challenges. You are trying to satisfy the different desires and motivations of individuals while delivering against targets. Much of the time you will have only limited authority and flexibility in terms of choices open to you, and the rewards and sanctions that you can deploy. In reality, you can't please all of the people all of the time, but management is about trying to make the best choices in a given situation.

This chapter explores ideas about how people are motivated to help inform your choices and how you express them. It begins with some of the attributes associated with management and the styles that characterise individuals and organisations.

8.1 Being a good manager

There are a number of functions a good manager should aim to deliver. The exact balance will depend on the organisation and their position within it. As they rise through the company the balance is also likely to evolve, but the basics are:

- setting and agreeing objectives – with the team and also higher management;
- motivation;
- communication – objectives and tasks down into the organisation and delivery of management reporting upwards;
- development of individuals;
- measuring performance; and
- identification of issues and risks.

These are the mechanical aspects of being a manager but the deployment of these factors requires an understanding of how to manage and motivate individuals/teams.

8.1.1 Five systems of management

Likert, an organisational psychologist, originally suggested systems of management to try to explain the continuum of management styles.[2]

Table 8.1: The continuum of management styles

System	Description
System 0	Highly fluid with little definition of roles and confusion through to complete chaos (in extreme cases).
System 1	Authoritarian management style based on fear and threats. This is all 'stick' and no 'carrot'.
System 2	A more benevolent approach with the use of rewards while still being broadly authoritarian. Policy comes down from the top of the organisation.
System 3	This is a more consultative approach with rewards and occasional punishments.
System 4	This approach encourages more participation with some group-based working and individuals belonging to more than one group to act as 'linking pins' – assisting in communication and coordination of information and actions.
System 5	This approach is more of a concept for the future where hierarchy disappears from organisations completely.[3]

Linking pins are integrated in System 4 and become vital in System 5. They are generally those who have higher influence, are more involved in the groups and coordinate across the groups to find solutions.

STOP AND THINK

There is no one right way for all situations. However, as a first step, it's useful to consider your own preferred style and how well that works in different situations.

Then consider the styles of those around you. Do they work well? When do they work and when do they fail to work as intended?

8.1.2 Task or relationship focus – Fielder's contingency model

Fred Fielder developed a contingency model of management effectiveness that considers a different angle on management.[4] Two main styles were identified:

- Task-motivated managers, who gain satisfaction from the successful achievement of tasks.
- Relationship-motivated managers, who gain satisfaction from having good relations with friends, colleagues and fellow employees.

Of course, few people are 100 per cent task-motivated or relationship-motivated. Most of us will fit somewhere between the two, but a fascinating and simple test of the preference towards one or the other is shown below.

EXERCISE

Ask a manager to identify their least-preferred co-worker. When they have done this, ask them to describe this person and their abilities across the different aspects of their role.

Typically, a manager who is more task-motivated will be critical of the person on most/ all aspects they mention. However, a more relationship-motivated manager is likely to rate someone highly in a few areas, even though they are their least preferred co-worker.

Fielder suggested that task-motivated managers tend to operate better when the situation is favourable or unfavourable (things going well or badly) and that relationship-motivated managers work when the situation is somewhere in between.

8.1.3 Decision making – Vroom and Yetton's leadership theory (with Jago)

Vroom and Yetton developed a categorisation that looks at the degree of participation in decision making for different management styles, and went on to suggest which styles would work best under which circumstances.[5] The styles were as follows:

Table 8.2: Vroom and Yetton's categorisation of management styles

Style	Description
AI	Solve problems and make decisions alone.
AII	Obtain information from workers and then decide (alone).
CI	Share problems with individuals and then decide as a result of that process of sharing.
CII	Discuss problems with group then manager makes decision.
GII	Work out solutions with the group.

You can see that the styles range from extremes of decisions being made practically in isolation (AI) through to the group-focused, participative style of GII.

The different styles can be matched to a range of situations as follows:

Table 8.3: Matching the styles to situations

Style	Focus of the situation being addressed				
	Acceptance	Reducing conflict	Fairness required	Goal concern	Acceptance is paramount
AI	NO	NO	NO	?	NO
AII	NO	NO	NO	?	NO
CI	?	NO	NO	?	NO
CII	?	?	NO	?	NO
GII	?	?	YES	NO	YES

Where a style is inappropriate for the situation, the option is marked NO. Where there is only one choice, the option is marked YES. Where a number of options are available, those options are marked with a question mark.

8.2 Motivation

It is useful to remember that not everyone thinks the way we do or is motivated by the same things. Understanding different forms of motivation and how individuals respond to them is important in getting the most from them. There are a variety of psychological theories about what drives individuals and it's interesting to explore them.

8.2.1 Needs theory

Psychologist David McClelland's needs theory provides insight into identifying and understanding what motivates individuals.[6] This understanding can then translate into ways to manage those with particular needs.

Table 8.4: What motivates individuals

Main motivator: the need for...	Characteristics of the Individual
Achievement (N-Ach)	These individuals have a strong need to define and then meet challenging objectives. This desire to achieve may avoid low-risk opportunities as they do not provide sufficient challenge. However, they may also avoid high-risk opportunities as the result may not be fully under their control. They require regular feedback on performance towards achievements, and their preference is to work on their own or alongside other high achievers, as those with different motivations do not share the same drive towards the objective.

Main motivator: the need for...	Characteristics of the Individual
Power (N-Power)	A person with this need is looking to acquire either positional or personal power. They want to influence others and exercise control through knowledge and/or the use of rewards and punishments – hopefully for the benefit of the organisation. Those seeking institutional power are seen as being more effective generally than those looking for personal power. They want to win – arguments, competitions, anything – and they enjoy the status that goes with the power.
Affiliation (N-Aff)	People with a high need for affiliation want to have good relationships with those around them. They want to feel liked and accepted. This desire drives them sometimes just to go along with the wishes of the group and they look to collaborate rather than compete. They may feel less comfortable with higher-risk situations as this may fracture the harmonious nature of their relations with others due to the increased stress.

Identification of the motivators can be used to help define roles and responsibilities for those in a team.

CASE STUDY

Don't over-promise and under-deliver

The Chief Commercial Officer (CCO) of a company was bored of his team over-promising to customers. At sale time, they would promise the service would start in three days, knowing it would actually take at least two weeks to begin. When asked why they kept doing this, the sales team told the CCO, 'That's what customers want to hear.' He just couldn't change this behaviour and it was the operations team that took all the angry phone calls from customers disappointed with the 'late' delivery of their service.

At the company dinner, the CCO stood up, praised his team and called the sales team up on stage to receive their reward, which would be an iPad for everyone (that's certainly what it sounded like to the audience). Sure enough, the first person did indeed receive a new iPad 2 and looked delighted. However, the next person on stage received an eye-pad (an eye-patch as we'd know it).

The CCO solemnly gave them to every other member of the team then stopped and said, 'I know you're disappointed because you expected one thing, you were promised one thing and you got another. Now imagine how our new customers feel when they don't get the service they have been promised. Don't over-promise and under-deliver again.'

While this may not have been the best approach, it was certainly a telling message to the team.

By understanding what motivates an individual, you can tailor your response to them when providing feedback or framing objectives.

The person seeking power

The person who is constantly organising the others is normally seeking power. If appropriate – in other words, if they are up to it – then these people should have the opportunity to manage others. This may be a temporary assignment or management of a project to see whether they are suitable for a full-time management role.

You can maintain this type of person's motivation by acting to improve their career prospects within the organisation. Tasks can be framed in this way to help motivate this type of person to deliver.

Feedback to this type of person should be specific.

The person seeking achievement

This person will have frequent discussions on their achievements relative to goals set for them – either providing updates on progress themselves or seeking clarification on their progress to date.

They should be given projects that are challenging without being impossible to achieve. This type of person may respond better to tough but clearly achievable objectives. They will require regular feedback and this should provide a clear view on what is going well and what can be improved. In this way, the individual can improve their performance which is entirely consistent with their drive for achievement.

The person seeking affiliation

The person who is relatively quiet in the group and generally agrees with the group probably has a high need for affiliation.

This can also influence the way you praise or criticise them. Doing this in a group will not be appropriate for someone with a high need for affiliation, as you are effectively marking them out as different. They don't really want that as it may threaten their status within the group. This is not to say that these people should not be praised or criticised, but you need to think about how you do it.

Put this person into a team or on group work where they can contribute within the context of an environment they find comfortable.

Feedback should be provided, wrapped along with some level of reassurance about their status in the group and the manager's confidence in them. It should probably also be given one-to-one rather than in a group.

Overall

In real life, it is impossible to provide individuals with work that is the right challenge and environment for them all the time. Compromise is required but if you begin to understand people's underlying motivations and preferences it means you can meet those requirements more of the time and avoid mismatching individuals to the wrong circumstances (for them).

8.2.2 Theory X and Theory Y

Douglas McGregor outlined two very different management assumptions about employees.[7] He referred to the two opposite views as Theory X and Theory Y, and assigned traits to each that are described in Table 8.5.

Table 8.5: Theory X and Theory Y

Theory X	Theory Y
People: ● don't like work; ● need to be controlled and directed; ● need security; ● are motivated by threats of punishment; ● are not ambitious; ● do not use their imagination; and ● avoid taking responsibility.	People: ● think work is a natural and normal activity; ● respond to recognition and encouragement as well as control; ● commit to the objectives of an organisation in line with the rewards offered; ● will accept responsibility and accountability in the right environment; ● can be creative.

The extreme differences in these views are starker in the twenty-first century. Although most people reading this book have more sympathy with Theory Y, Theory X should not be discounted. Rightly or wrongly, workers in some countries are managed in line with Theory X. Sweatshops, for example, are likely to be almost pure Theory X management in action.

8.2.3 Herzberg's hygiene factors and motivators

Clinical psychologist Frederick Herzberg looked at the motivation of workers in the US. His work was similar to the work of McGregor but created an interesting distinction between those factors that have to be present (hygiene factors) and ones that will provide additional motivation (motivators).[8]

Table 8.6: Hygiene factors and motivators

Hygiene factors	Motivators
● Salary ● Benefits ● Company policies ● Relationships with colleagues ● Supervision/management	● Achievement ● Recognition ● Responsibility ● Promotion ● The work itself

Delivery of the hygiene factors is the basis for satisfaction. We want a reasonable salary for the work we do, but without this we will feel dissatisfied or exploited. We expect fair policies and relationships that are generally respectful and not abusive. If we have these, the theory is that we will be satisfied.

Motivation requires the addition of some of the other factors such as recognition for the work we do.

However, if the hygiene factors are not present in an acceptable way, it is unlikely we can be truly motivated.

8.2.4 The impact of morale on performance – the three-factor theory of motivation

Is morale the key to performance?

In *The Enthusiastic Employee*, Sirota *et al.* suggest that a company with enthusiastic and motivated employees will outperform typical organisations.[9] Their work covered more than 200 companies and two million employees. They summarised their findings in three factors that need to be present to maintain the enthusiasm of employees.

The initial point would be that most of us start a new job or assignment with good motivation. It's an opportunity for something new, a clean slate after past problems and mistakes, and a chance to shine. However, that motivation is often eroded over time.

The book suggests that the goals of employees and management are actually not far apart. The challenge is ensuring management do not destroy the motivation of employees. If the company can identify what employees want and deliver it, employee satisfaction becomes enthusiasm. The results of this enthusiasm are significant competitive advantages for the companies that can maintain this energy in the long run.

The theory proposed by the authors suggests motivation comes from the following three factors.

Table 8.7: The three-factor theory of motivation

Factor	Description
Equity	People want fair treatment at work. This breaks down into a number of areas, including: • job security (except in cases of genuine poor performance); • fair compensation; • respect – eliminating indifference towards employees and disrespectful treatment, e.g. humiliation; • expanding on the respect principle, workers should have safe working conditions (in psychological as well as physical aspects); and • best company policies and practices.
Achievement	People want to do work that is important and receive the correct recognition for success. • Enable people to succeed by creating the right environment. • Drive this through effective team building, good delegation (of tasks and authority) and flattening the organisational structure. • Pride in the company – driven by the actions of the company. • At the opposite extreme, avoiding unethical organisational behaviour which will damage employees' opinion of the company.

Factor	Description
Camaraderie	People want to enjoy themselves at work – based on the relationships and culture around them and making them feel part of the success of the company. They don't want to go to work for conflict. ● Reward the 'right' behaviours. ● Work more cross-functionally. ● Managing conflict collaboratively. ● Define rules for behaviour across teams. ● Building partnerships to deliver against objectives.

In a change from other management theories, the book says that pay is actually important in helping to define status – reflecting respect from the company and a visible sign of achievement.

8.3 Motivating

Now we've had a look at some of the theory, let's use that to look at how you might actually motivate an organisation using the five-stage process described below. It begins by questioning what your own views on motivation are, as these will affect how you think about the motivation of others.

8.3.1 Stage 1 – What are your own assumptions?

The first step is to consider your own views on motivation. We tend to believe early on in life that other people think and react in the same way that we do. We may figure out the fact that this isn't true on our own or may continue wondering why conflicts and misunderstandings of our motives go on around us until much later in life. In terms of motivation, the first thing to consider is how you like to be motivated and how you believe others are motivated.

Consider the models described previously and whether you ascribe to beliefs that employees are looking for responsibility and satisfaction or need to be carefully managed/controlled. Whatever you think, one thing will be true.

Your assumptions about the motivations of those you work with will impact how you treat them.

8.3.2 Stage 2 – Identify demotivators

Stage 2 is to look at the major areas of dissatisfaction and the factors that are damaging motivation.

This dissatisfaction may be driven from a lack of the equity factors in the three-factor theory or you could look at Herzberg's theory to see what might be missing.

A logical approach is first to consider the potential causes of dissatisfaction that you can see in the situation against the background of the different hygiene and motivation factors described previously.

Once you've given this some thought, you need to then do the obvious thing and get some feedback from the employees. This could be done one-to-one or you could set the identification of dissatisfaction factors as a task for a small group. This needs to be done carefully as, if they identify many causes that are then not addressed, this may actually serve to demotivate them. They might also not be aware of things being bad until they start to think about them, so be careful how you frame any such task.

This identification is a useful step because when you think about positive actions to improve motivation, it is easy to forget the negative influences that are in place. It's therefore important to look at these in isolation so that they are not missed.

8.3.3 Stage 3 – Identify and implement positive motivators

Stage 3 is to identify the positive motivators for the individuals and groups under your control.

This should be done using a balance of the understanding of the situation facing the organisation, the existing issues and the current causes of dissatisfaction. You also need to take into account the different types of motivators described previously.

Ideal positions for the company can be defined and then compared to the current status to identify gaps. Plans can then be put in place to address these gaps at a company level.

8.3.4 Stage 4 – Motivating at the individual level

This final stage looks at the motivators and needs for individuals, matching the individual preferences with the best approach possible under the current circumstances. In particular, the three-factor theory and McLelland's human motivation theory can be very useful.

8.3.5 Stage 5 – Monitor and amend as necessary

The best intentions and plans will nonetheless create unintended consequences. You need to look at the results and consider whether the organisation is seeing the results you expect. In particular, you need to consider at an individual level whether your actions have resulted in an improvement of motivation. In a small organisation or team this may be relatively simple but some of these improvements have been applied widely across the organisation. A better approach is to carry out employee surveys.

Tesco knows that 69 per cent of its employees find work interesting[10] and 72 per cent of Cooperative Group employees feel engaged with the business in terms of behavioural and emotional commitment.[11]

CASE STUDY

Paying attention makes a difference

The Hawthorne Experiments were carried out at a Western Electric plant in Illinois during the late 1920s and early 1930s.

The idea was to try to find the optimum work conditions by varying things such as the lighting level, length of breaks and the hours in the working day. The first experiment was carried out in the relay assembly room and over the period, most changes improved output. Even reversion to the original conditions would see output increase.

The impression is that people change their behaviour and potentially improve performance because they are being studied. There has been a lot of discussion about the real reasons behind the improvement but conventional wisdom, and perhaps common sense, suggests the improvement was partly down to the workers having someone interested in what they were doing, asking for their suggestions and responding to these.

A second experiment was carried out in the bank wiring room and was a classic example of unintended consequences. Financial incentives for performance were put in place but output actually went down!

The belief is that the informal groups created by the workers held more influence than management and the financial incentives were viewed suspiciously as a potential forerunner to firing some of the workers.

8.4 Management and groups

8.4.1 Benefits of groups

Intuitively, groups should provide the ability to generate better solutions than individuals alone. This is the concept of synergy, where the overall performance exceeds the 'sum of the parts' in the group.

This is particularly true when the group contains members with discrete skills and experience. They can provide a perspective on aspects of a problem that an individual could not achieve. However, if this specialist knowledge does not form part of the discussions, then the value of the group will be less strong.

The exercise of brainstorming also works better within a group as one person's comment can stimulate the thinking of the others and the ideas can build one upon the other.

SNAPSHOT

A telephone company in Canada faced severe problems as ice forming on wires would eventually build up to a point that the wire would snap. The company conducted a brainstorm to try to find a solution.

One person suggested getting polar bears to shake the telegraph poles as this would also shake the snow and ice from the wires. There was probably laughter at this suggestion, but the

SNAPSHOT

idea wasn't shut down. The question then arose: how to encourage the polar bears to shake the poles? The suggestion was to put food on top of the poles as the polar bears would shake the poles to get the food down. The group carried on and thought about how they could get food on top of the poles. At this point, someone suggested that you could use a helicopter to place the food on top of the poles.

The discussion had obviously got quite silly by this stage, but the group then realised that the helicopter dropping the food would itself blow the snow and ice from the wires. The food and polar bears were actually unnecessary – all they needed was a helicopter to fly along their wire routes.

8.4.2 Limitations of group decision making

There are, of course, a few downsides of decision making in groups.

'Group think' describes the way that a group may come up with a poor decision because, in part, no individual feels enough responsibility for the output that they create. The 'blame' for any such decision will be spread across a group and this lack of identification with one or two decision makers allows the group to develop solutions that an individual might reject out of hand.[12] The group may also be influenced by opinions provided by senior management prior to or during discussion of the topic, or fail to consider alternatives fully.

Potential solutions to this include encouraging all participants to review progress critically with one or more external experts present on major discussions to provide detailed information as well as an independent perspective.

Examples of group think include the decision to launch the Challenger space shuttle on its ill-fated mission.[13]

'Risky shift' is a phrase that denotes the dilution of responsibility from the individual to the group and the dangers in this transition.

Groups can also suffer as a result of time wasting and focusing on trivial matters to the detriment of getting on with the job at hand.

8.5 Understanding people and situations

As a final part on management as a distinct skill (as opposed to the tools and techniques found throughout this book), we'll consider some ways to improve understanding of our own decision making and firstly, how we perceive others' motives and actions.

8.5.1 Individual competence

It is sometimes difficult to understand how people can be so poor at something and yet not realise. Watch any reality talent show and you'll see the tone deaf proudly proclaiming themselves the next big thing in pop music. Management can be the same challenge. People don't necessarily understand their own ability (good or bad) and it's useful to look at the way that competence develops over time. This, of course, assumes it does develop!

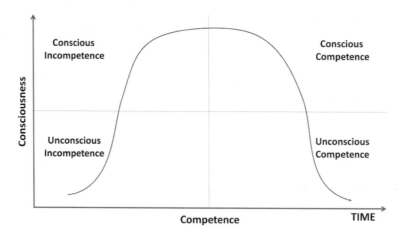

Figure 8.1: Competence development model

Figure 8.1 illustrates how individuals develop competence in an activity. Think of a young child playing a piano. They smash away at the keys and don't ever think to themselves that they are playing badly because they don't know what good playing is.

We may similarly be unaware that we are performing part or all of our work badly. It may simply never cross our mind. This can range from missing defective parts on a production line through to demotivating individuals through consistently negative feedback. We're doing a bad job and we don't even know it. This is unconscious incompetence in action.

If we are made aware of an issue then we may monitor it to try to eliminate it, or at least reduce the incidences of it. This is the beginning of conscious incompetence. We know that we're not doing a great job at something and we are aware of the mistakes as they happen.

This awareness of our limitations can prompt us to improve. This might be through training or practice, but noting the instances of mistakes and errors will help to reduce those until we may achieve conscious competence. In this state, we are pretty good at something and we know it through the absence of the mistakes and weaknesses that may previously have been very obvious.

As actions and habits become automatic, our awareness of them may fade so much that we don't even register the good performance any more. This is the unconscious competence and it's the drive to work you take, where you get out of the car and can't even remember the journey. Our subconscious is on 'auto-pilot' and we achieve our objective without much conscious effort.

If nothing else, this serves as a useful reminder that different people will be at different places on this development curve. In particular, the unconsciously competent person may struggle to sympathise with those less able and may certainly struggle to teach what they do as a lot of the ability is, as the description suggests, unconscious.

8.5.2 Working with perspectives

In neurolinguistic programming, a valuable exercise is to consider the viewpoints of both parties in a discussion or dispute from a number of perspectives.

The first-person perspective is how you think, feel and respond from your viewpoint in the interactions.

The second-person perspective places you as the person you are communicating with or with whom there is a problem. This provides an interesting point of view as you try to understand how it feels to be on the other side of the discussion/argument/transaction.

The final perspective is third person, where you stand back and look at the interaction between both parties, considering more deeply what is going on in both directions and trying to identify dispassionately some of the issues or concerns.

Often by putting ourselves into the shoes of other people, we can see our own behaviour and approach things in a different light.

An extension of this thinking can be done with a team.

EXERCISE

The key stakeholders connected to a particular issue are identified by the group. These are noted on Post-its and then placed one in front of every person in the group. In addition, a flipchart page is stuck to the wall and labelled for each stakeholder.

The group sits down and each person considers the situation from the perspective of the stakeholder defined on the Post-it in front of them. In turn, each person goes up to the flip chart page for the respective role and notes any insights they have about what is important in the situation for that particular role.

Each person has to find something new to add to the list for the role they are considering when it is their turn.

The trick to making this work is thinking and phrasing things as if you are the person in the role defined on the Post-it in front of you. Remain thinking like that until you change to the next 'role'.

To kick-start thinking, people can consider some generic questions about the issue being considered.

For example:

- Why is this important?
- What happens if we don't do this?
- What is my role in this (as the person marked on the Post-it)?
- Who and/or what are pushing for things to change?
- Who and/or what are pushing for things to stay the same?
- What is unique about this role's perspective on the issue?
- What can this role do to improve or advance the situation?
- How is this role reliant on other people?

8.5.3   Ladder of Inference

The concept of the Ladder of Inference was developed by Chris Argyris and then appeared in Peter Senge's book, *The Fifth Discipline*.[14] It is a fascinating insight and maps the way that we move from concrete information and experience and evolve that through to actions.

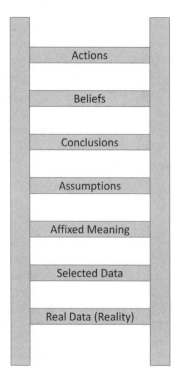

Figure 8.2: Ladder of Inference

Let's look at the lowest rung first and move step by step to the top.

Table 8.8: Rungs on the Ladder of Inference

Rung	Description
Reality – real data and experience	This is reality – not subjective, not interpreted. This is what actually is happening.
Selected data and experience	From the full set of reality, we pay attention to only part.
Affixed meaning	We take the selected reality, interpret it and then affix meaning to it.
Assumptions	From the meaning we have affixed, we develop assumptions.
Conclusions	From these assumptions, we form conclusions.
Beliefs	These conclusions become beliefs.
Actions	We then act on the basis of our beliefs.

The following example shows how people can step through the ladder of inference and, in this case, get the wrong answer.

STOP AND THINK

Robert was asked to join a new department run by Mark. Although initially enthusiastic, Robert eventually turned down the offer. The following is Mark's ladder of inference about the reasons.
1. Mark is disappointed. He wanted Robert to join him (reality).
2. Mark focuses on the reasons why Robert is not changing teams (selected reality).
3. This is another example of Mark being 'attacked' by the head of Robert's current department, who must have ensured Robert would not switch (interpreted reality).
4. Robert is staying where he is because he felt his current manager has more influence (assumption).
5. Robert is playing a political game (conclusion).
6. Robert is disloyal to Mark (belief).
7. Robert should be made to regret his actions through being frozen out of projects run by Mark (action).

In fact, Robert had considered the opportunity and wanted to join Mark's team. However, as he was the strongest fee earner in his department, his current boss threatened to resign if Robert changed departments, as losing Robert would create huge issues for the current team.

Robert chose to stay where he was through personal loyalty and because he realised the damage he would do to his current colleagues.

Mark was plainly wrong and Robert (as he'd appreciate later on) was gullible for being emotionally blackmailed so easily.

One interesting feature of this model is that it can short-circuit and start to reinforce itself.

Once someone reaches the belief point, this can influence the way that they select where they pay their attention (selected reality). That is likely to lead to a reinforcing cycle where the person only pays more and more attention to the things that support their view (belief) of the situation. In psychological terms, this is similar to confirmation bias, where someone lends more credence to facts that support their opinion.

Being aware of this pattern can help you to understand better where your own interpretations may be going astray.

EXERCISE

To use this model on your own thinking, consider a decision that you are contemplating.
As a first step, identify where you are on the ladder:
● Collecting data?
● Selecting data?
● Interpreting data?

EXERCISE continued

● Looking at potential assumptions or considering ones you have already made?
● Formulating conclusions or evaluating them?
● Defining a course of action?

Secondly, once you have worked out the rung you are currently 'on' then trace your path backward down the inferences you have made at each step. At each point on the ladder, you can consider both the drivers for each inference and whether there were other alternatives at that point. Stepping down from the top, you can pose questions such as the following.

Actions	Why did I select this action?
	What else should I have considered?
Beliefs	What beliefs led to selecting that action?
	Where does that belief come from?
Conclusions	How did I come to that conclusion?
	Does it make sense?
	Is the conclusion sound?
Assumptions	What are the assumptions used?
	What has been overlooked or ignored?
	Why were these assumptions selected?
Affixed meaning	What meaning have I attached to this data?
	How else could it be interpreted?
	Why did I look at it this way?
Selected data	Why was this data selected?
	Why was other available data ignored?
	What else should be considered?

Summary

In general, management is a mix of different skills and focuses to help develop and deliver objectives for individuals and groups. This will require monitoring en route to correct mistakes and misconceptions, as well as support to provide the necessary knowledge and resources.

Management is particularly about getting the right performance out of individuals. This is a complex area but having a motivated team is more likely to deliver good results. There are a variety of different models of motivation and care should be taken to try to recognise the different motivators that work best for different people.

What's next?

We've talked a little about some of the skills of a manager in understanding and motivating individuals and groups. The next chapter will consider the more elusive concept known as leadership.

Notes

1. *Concept of the Corporation*, Peter Drucker, Transaction Publications, New Jersey, 1996.
2. 'System 4: A resource from improving public administration', Likert, R. (1981), *Public Administration Review*, 41(6), 674–8.
3. 'Managing without a boss: System 5', Likert, J.G. and Araki, C.T. (1986), *Leadership & Organization Development Journal*, 7(3), 17–20.
4. *Leader Attitudes and Group Effectiveness*, Fred Fielder, Greenwood Publishing Group, Connecticut, 1981.
5. *The New Leadership: Managing Participation in Organizations*, Vroom and Jago, Prentice Hall, New Jersey, 1988.
6. *The Achieving Society*, David McClelland, Simon and Schuster, New York, 1967.
7. *The Human Side of Enterprise*, Douglas McGregor, McGraw-Hill, New York, 1960.
8. *The Motivation to Work*, F. Herzberg, B. Mausner and B.B. Snyderman, John Wiley & Sons, New Jersey, 1959.
9. *The Enthusiastic Employee*, Sirota, Mischkind and Meltzer, Prentice Hall, New Jersey, 2005.
10. *Tesco Annual Report 2011.*
11. *Cooperative Group Annual Report 2011.*
12. *Victims of Groupthink*, Irving Janis, Houghton Mifflin Company, Boston, 1972.
13. 'Twenty-Five Years of Groupthink Theory and Research: Lessons from the Evaluation of a Theory', Turner and Pratkanis, *Organisational Behaviour and Human Decision Processes*, February/March 1998.
14. *The Fifth Discipline: The Art and Practice of the Learning Organisation*, Peter Senge, Doubleday, New York, 1990.

9
Leadership

Leadership is the art of getting someone else to do something you want done because he wants to do it.[1]

Dwight D. Eisenhower

People ask the difference between a leader and a boss... The leader leads, and the boss drives.[2]

Theodore Roosevelt

9.1 The characteristics of leadership

9.1.1 Defining leadership

The management thinker Peter Drucker created an interesting distinction in thinking about management and leadership.

Effectiveness is doing the right thing. Efficiency is doing the thing right.[3]

This creates an interesting contrast between the more strategic view of 'effectiveness' and the more immediate focus of 'efficiency'. Both play an important part in management as getting only one right is not good enough. Doing the wrong things really well or screwing up the right things won't advance the organisation.

Stephen R Covey put it beautifully:

Management is efficiency in climbing the ladder of success; leadership determines whether the ladder is leaning against the right wall.[4]

Professor Warren G. Bennis had a slightly different take, putting responsibility for doing the right thing on to leaders.

Leaders are people who do the right thing; managers are people who do things right.[5]

It is clear that there are significant perceived differences between the manager and the leader although there will be overlaps between the two according to the individual's viewpoint.

Attributes of leadership

Let's start with some generic attributes of leadership.

- **Vision** – The leader is seen as creating an inspirational vision of the future for the organisation.
- **Building the team to deliver the vision** – developing their capabilities (through selection, coaching, mentoring, training, gathering of experience, learning, recruitment).
- **Motivation** – managing the environment so that individuals and groups receive the appropriate rewards and recognition for their efforts, such that both the effort and achievement levels remain high.
- **Inspiration** – stimulating individuals to an increased level of belief and subsequent activity.
- **Monitoring** – measuring progress against the vision and ensuring that the organisation delivers.

Creating the environment in which the team can succeed

It's a tough challenge to deliver successfully even a few of those attributes, but it's also true that some will be more important than others in an organisation at a particular time.

The following scorecard is one approach I've developed to consider both the relative importance of these attributes but also how well they are being delivered.

9.1.2 The key leadership focus scorecard

Take a moment to think about either your own style or those of the leaders in your business.

How much time is spent on each part of the previous list of attributes? It's quite typical to focus more on areas that are particular concerns for the organisation at the time, or on the things that are more 'interesting'.

Secondly, what do you consider the correct level of attention should be for each factor?

EXERCISE

Pick one of the leaders in your own organisation or yourself if appropriate.

On a table like the one below, fill in the current score for each attribute according to how well you think they are doing (the 'How is it going?' column). You score them (out of 10) on delivering against each attribute.

Then mark down the amount of time spent on each attribute as a percentage.

The first column (Now) is how they are currently dividing up their time. The final column on the right (Ideal) is the percentage of time you think should be spent given the situation in the organisation and the challenges it is facing.

EXERCISE continued

Key leadership focus scorecard	How is it going?	Where is effort being spent?	
Focus area	**Current score (1 (low) to 10 (high))**	**% of time spent Now**	**% of time spent Ideal**
Vision			
Building			
Motivation			
Inspiration			
Monitoring			
Creating the environment			

What do the results mean? Only you understand the organisation being led and so only you can really say how well or badly the leadership fit is to the situation. However, big gaps between the way time is being spent and how you ideally think it should be spent will highlight areas for potential improvement.

As mentioned earlier, our preference is often to do things that interest us rather than the things we must or should do. Don't be surprised if the scores in the table above are skewed towards the preferences of the person in question. Circumstances can catch up with us during the year and knock us off track. A big gap between the 'Now' and 'Ideal' may indicate serious fires to put out in the business. Those are important but leadership is about the longer term and perhaps fire fighting (and preventing fires) should be delegated further down the organisation.

9.1.3 Big Hairy Audacious Goals (BHAGs) versus 'sensible' targets

> Never give an order that can't be obeyed.[6]
> Douglas MacArthur

General MacArthur presumably had never heard of BHAGs but was smart enough to understand the dangers they can create! The concept of BHAGs can be very badly applied. MacArthur's point was to maintain credibility as a leader by never demanding more from someone than they could deliver. This didn't mean the order wasn't a stretch, or that the person receiving the order sometimes did not believe that the order was possible. It meant MacArthur believed it could be done and knew the damage he might suffer as a leader if his orders were unattainable.

Collins and Porras came up with the term Big Hairy Audacious Goals.[7] It's an interesting concept but is one that is misapplied by people who don't understand it. Sometimes, it allows a lazy manager to congratulate themselves for setting the most ridiculous set of targets for their team.

Rather than accept they have asked the impossible, these managers are thinking they are clever by setting BHAGs. For the most part, their team isn't thinking the same. They may be saying yes and smiling but some will be firing CVs out of the printer while others will be hoping the target will change before delivery. All are likely to know the audacious goal being set is impossible.

BHAGs themselves are a perfectly acceptable way of providing a stretch target. President John F. Kennedy told Congress the key facts of his audacious goal to land a man on the moon in just 25 seconds of a speech.

> First, I believe that this nation should commit itself to achieving the goal, before this decade is out, of landing a man on the moon and returning him safely to the earth. No single space project in this period will be more impressive to mankind, or more important for the long-range exploration of space; and none will be so difficult or expensive to accomplish.[8]

However, President Kennedy followed up that introduction by further detailing the practical steps and support that would be provided to achieve this incredible feat. As President of the most powerful country in the world, he had the resources at his disposal to make this goal happen but nonetheless, it remains one of the most extraordinary audacious goals in history.

In business, setting a BHAG can work well for an organisation – for example, Nike's aim to 'crush Adidas' or Tata's vision to provide cars at a price almost all can afford (the Nano). However, the damage to motivation in a business can be serious if the goal is not sufficiently well thought through and communicated.

For example, if you tell me my target is to do the near impossible in a year and communicate that in a way that I feel my job depends on achieving that target, you're unlikely to get the right result. If feedback is acceptable and normal in our relationship, then I might debate the attainability of the target to try to get something more sensible. If that kind of open communication doesn't exist in the organisation, then I'm likely to stay quiet and you might assume that I agree.

If the target remains near impossible, some of the team may buy into it initially while others will be on the fence or actively seek work elsewhere in the company or outside. The problem is the subtle sabotage that occurs. If something is plainly impossible, the team won't do their best and put in the extra effort that might be needed to achieve it. They will leave at 5pm on a Friday night even if an important task has just landed on their desk for their urgent attention. If they believe the project is doomed anyway, they will consciously or unconsciously hold back and not go the extra mile required to deliver the biggest and most ambitious projects.

However, if the BHAG is pitched to them as an interesting thing to do – something to explore and try hard to see if it is possible – then the psychology is different. This will inspire some and will avoid the potential demotivation and panic that can occur when a BHAG is imposed with no apparent choice or discussion around it.

Leadership should be about inspiring people to greatness – not trying to scare or back them into it.

CASE STUDY

The Leadership of Jack Welch, Chairman and CEO at General Electric[9,10]

Jack Welch was named 'Manager of the Century' by Fortune Magazine for his leadership as Chairman and CEO at General Electric (GE) from 1981 to 2001. He became synonymous with the exceptional results at the company during his tenure as well as for the clarity of his management thinking and approach.

He oversaw a quadrupling of revenues during his tenure and the company's rise to become the most valuable company in the world at the time.

His principles were simple but underpinned the success of the company. The most controversial was perhaps the fact that the bottom-performing 10 per cent of employees would be asked to leave the company each year. At the same time, the top 20 per cent would be rewarded with share options, bonuses and other incentives. This was consistent with his belief that the people in the business are the most important asset as they are the ones delivering the results.

He saw his job as selecting the right people and providing the support they need to succeed.

The overall streamlining of the business earned him the nickname 'Neutron Jack' – after a neutron bomb which leaves buildings standing while decimating the human population.

Welch is also noted for the introduction of the Six Sigma quality approach in the 1990s while creating a more streamlined and less bureaucratic company.

One key to the reshaping of the company was the refinement of the portfolio of business units over time. Welch wanted to be number one or number two in a market and companies with lower positions were liable to be to be treated in line with a key Welch phrase: 'Fix, close or sell.' Welch's view was that any company that was not in the top two in a market and that lacked any advantage based on technology should be heavily scrutinised.

As a leader, Welch has been praised by colleagues for his consistency and he said,

> You don't get anywhere if you keep changing your ideas. The only way to change people's minds is with consistency… the more simply your idea is defined, the better it is.

As evidence of a different aspect of this drive for consistency, many of the key messages and core values for the company would be printed on a values card given to all employees. One such message perhaps sums up one of Jack Welch's key strengths.

> Create a clear, simple, reality-based vision… and communicate it to all constituencies.

9.2   Power

Leadership is about the use of power. That power may relate to an individual's position in an organisation, or be derived from their personal characteristics and skills. This section will consider different forms of power in organisations.

9.2.1 Sources of power

A widely used scheme for categorising different sources of power was developed by French and Raven in their studies of social power as far back as 1959.[11] The original five sources were later expanded to seven.[12]

The seven sources of power can be divided into two logical groups – positional power and personal power.

9.2.2 Positional power

These sources of power are called 'positional' because they are given to an individual by the organisation as a result of the position they hold in the hierarchy. They do not relate to the individual, but to the formal position they are appointed to.

Table 9.1: Types of positional power

Type of power	Description
Legitimate power	This derives from a person's formal position in an organisation and the authority that is delegated to them. In good organisations, the way that power is distributed down into the management hierarchy will be clear, unambiguous and consistent with giving managers the tools they need to achieve their own and their group's objectives.
Reward power	This refers to the discretionary rewards that are under the control or influence of the manager. It will range from obvious rewards to do with promotions, salary increases, job titles, bonuses and holiday rights, through to secondary rewards such as where people sit, flexibility of working hours and awards.
Coercive power	In the same way that managers can use their legitimate power and authority to reward, they can also use the same source of power to punish. Coercive power is the ability to withhold rewards or worsen the working situation for an individual or group. This can be through changes to working practices and environment, to withdrawal of privileges and finally on to the toughest of sanctions (e.g. formal warnings, demotion or even being fired).

9.2.3 Personal power

In contrast to the sources of power above, the sources of personal power are all about the individual rather than the position they hold in the organisation.

Table 9.2: Types of personal power

Type of power	Description
Expert power	This source of power derives from the specialist knowledge and/or experience that an individual possesses. It has to be relatively scarce or the expertise will not have any value and hence power. This type of power can lead to promotion to a specialist role where the expert power is then complemented by positional power.
Referent power	Referent power derives from admiration for an individual. That can be because of their personality, achievements, approach or management style.
Connection power	The ability to learn from, leverage and refer to an external network that provides value to an individual within the context of the organisation is called connection power. It's a network of contacts that may also have what would be called 'the old school tie' effect in the UK or *wasta* in the Arabic world.
Information power	In theory, a manager should know more about what is happening in the organisation than the people who report to them. However, at any level in an organisation, there are those who are better at gaining information and these may be able to use this resource/skill as a source of power or influence.

9.2.4 Personal leadership

The first person that you need to think about leading is yourself. If you apply long hours and all your effort at work, but ignore considering your own future, you are unlikely to realise whatever dreams you have.

STOP AND THINK

Think about this for a moment. You are 70 years of age. You are looking out of a window. What can you see? The slopes of a mountain? A river at the end of a garden? A harbour with your yacht moored there?

Why I'm writing this is because you need to start with the end in mind. That's as true of your life as it is for work objectives. What can you hear? Are there children there? Do you want to have kids? If you'd achieved all you wanted by then, what would that be? Lecturing at a university, owning your own company?

This is the only point in the book where I'll do this, but I'm telling you to put the book down for a moment, get a coffee if you like and just focus on you and what you want. Take as long as you need.

. . . .

Welcome back!

So, if you know the end that you want, you next need to realise that planning for it starts today. That's the same if you're 20 or 65. There is the place you want to be and the distance you need to go to get there. You might be very close or seemingly miles away, but what you want to achieve for you will not come by accident and you probably need to start planning and thinking about it very soon (if not immediately).

To get that CEO post you probably need to be a general manager in a company like Xyz Inc. How do you get that job? What will it take? Who can help you?

To write that book you'll need to find some time. Are you going to take a holiday or get up early and write until it's time for work?

The next thing you'll have to think about is who you are and what you can presently do. To kick that off, we'll look at leadership/management styles as you can then consider which ones apply to you and how you use them under different circumstances.

9.2.5 Leadership/management styles

To kick off, we'll·look at three generic styles that most managers will use at different times and depending on the circumstances.

Table 9.3: Generic management styles

Style	Description
Transactional	This focuses on the use of reward and punishment to motivate people. Management becomes the application of these at a high level, or day-to-day aspects of these two extremes, to keep the operation going. That will include providing feedback and assisting in obtaining the resources/knowledge/ training needed to succeed.
Transformational	This is what is often termed 'leadership' – inspiring individuals or teams to perform. This style of leadership requires high visibility and significant face time. This time will be spent explaining, cajoling, persuading and otherwise working to ensure that the future vision is achieved.
Laissez-faire	Derived from the French to leave something alone, this style sees the manager only slightly involved in the actual act of management. For the most part, the manager just lets people get on with what they are doing. In a strong organisation where objectives are clear and employees are experienced, this style can be appropriate as the manager minimises 'unnecessary' interventions with the team. However, if the team is inexperienced or objectives are unclear (or both), then this style is completely inappropriate. Similarly, if the company's situation moves very fast, this style risks failure to communicate changes in objectives and priorities.

Few people adopt one style all the time. The trick is to use whichever style is appropriate at the time.

9.2.6 Desired leadership behaviours

The transformational style has been described in numerous different ways over the years and the following elements seem the most important to consider. Leaders:

- demonstrate the behaviour they want to see from others;
- encourage creation and consideration of new ideas;
- look after the well-being of their team;
- manage pressure from shareholders or more senior management (i.e. they are the lightning rod for their team); and
- inspire and motivate individuals.

That is a significant set of attributes, but transformation doesn't happen easily. If you are going to move people out of their comfort zone and change behaviours, you can do it in the short term through transactional means – threats or rewards. However, you're not impacting the culture within the organisation. To change behaviours and beliefs more permanently, then transformational leadership will be required. This is discussed in more detail in Chapter 10.

Leadership can be described in a number of different ways.

Table 9.4: Descriptions of leadership

Approach	Description
Behaviour	This approach looks at the behaviour exhibited by leaders.
Personality/traits	This considers the personal abilities and characteristics of the leader.
Contingency	Here, the approach employed varies depending on the circumstances. For example, it can be very interesting to see how the leadership style changes when a person is under pressure.
Power	This looks at the use of different forms of power and influence to achieve what they need.

9.2.7 Ten characteristics of leaders

The following characteristics have been associated with leaders in an organisation in management thinking:

1. Problem solving
2. A variety of interests and a sociable nature
3. Positive attitude to subordinates
4. Self-confidence
5. Self-discipline
6. Enthusiasm
7. Manners
8. Communication
9. Drive to achieve
10. Emotional stability

You may already be thinking about leaders you've encountered and are questioning whether they have some of those characteristics. However, if you wanted to define what a leader should be like, you'd probably draw up a list similar to the one above.

The more of these characteristics an individual possesses, the more likely they will be able to fulfil a leadership position well.

9.3 Leadership strength

The leader has to be practical and a realist, yet must talk the language of the visionary and the idealist.[13]

Eric Hoffer

Hoffer's statement is put into sharp relief by the principles in the following story.

9.3.1 The Stockdale Paradox

In *Good to Great*, Jim Collins describes the Stockdale Paradox.[14]

During the Vietnam War, Admiral Stockdale was held for eight years in captivity. This was undoubtedly a very challenging situation and Stockdale himself was repeatedly tortured. Against this terrible backdrop, he noticed the differing fortunes of those around him and how this related to their mindset.

Those who were very optimistic held on to hope like a lifejacket – saying that they would be out by Christmas but then having their hopes dashed when Christmas rolled around and they were still in captivity. Then they might say it would be Easter when they were freed and the same disappointment would strike them when they were still held on that date. In fact, these people were not facing the reality of the situation. Their optimism was a way of avoiding the terrible reality of the situation and when finally they had to face up to their true situation, they crumbled.

Some who faced up to the reality immediately presumably would have cracked quickly but Stockdale managed to walk the line between ignoring the situation and collapsing under the strain.

Stockdale himself was fully aware of his situation but instead of hiding from it, he worked hard to support the morale of the men. He said:

You must retain faith that you will prevail in the end, regardless of the difficulties. AND at the same time... You must confront the most brutal facts of your current reality, whatever they might be.[14]

That is an amazing challenge for a leader but one that is also valid for the tough times in a business. Too many managers ignore the reality and hope for a miracle to save the situation. Others can't confront the problems and succumb to them, losing the confidence and backing of their team.

9.3.2   Strong leadership every day

If things are bad, you as a leader cannot simply hope they go away or wait for some miracle to make things right. Those may not be conscious thoughts but you see this type of thinking in some companies.

Nick Leeson caused the collapse of Barings by taking increasingly large trading gambles in an effort to recoup previous losses. He was hoping that one last big gamble would clear away his previous debts.

Other managers are ignoring problems because raising these as issues would draw attention to them or highlight their own failure. They therefore drift along with projects, departments and even businesses that are in serious trouble (or worse), and are not willing or able to admit the truth of the situation.

It's a trap people can fall into when they know things are bad but there is no apparent solution. They'll talk up the situation and act as if things are fine because of the cost of admitting the truth – whether that is the psychological cost or in terms of damage to their reputation.

To be a top leader, you need to be able to confront the harshest reality about your situation with clarity. However, as with Stockdale, you have to combine that with the personal strength, courage and commitment that the organisation will overcome the adversity.

If you're facing the senior management team, the workforce, the unions or the media, any sign of weakness or hint that you do not have the courage of your own convictions will undermine your message.[1] That doesn't mean you're not honest about the situation. What it does mean, though, is that possessing the belief that you can overcome the difficult circumstances while fully recognising how hard things are is a rare and valuable attribute for a leader.

On a personal level, the Stockdale Paradox is a useful tool to remind us that when we're aiming for the toughest targets or following the hardest routes, we should not forget the occasional reality check on our progress. Only by recognising where we really are can we then plot a new path to get to our destination.

Summary

Leadership is a challenging combination of different attributes from vision through to creation of the environment in which that vision can be delivered. Through the life of an organisation, and as the external environment changes, the required mix of these attributes will change.

Leaders bring with them a combination of personal qualities and experience that give them what is known as personal power. This is then combined with the positional power they hold in the organisation.

It is important to understand our own strengths and weaknesses, and recognise how we cope with difficult times in an organisation. The ability to confront challenges while still showing positive leadership is a rare but incredibly valuable characteristic.

What's next?

The next chapter looks at change management. Changes provide both opportunities and also a real need for leadership, and the chapter looks at the other elements in completing a successful change programme.

Notes

1. *The Federal Career Service: A Look Ahead,* Society for Personnel Administration, 1954.
2. *Social Justice and Popular Rule: Essays, Addresses, and Public Statements*, Theodore Roosevelt, Ayer Co Pub, New Hampshire, 1923.
3. *The Effective Executive – The Definitive Guide to Getting the Right Things Done*, Peter Drucker, HarperBusiness, New York, 2006.
4. *The 7 Habits of Highly Effective People,* Stephen Covey, the Free Press, New York, 2004.
5. *Leaders: Strategies for taking charge,* Warren Bennis and Burt Nanus, HarperCollins, New York, 2003.
6. *Wisdom for the Busy Leader*, Pat Richie, Xulon Press, Maitland, 2007.
7. *Built to Last: Successful Habits of Visionary Companies,* Collins and Porras, HarperBusiness, New York, 2004.
8. 1961 speech to the US Congress by President John F. Kennedy.
9. *Winning*, Jack and Suzy Welch, HarperBusiness, New York, 2005.
10. *Jack: Straight From The Gut*, Jack Welch, Headline Publishing, London, 2003.
11. *Studies in Social Power*, Dorwin Cartwright, Research Center for Group Dynamics, Institute for Social Research, University of Michigan, 1959.
12. *Management of Organisational Behaviour*, P. Hersey and K. Blanchard, Prentice Hall, New Jersey, 2007.
13. *The True Believer: Thoughts on the Nature of Mass Movements*, Eric Hoffer, Harper Perennial, New York, 2009.
14. *Good to Great*, Jim Collins, Random House Business, New York, 2001.

10
Change management

If you want to drive change, it's not a passive event.[1]
Jeffrey R. Immelt, Chairman of GE

10.1   Introduction

Jeffrey R. Immelt, Jack Welch's successor as CEO at GE, praised Welch's leadership. He cited the case of becoming a Six Sigma quality business, one where there are less than 3.4 Defects Per Million Opportunities (DPMO). From kick-off in 1995 to the target date of 2000, this objective was part of most meetings and took up half of the annual personnel review.[1]

Immelt said, 'If a leader wants to drive change, he or she must intervene.'

Companies are continually changing for many reasons such as:

- opportunities to become more efficient;
- an external driver creating pressure on the company (e.g. economic forces or a new competitive threat);
- a need to evolve or radically change the culture in the organisation;
- new technologies to integrate; and
- a need to improve internal processes.

The volatility of the economic climate means that serious external changes are likely to hit organisations even more frequently than in the past.

The change may also be smaller and more subtle in the organisation. Not every change is part of a designated programme.

You'll also sometimes hear people explain how they change things but they do it without the need to manage it formally. It may be true in exceptional cases but drifting through a change and hoping you get to the right result is more a triumph of hope over expectation.

The principle of a change process is deceptively simple.

1. Identify where you are now.
2. Define where you need to be in the future.
3. Plan how you get there.
4. Implement the change.
5. Monitor progress.

6. Course-correct as needed.

7. Finish.

Given how simple that is, it is quite extraordinary how badly change programmes can go.

STOP AND THINK

How many change programmes have you been involved in?

You may have started thinking about the obvious programmes that had change in the title. Now think about any mergers, acquisitions, divestments, system integration projects, changes to working practices, office moves, centralisations or decentralisations you've been part of. Each one of those is a change process.

Now ask yourself how many of those went well. I've asked this question of hundreds of executives, partners, directors and CEOs, and only a handful have ever claimed to be part of a successful change process.

Change is not easy and if you want to successfully run a change programme, you need to plan and execute it very carefully. Some types of project can be badly run and still succeed (for example, you can overrun on cost while developing a new product, but the product itself can be fine). However, change projects are not like that. If they are run badly then the results are likely to be very poor – either not achieving the targets or in collateral damage to morale and performance en route.

This chapter will outline some of the high-level principles involved in managing change successfully, then go through the anatomy of an organisation-level change.

10.2 Types of change

10.2.1 What's the objective?

Beer and Nohria from Harvard Business School came up with the terms Theory E and Theory O to define two extreme ends of the change spectrum in a business.[2]

Theory O is about organisation and looks at trying to achieve cultural change to improve performance. Changing culture is a long-term objective and one that takes years rather than months. However, Theory O describes the efforts to better integrate employees with the company's goals – training and empowering them to work in new ways. Although initiated at the top of the organisation, the longer-term benefits of this type of change programme are that the improvements can come bottom-up through the organisation.

Theory E is about economics. This is a shorter-term objective targeting the improvements in the returns for shareholders. It is particularly focused on reshaping an organisation through rightsizing, divestments of unprofitable parts of the business and general measures to cut costs.

In reality, a combination of the two styles may be more effective in the medium term for an organisation.

SNAPSHOT

Managing Change and Transition quotes the revolution at GE under Jack Welch as an excellent example of a project that combined elements of both 'O' and 'E'. In the short term, Welch looked hard at the company and divested business units that were not profitable or that were not strong enough in their own market. This is pure 'E'.

Once the company was in a better shape for the future, the focus switched to many activities that are more classically 'O' based. For example, the 'Work Out' programme involved workers at all levels in the company, identifying and resolving issues within the business.[3]

10.2.2   Comparing Theory E, Theory O and combined projects

The following table, based on Beer and Nohria's work, expands on the difference between the discrete approaches and combining them. The categories are amended from their article based on experience from real change implementations.

Table 10.1: Comparing Theory E, Theory O and combined projects

	Theory E	**Theory O**	**Theory E and O combined**
Goals	Maximise shareholder value. The focus is on financial results which will improve the metrics used to value a company and therefore increase the value of shares and/or allow bigger dividends to be paid out.	Develop organisational capabilities. This means people-based improvement of the skills and competences – as well as the cultural and organisational influences that drive behaviour.	Combines the shorter-term, economic focus of Theory E with the longer-term, capacity building from Theory O.
Leadership	Management and direction of the changes come from the top.	More participative approach with bottom-up input on the relevant changes needed and creation of potential solutions.	Some parts of the decision-making processes (on shorter-term efficiencies and cost savings) may become more participative but the big strategic decisions probably remain driven by management.

	Theory E	Theory O	Theory E and O combined
Focus	Hard elements of the organisation (structures, SBUs, systems, processes).	Softer elements linking to culture and employee behaviour.	Should be the optimum approach as the hard and soft elements of an organisation are never entirely discrete and considering the O and E elements together should deliver better overall results.
Process	Should be carefully planned and structured.	More fluid as solutions develop during the programme and are liable to evolution as actual behaviour is compared to what is intended.	Both elements should combine to inform the overall shaping of the change programme.
Rewards	Can be based on purely financial metrics.	Reward changes in behaviour.	Combined approach.

10.3 High level fundamentals of change management (unfreeze – change – refreeze)

Psychologist Kurt Lewin developed the simple unfreeze – change – refreeze analogy to illustrate the life of a change programme.[4]

An organisation that doesn't understand the need for change will be 'frozen'. Any attempts to reshape it will be very difficult and met with significant resistance. Changes will be resented and seen as management meddling unless the reasons underlying the change are properly understood. You need to unfreeze the situation, make the change and then refreeze it in order to restore stability to the organisation.

10.3.1 Preparation

Serious changes in an organisation can be kept quiet during the planning phase for only a limited period of time. You might get four weeks in which things can remain secret but the longer you plan before getting into a managed unfreeze phase, the more you risk things unfreezing themselves as the news leaks out and you face potentially significant unintended consequences.

10.3.2   Unfreeze

Before you 'unfreeze' the situation, there will be little appetite for change. If you put a (hypothetical) frog in a pan of water and gradually increase the temperature, the frog will allow itself to boil to death. However, if you drop the frog straight into boiling water, it will jump out immediately.

Something has to happen to unfreeze the situation and allow change to take place.

The first step is to ensure that the organisation understands the need for the change. This is described in different ways. There is the classic 'lion in the room' or the creation of a 'burning platform' to create the urgency needed for the change. In both cases the urgent nature of the danger means you would move without question. If you compare that to what happens when a fire alarm goes off in your building, there is nothing like the same sense of urgency. The typical reaction seems to be to stare at each other asking if it is a drill and expecting the alarm to be turned off.

There is one rule for predicting people's behaviour when faced with a change: For people to change, the pain of staying in the same place has to be greater than the pain of undertaking the change. If it isn't, they probably won't.

The important thing is to ensure that people understand that the current way of working cannot or should not continue. This is equally true whether the company is prospering and is, for example, undertaking a merger, or is in trouble and needs to reorganise.

This unfreezing process essentially creates stress for those in the organisation and suddenly outcomes that were previously unlikely become possible. Staff members who were previously happy to remain in the company might now start looking for a job. Highly productive individuals may become almost paralysed by concerns over what is happening. Casual conversations and gossip will all turn themselves to what is happening with the change programme and rumours will crop up out of nowhere.

The simple truth is that some of us can endure significant and ongoing change while others find it incredibly challenging to endure.

You want your organisation to be back to normal as fast as possible so the change phase in Lewin's three-stage model needs to be done well and done quickly. Once a change programme is underway, it should be completed in the shortest time possible that allows it to be achieved successfully.

SNAPSHOT

One organisation spent time explaining the reducing cash in the organisation to their employees. The management team ended the presentation and invited questions but had not done their homework on how to respond. Employees suggested cutting external sponsorship of events, management salaries and then descended into unfair criticism of past programmes. The management team were unprepared for the direction that the meeting took and were unable to rebut these criticisms.

In fact, sponsorship was a fraction of 1 per cent of the overall revenues, and the past programmes were of course irrelevant in discussing the future of the organisation.

10.3.3   Make the change

The change phase is where things start to happen. People start to work towards the objectives and can start to see the light at the end of the tunnel.

10.3.4   Refreeze

Remember the organisation, or a part at least, has been put into a state of flux. The refreeze is where you stabilise things.

This means people understand what they have to do and are already doing it. It means the change is over and so this needs to be clearly signalled to everyone. If you don't do this then you risk the stress and uncertainty continuing. You want all the unwanted side effects of unfreezing the situation to be over.

To mark the completion of the programme, there should be an event of some sort. That might be a celebration dinner or just a meeting of all the staff, but the message has to be clear. The change programme is complete and it's back to business as usual from that point onwards.

That's a high-level look – now let's disassemble the parts to understand better what happens during the process.

10.4   The context for change – are you ready?

Let's consider the 'lion in the room' in the context of an organisation and the psychology of individual employees. Highly successful companies making big profits are less likely to recognise let alone implement any major changes. 'If it ain't broke, don't fix it' will be the mantra and this may be fine for a period. However, the success often masks the need to be more competitive.

At the height of their domination of the photocopier market, Xerox realised their cost to manufacture one of the machines was actually higher than the sales cost of their new Japanese competitors. Suddenly a lion!

Kodak's high profits in the film era are said to have masked the underlying inefficiencies in the business.

For these and similar businesses, there is no lion in the room when times are good. There is no screaming need to fix things and so things don't tend to change.

However, it's also not enough that the senior management alone understand the need to change. For every person in favour of change there will normally be at least one against and more who just aren't that interested. It is vital that the message that change is needed and desirable is clearly shared across the organisation!

This shouldn't be a vague promise of good times ahead or unstated concerns over the coming months. This has to be a clear and unambiguous statement of the need for the change along with supporting evidence to absolutely minimise the number of people that don't understand (or don't want to understand) the need for things to change.

If you're sat in an office, in a remote site within an organisation, then why would programme X affect you and, more importantly, why should you contribute to making it work? The answer is that every relevant person needs to understand that things can't remain as they are and they must contribute to make the change work.

10.5 Are you ready – credibility and respect

The next question is: who is going to lead the change? That doesn't automatically mean the CEO or Managing Director. They are the head of the executive team and their job is to manage. Their influence on the change process is obviously enormous – the buck stops with them! However, they may not be the best person to be the visible face of the process.

For every inspirational leader like Steve Jobs, there will be many more CEOs who are exceptional at their jobs but who are not remotely charismatic or inspirational. The same is true of business unit leaders and managers throughout the organisation. At whatever level the change is going to take place – whether it is a minor change to a business unit or a company-wide transformation – the change process needs to have the right leader.

Let's cut to the heart of this. The change process involves trust and respect. That is never automatically given and is a fragile thing that can easily be destroyed. Someone new to a company may not have earned enough trust to be the leader of the toughest change programme. Equally, someone may not have the personal credibility to carry off a serious change if they:

● are relatively unknown;
● are too junior in the organisation;
● have previously manipulated people or lied within the organisation; or
● have a poor reputation.

The strange thing is that someone relatively junior in an organisation may possess all the traits needed to carry off a challenging change process, but the audience of employees and other stakeholders may not believe they carry the power needed to back up their words. If you don't believe someone has that power, you are likely to discount much of what they say because they are relying on someone else to deliver on what is being said.

10.6 The story has to be right

The content and style of any presentation about change needs to be considered very carefully as you are trying to be very clear and compelling. This is particularly true of the first time that a major programme is introduced within the company. First impressions will count!

This is also the first opportunity with the larger audience to illustrate the approach that will be taken in the change process. For example, talking about a highly participative process should be done in a highly participative way. This means that you are acting in a way that is consistent with the words the audience is hearing. If you describe the same process by simply telling the audience and invite no questions or input from them at any point, they are liable to question whether the change programme itself will be any different.

There is a delicate trade-off between creating a sense of urgency and spreading panic in an organisation. It is also important to bear in mind that information you provide to the organisation could be used by your competitors to generate negative publicity in the market.

SNAPSHOT

A company that was experiencing a slowdown in revenues and a more severe reduction in its margins wanted to explain this to the workforce to help justify and launch a serious package of changes. Their initial idea was to explain that the ship was sinking. However, although this provides a clear sense of urgency to the organisation it also provides ammunition to the various competitors and other forces seeking to criticise the company.

A better wording in this case was to explain that if the ship continued on its current course it would run aground. Also, the ship was low in the water because of all the inefficiencies and challenges in the market and so would be at risk in any future storms.

The program would change the direction of the boat so that it no longer risked running aground and also restored it to sitting high in the water so that it would be better able to cope with any severe weather in the future.

The company has started to share this message and is entering full implementation.

10.7 The enemies of change

10.7.1 Complacency

In the battle to win the hearts and minds of employees (as well as other stakeholders), problems can be caused by lots of things that seem to contradict the way you are explaining the situation.

When things are going badly, people may still believe they don't need to change for a variety of reasons.

In part this is like being in denial about bad news. They may modify their view in the short term or may hold on to the incorrect belief for far longer. Table 10.2 shows a few examples.

Table 10.2: Reasons for complacency

We don't need to change because...	Why does this thought occur?
Things are fine.	If the company hasn't been communicating effectively with employees, then don't expect them to realise how bad things might be.
The company is state-owned and they won't let us fail. They won't let jobs be lost.	This may be true. However, state-owned corporations frequently go bust because the hard decisions aren't taken either in time or at all.
We've been in trouble for years and nothing bad has ever happened – there haven't been any layoffs or problems.	The lack of previous action may have made the current situation far worse but yes, if negative consequences have never occurred, then the company may suffer from having cried wolf in the past.

We don't need to change because…	Why does this thought occur?
There's plenty of fat in the organisation.	Possibly true – but that's probably why the organisation is in trouble.
It won't be me. / It won't affect me.	Wishful thinking, denial, fear of change and other reasons can lead people to ignore seemingly overwhelming evidence in front of them.
Changing what I do won't affect things, as I'm only a small part of a huge organisation.	If everyone thinks this same thought then nothing would ever change. It's all the little changes that add up to the big results.
It's just another change programme – we've seen it, heard it and done it before – and nothing ever really changes.	This is the result of 'change fatigue' caused by the numerous change programmes that are abandoned, unfinished or just don't meet their objectives.
We should cut management salaries first.	This is classic *1984* – do it to them first. However, the potential saving from that type of cut is unlikely to change the underlying problems by more than a small amount.
We should do [*insert some minor action*] first.	This is often some minor action that again won't change the underlying problem enough but people may hope it will avoid the change they fear.
This isn't the right thing to do.	If you haven't been part of choosing a solution to a problem, you are less likely to accept it. This can be pure 'not invented here' syndrome.
Why should we do what they say?	Some people don't like being told what to do (and as above this will be worse if they have not felt part of the definition of the change).

One simple rule does seem to hold true – the better things are going in an organisation, the harder it is to justify change.

10.8 Classic mistakes and problems within change programmes

10.8.1 One size doesn't fit all

Top-down change doesn't enable the management team to fully exploit the learning, experience and ideas from across the organisation

A top-down management approach works on cost cutting and similar projects as you reconfigure the company in line with a particular strategic set of decisions. It won't necessarily ensure the commitment across the organisation in a way that a more bottom-up approach can deliver.

You cannot just change one element and assume it will fix everything else

Change is about evolving some or all of the elements of the business (e.g. systems, metrics, roles and responsibilities). These elements are linked to one another and interact with each other in a complex fashion. If you only change people's job titles and nothing else changes, they will turn up to work on Monday morning and do exactly what they have always done.

You can't change overnight

The complexity of the interactions means you have to carefully plan each move to maintain momentum and avoid mistakes. Constant course corrections will be required on the way to completion and monitoring the actual versus desired results should indicate whether the changes are delivering the expected outcomes.

Things evolve

The external situation may alter radically during the course of a change programme and so the organisation needs to be aware that what they start may need a major change of direction or even be completely stopped if it is no longer relevant and appropriate to the circumstances for the organisation.

Not everything goes according to plan

Actions will take longer than expected and new problems will surface. The process needs to survive these challenges and not lose momentum.

The board and/or shareholders need to be managed too

It's not just employees you need to educate/persuade about a change. The external stakeholders and board have different agendas from the executive team and even from one another and so need careful management. Most changes will result in a dip in performance before things improve and you certainly want to forewarn the board of this type of impact rather than surprising them.

SNAPSHOT

The biggest investment and change in the history of one company in Europe was designed to transform their competitiveness and create a significant barrier to entry. Changing the way they delivered broadband services to consumers and businesses would make the investment prohibitive for any competitor trying to enter the market.

However, no effort was put in to 'manage' the board and the change/investment appeared as item seven on the agenda for the board meeting.

The board were unhappy at not being more fully consulted and fired back question after question about the change that the management team were not fully prepared to answer.

It took another three months, a 200-page document full of detailed answers to the board's questions and a great deal of careful negotiation and discussion to recover the situation and get them to agree to the investment.

When a significant change programme is announced and the reasoning explained, there is also a tendency to look to the past and find reasons that the company is in the current situation. The blame game can be addictive and people may endlessly rehash old issues and decisions. The simple truth is that past decisions cannot be undone, but the organisation needs to face where it is today and be ready to deal with tomorrow.

10.8.2   Things will get worse before they get better

It is worth remembering that the first impact of announcing a serious change programme will be a drop in productivity in the organisation. This is tough but natural, as people discuss any briefings they have received and speculate about what the impact will be for them, their departments and the company overall. The better and more compelling the brief provided, the more quickly the organisation will return to some semblance of normality.

10.8.3   Four steps forward, one step back

Ideally we would like progress to be smooth and to follow a consistent upward path. However, it's like quitting smoking or losing weight or going to the gym regularly – sometimes we all slip back a little. Behaviours in any change programme are the same. This would be more serious in cases where behaviours are not being monitored.

   The reason the focus here is on behaviours is because systems and metrics and processes don't suddenly decide that they preferred things the old way. It's people who revert back and so behaviour is what needs to be understood and the impact of change monitored.

10.9   Models of change

Let's turn our attention to the impact of change on individuals in an organisation and explore why performance typically drops away at the start of a managed change process.

10.9.1 The Satir change model

Psychologist Virginia Satir's model developed an interesting way of viewing the psychology of people during a change process and was based on clinical studies.[5]

   The following table shows the process slightly refined to focus on change programmes.

Table 10.3: Satir's change model

Stage	Description
Status quo	This is the current situation before the triggers for the change are applied. Things are familiar, people know how things work and whom to talk to in order to get things done. Most people are inside their comfort zone at this point.
Foreign element	This is the trigger that changes the situation – meaning the status quo will no longer be maintained. This element causes the 'unfreeze' that then continues into the chaos phase.
Chaos	Once the foreign element or trigger is widely recognised across the company, the status quo will be abandoned and there will be stress, anxiety, worry, and feelings of vulnerability and anger. During this time, individual and overall performance within the company will drop.
Integration	In this phase 'transforming ideas' appear and people work out how those ideas can fit into the overall system and how they will work in the new situation.
Practice	During the practice phase, people are getting used to the new reality that faces them and acting in a way that is required in this new phase. They will typically need appropriate encouragement and support to keep going with changes that have been made.
New status quo	Finally, the performance dip experienced during the process will have disappeared and, if the transforming ideas have been well chosen, performance may likely exceed what was being achieved at the start of the process.

10.9.2   The team formation process

The Satir model is similar to the team formation process suggested by educational psychologist Bruce Tuckman in 1965.[6] This is a mini-change process that almost everyone has experienced on a number of occasions.

Table 10.4: Tuckman's stages of group development

Stage	Description
Forming	This is the creation phase for any team.
Storming	Once a team has been created, the problems begin. People have their own expectations, habits and ways of working. These aren't initially going to fit well with the other people in the team. This normally creates tensions, discussions, arguments and other simple forms of conflict within the team.
Norming	Unchecked, the storming will continue and some teams never actually get beyond this stage. Norming describes the creation of a set of agreements and expectations about behaviours and actions within the team. It is the process of negotiation and compromise allied to improved understanding of the way everyone works and thinks.

Stage	Description
Performing	If the team gets past the norming phase, this performing stage is when it really starts to deliver. The team knows how to operate and is past the internal conflicts for the most part.
Mourning	This phase is sometimes added to the original steps as it describes the period after a team stops working together. Individuals may miss their colleagues and/or the excitement of working towards an objective with the team. This sense of loss is sometimes referred to as mourning.

10.10 Rewards and metrics

Behaviours are closely linked to the metrics used to measure performance and so also to the rewards given to groups and individuals. As a rule, metrics designed to underpin a cost-cutting programme will naturally need to be more aligned to financial results. Where cultural change and new behaviours are required, the metrics need to be more aligned towards adoption of new behaviours.

At the start of any transition process, the metrics and rewards are very unlikely to be suitable to support the changes that are being targeted. This means that the metrics and reward structure will need to be realigned as part of the overall process. In fact, in longer-term change processes, you may need to have adjusted metrics during the process and then change them again once the process is complete. This final set of metrics and rewards is designed to maintain the 'steady state' and also can serve as another indicator that the organisation is in the 'freeze' phase.

10.11 Psychodynamics

This is the study of the psychological processes that we undergo during a change focusing on the feeling and emotions that individuals go through.

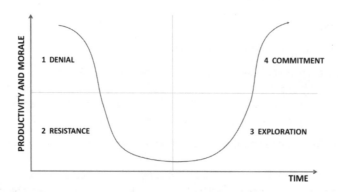

Figure 10.1: Four-stage change curve (derived from Kübler-Ross' Five Stages of Grief)

Figure 10.1 shows a simple but interesting viewpoint on the stages that individuals will experience as they go through a change process. It is based on Elisabeth Kübler-Ross' work identifying the Five Stages of Grief,[7] developed from work with terminally ill patients.

It might seem strange to compare organisational change to that of grieving, but remember that although it is thankfully much less traumatic, people still experience loss during change. That might be a loss of certainty, status, comfort, reassurance or many other tangible and emotional elements. However, they are lost (even if only for a short period) and this loss is something like pure grief.

Denial sets in as the change will unsettle their 'world' and potentially move them out of their comfort zone.

This is followed by resistance where attempts are made to counteract the forces creating the change.

When resistance is exhausted or the person recognises that they may not be able to fight against the changes, exploration will take place. Here a person considers what is happening and starts to consider the impact on them and how they will feel about it and also adapt to it.

Finally, the hope is that individuals will quickly enter the commitment phase where they are genuinely committed to the new status quo, or at least have recognised that this new reality has to be faced.

Figure 10.2 shows a more detailed version of the previous change curve – illustrating some of the more subtle emotional transitions that individuals will make over the lifetime of the process.

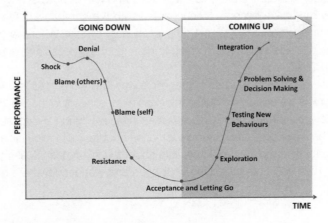

Figure 10.2: Transition curve during change process

10.12 Hubbers, saboteurs and fence sitters

10.12.1 Hubbers

As you consider the problem of communication within a change programme, you particularly need to consider how you efficiently keep the employees and other stakeholders up to date. You can't personally talk to everyone every day. You do want to ensure that they have the right message and also capture any concerns and stop any incorrect rumours before they cause damage.

The natural networkers in the organisation can be incredibly useful in a change process. We'll call this group hubbers,[8] as they sit at a hub of communication radiating out into the organisation. They have the strongest connections across the organisation and are pretty easy to identify. These people typically:

- tend to know the gossip first in the company;
- are the organisers of social events; or
- have been in the company for a while – perhaps working across a number of different departments.

There are no hard and fast rules but if you take five minutes to think about it, you can probably list half a dozen people that could help disseminate messages about the change programme, as well as provide feedback on how things are being perceived across the organisation. This feedback may not always be accurate, but it's better to have too much information than too little.

At their best, hubbers act as informal champions for the change process and are tremendously beneficial.

10.12.2 Saboteurs

At the opposite extreme are the saboteurs, individuals who will act against any management-led programme. They may have become disenchanted with the company, hold a grudge against someone in the management team or just be exceptionally cynical. Whatever the reason, these people need to be managed as they are going to damage the process and undermine what the team is trying to achieve.

Worse than this, they are going to do damage in a way that is often hidden. Although some of their hostility or cynicism may surface during information meetings and the like, the most damage is going to be below the surface during informal meetings, over lunch and at the coffee machine. They are likely to be making up false rumours, creating doubts, rubbishing claims and otherwise spreading misinformation and you will know little about it until someone asks you about one of these fake facts. Then you'll be scratching your head and wondering where on earth that idea surfaced from.

10.12.3 Fence sitters

The third group are the fence-sitters. At the start of a change process, they are happily minding their own business and probably imagine that they won't be affected by the programme. They may have a vague awareness that things need to change but are uncertain how this should happen and probably hope it won't impact on their life too much. There's nothing wrong with this view – the fence sitters are normally the majority as you enter a change process. The recognition of the reasons to change balances unsteadily with their desire to continue as they have been and only a compelling message will help sway them to become more supportive of the change.

10.13 What you should do

10.13.1 Communicate, communicate, communicate

You need to prepare carefully before you announce the change programme. As has been said, you can assume there's a certain amount of time during which a change programme can remain secret. This isn't going to be months but you need to spend this time wisely.

However, during this time you need to absolutely make sure that you have an effective and comprehensive communication plan. When you announce what is going to happen you need to understand what the precise message is for the employees.

You also need to understand what message they should be passing on in their conversations with family, friends, customers and even the press to ensure everyone remains on message. The communication plan also needs to include how you handle objections, questions and concerns. You don't want to have somebody asking the difficult question in front of the whole organisation and then not having a good answer.

Ensuring that the key communicators (hubbers) are enlisted in the process will help maximise the efficiency of sharing information across the organisation.

10.13.2 Carefully plan each phase

Any diagnostic, implementation planning and eventual implementation phases need to be correctly structured at a high level and then broken down into the appropriate work packages and tasks/ actions. Using RACI matrices (see pages 62–63) is particularly helpful as it allows the definition of those responsible, accountable, consulted and informed for each task. This allows team members and also employees to review the actions assigned and identify any errors or omissions.

10.13.3 Ensure there are quick wins

To underpin the ability to achieve the long-term objectives of the change programme, it is really helpful to identify and then deliver quick wins. These may be pilot processes that start to deliver benefits from early in the project, improved customer satisfaction numbers, better feedback from suppliers or improved defect rates. The 'what' is less important than the fact that there are positive results early on. This will hopefully encourage those in favour of the process, convert some of those who are neutral about it (fence sitters) and discourage some of the naysayers and saboteurs.

SNAPSHOT

The Head of Sales in a Swedish company realised how important it was to show progress towards the objectives as this would help maintain the motivation of his team. However, he also knew that the systems were so poor he couldn't accurately measure anything. His solution was to put a large, clear plastic tube in the reception of the company and the sign above it said it would have a tennis ball in the tube for every '1,000 new customers'.

10.14 Structuring a change process

Drawing the strands together of the do's and don'ts of a change process, John Kotter suggests an eight-step strategy for managing change (1995). It summarises a lot of what has been discussed in this chapter very neatly.

Table 10.5: Managing change (Kotter, 1995)

Change step	Description
1. Establish a sense of urgency.	Share information about the current situation and competitive realities. Consider scenarios that map what may happen in the future to increase belief in the need to change.
2. Create a guiding coalition.	Put together a team that can work well together but which also has sufficient power to deliver key parts of the change. This team should be a role model for new behaviours.
3. Develop a vision for the change.	Create a vision for the change and how it will be achieved.
4. Communicate the change vision.	Communicate, communicate, communicate! Do this in a variety of ways to try to ensure the message is received and understood as widely as possible in the organisation.
5. Empower everyone to act on the vision.	Let people challenge the status quo and drive through barriers that are blocking progress.
6. Produce quick wins.	Ensure these are widely publicised within the organisation with visible rewards for individuals.
7. Consolidate gains and produce more change.	Refresh the process with new projects and people in the process.
8. Set the new ways as part of the culture.	Create a strong link between behaviours and success in the organisation.

Summary

The drivers for change in organisations are becoming both more frequent and more important to respond to correctly under the prevailing economic climate.

Although it seems as if it should be simple, the complexity of changes and the impact on individuals' performance and psyches make it difficult to get right.

The change process must be underpinned by clear justifications that motivate as many people as possible in the organisation to pursue the change positively. However, once this state is achieved, it is vital to change and then return to the new status quo as quickly as possible. Along the way, the organisation should focus as hard as possible on delivering clear communication to continually reinforce the reasons for the change, show progress along the way and provide whatever reassurance and support may be needed.

Once completed, the aim should be to return to normality and clearly demonstrate that the change is completed internally.

What's next?

The next chapter will look at the fundamental elements of project management in some detail.

Notes

1. *Jack Welch and The GE Way: Management Insights and Leadership Secrets of the Legendary CEO*, Robert Slater, McGraw-Hill Professional, New York, 1998.
2. 'Cracking the code of change', *Harvard Business Review* 78 (May–June 2000).
3. *Managing Change and Transition*, Michael Beer and Nitin Nohria, Harvard Business Essentials, Boston, 2000.
4. *Change Basics*, Linda Russell and Jeffrey Russell, ASTD Press, Alexandria, 2006.
5. *Making Sense of Change Management: A Complete Guide to the Models Tools and Techniques of Organizational Change*, Esther Cameron and Mike Green, Kogan Page, London, 2009.
6. *Effective Group Coaching*, Jennifer Britton, John Wiley & Sons, New Jersey, 2011.
7. *On Death and Dying*, Elisabeth Kübler-Ross, Routledge, London, 2008.
8. John Jeffcock on change management, Winmark Europe.

11
Managing projects

11.1 Introduction

This chapter will look at the fundamental elements of project management in some detail. That includes:

- diagnosing the state of an existing project;
- creating objectives;
- developing milestones;
- managing risks; and
- managing issues.

Although this represents only part of the world of project management, it focuses on the key areas where things tend to go wrong.

We'll start with an important question.

11.2 What is a project?

There are some characteristics that hold true for all projects.

11.2.1 A project has a temporary organisation

This means that the group of people working on the project, whether full or part time, have been brought together to execute the project and will not exist as a team beyond it. This is true even if the project has a duration running into years. For example, the people building the Channel Tunnel that links England and France were brought together for this epic project and were then broken up as a team when it was completed.

11.2.2 The project itself is unique and not a recurring activity

If a project repeats then it is actually a process that you can measure and improve each time you run it. Projects are more challenging because their unique nature means you have not seen the particular set of circumstances and problems before.

To illustrate the difference, the design and development programme for the 'super-jumbo' Airbus A380 was a project. Manufacturing A380s is an impressive, but nonetheless repetitive, set of tasks that constitute a process – repeating each time a plane is built from scratch. Designing the A400 will be a new and unique project.

11.3 Why is it vital to manage projects well?

Managing a project well should provide you with critical information to help make decisions and keep the project on track. This information includes:

- Feedback on progress of the project against initial plans – where are we against where we expected to be?
  - Estimated completion dates for key milestones.
  - Estimated overall completion date for the project.
  - Estimates of the ongoing resource requirements – what resources do we need now and what resources are assumed in the project in the future to achieve the current milestone and completion dates?
- Management of risk and uncertainty:
  - What are the risks identified in the project?
- What is their potential impact and what is being done to minimise or eliminate them?

11.4 Diagnosing the state of an existing project

If/when you are given a project to take over, or are put in charge of people running multiple projects, you have a short period of grace where you can signal any serious issues or problems to senior management. However, you need to know as soon as possible whether there is a disaster in the making. Wait too long and if things have gone wrong they will be blamed on you.

There are two important factors that you will need to understand to identify if there are major problems with the project:

1. You need to know if the team is competent enough in running a project to know where they really are.
2. If the team knows what they are doing, then do they actually believe the project is on track?

It is important for a project manager to motivate the team to work with them. I know that seems a strange concept. They're being paid so they should be professional, right? Unfortunately, this is not always the case.

If the team has experienced difficult projects with ineffective management, dates imposed arbitrarily, problems ignored and inaccurate plans, they will need some convincing that this project is going to be different with you as project manager. I repeat – it is vital that you are able to motivate the team.

11.4.1 Talk to the previous project manager

The first person to speak to, if possible, is the previous project manager. They can be an invaluable source of advice and tips about dealing with the project team, senior management and any customers involved. Essentially they can tell you where the icebergs are.

If your predecessor describes a series of problems, you already have a partial answer as to the state of the project. It may be in trouble and you need to make sure this is clear for senior management either as you take it over or as you decide not to take it on (if that luxury is open to you). Do bear in mind though that the previous project manager may not have been competent nor had enough time to manage things properly. They may therefore be trying to justify their being replaced by exaggerating problems.

If the previous project manager says everything is fine and on track, that may be good news but you can't simply assume they are correct – you need to keep investigating.

11.4.2 Talking to the project team

Next it's time to talk to members of the project team. Remember that this can only confirm there are problems with the project at this point – you cannot prove it is going well.

Assessing a project seems to work best when done informally. Just go around the project team and try to have a word with them while they are alone. It's a good time to introduce yourself and you can then get to the following questions.

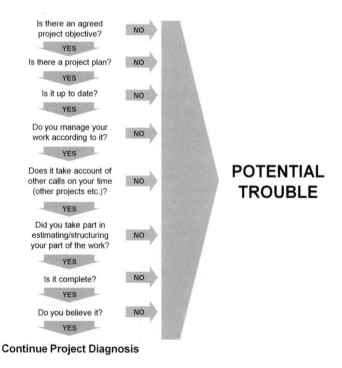

Figure 11.1: Project diagnostic approach

I developed the quick diagnostic in Figure 11.1 as a fast mechanism for getting to the truth of the situation. If you get a 'NO' at any point then you need to investigate further.

11.4.3   Is there an agreed project objective?

You're looking for evidence that the team is working to a clear statement of the objectives of the project. If this is entirely absent, it's unlikely the project can ever succeed.

If only a few of the team understand the objectives, you need to consider how the project is being run. However, it is not a problem for some team members to be unaware of the objectives if the project is being managed in line with them. If someone isn't familiar with the objectives for the project, ask them:

- What are the targets for the project?
- What targets are you working to personally?
- How is the work you do specified?

You will find some team members are directed completely by others so they do not understand the 'big picture', but what they do is in line with achieving success for the project. That is not a reason to press the panic button, but you do need to work out where the direction is coming from and ensure it's consistent with the objectives.

If there is no evidence of an objective (no paper description or evidence of the team following one), then you know there is a problem.

11.4.4   Is there a project plan?

If no one has sight of a project plan, the project will be in trouble. Without one, the team can't review against progress, identify problems early and resolve them before they become crises. It's like trying to get somewhere without a map. You have no idea where you are in relation to your destination so don't know if you're running late and need to speed up.

11.4.5   Is it complete?

If the project plan is not complete, again there is a problem. That does not mean that you have to plan everything to intricate detail three years in advance – that would indicate a different problem. However, there should not be any missing segments of work or major tasks that are not on the project plan but which are due to occur in the near future. If there are gaps, the plan is unlikely to reflect the true picture of the project.

If you find gaps, try to understand why and get some idea of the likely impact.

11.4.6   Do project team members manage their work according to the plan?

There may be a complete plan, but if team members are essentially ignoring it, that part of the plan does not represent reality. A plan that does not reflect what people are doing should be treated very suspiciously.

11.4.7 Does it take account of other calls on team members' time?

The plan may be complete and people may be deciding which tasks they are doing on the basis of the plan, but does it reflect their real availability? There are many small tasks we need to do that would take five minutes to complete but are left for months because there are other calls on our time. Tasks within projects are just the same. There may be a task clearly assigned to someone, but that does not mean they will do it when you expect them to.

If you don't know what else that person is doing, you have no means of knowing when the task will be done. You can't run a big project with everyone telling you when they'll do every task because:

- they'll be wrong sometimes;
- there will be way too much information for you to handle; or
- you'll be relying on their ability to estimate how long their current workload will take and so will be at the mercy of the massive variation in people's ability to estimate. You'll have ultra-conservative estimates alongside hopelessly optimistic ones.

If you're the project manager, you need to take control of estimation so you are satisfied with the information in the plan.

11.5 Digging into the plan

If you've had reasonable responses from the team, you can start looking at the plan. It is far easier to investigate the electronic version rather than a printout. If you aren't familiar with the software being used, ask someone to help.

11.5.1 Are the key dates achievable and consistent?

You should look at dates for both milestones and for the end of the project. Consider whether these dates appear realistic and whether they meet internal/external constraints and require-ments for the project such as:

- contractual obligations;
- dates for handovers to other departments (e.g. development to industrialisation); and
- market windows (e.g. getting a product in time for a particular event – Christmas, the Olympics, etc.).

11.5.2 Are external inputs into the plan on course?

If there are key elements within the plan that are delivered from other projects or from outside the organisation, are these on target?

Talk to the relevant external project manager to get feedback on whether their part of the project will be delivered on time.

11.5.3 Does the high-level structure of the plan appear logical?

In project terms, you are looking for logical problems like the roof of a building being put on before the walls are erected. Check through and see if there is anything obvious that jumps out as being strange. Ask more questions to clarify any concerns you have. You won't be able to spot every error in project logic, but you'll catch some and also signal to the project team that you are keeping an eye on everything.

11.5.4 Is the resourcing realistic?

By talking to the team you have already identified if the time available to work on the project is realistic. However, this is a second type of resource problem.

CASE STUDY

Carlstedt Elektronik – Sweden

I went into a development programme once and looked at the project plan for a new type of computer processor. It looked good at first glance but had a fundamental flaw about availability.

The resource plan for the first person I checked had 56 hours of work planned for the following Monday. It was clear that this unreality was repeated throughout the plan. No one bothered checking and the project manager was both new to the company and completely inexperienced. When the real availability for the team was used, the overall duration lengthened by 700 per cent before any optimisation.

The final version of the plan ended up 250 per cent longer than the team thought when I arrived.

Assuming someone can put in a full 8-hour day of moving project tasks forward is unrealistic but letting the plan suggest they'll do 56 is insane. The result of this type of error is that the end date will be wildly optimistic even though the plan apparently looks sensible. People will not be able to get through the work as fast as the plan suggests and it will be significantly late.

You need to look at the resource usage to see if individuals or groups are over-allocated with work. The usage can be displayed graphically by project management software as shown in Figure 11.2.

The bars above the 100 per cent usage line (shaded slightly darker) show that the resource 'RJ' has more work to do on every day of the project. There will normally be a number associated with this over-allocation. In the diagram above, the highest bar is actually a 600 per cent allocation of work to the resource.

An individual should never be allocated more than 100 per cent for any day.

If you spot significant over-allocation of resources in a plan, it is a sign that you need to review the plan in detail. The only thing you know with certainty is that the duration of the project is going to increase as a result of any corrections.

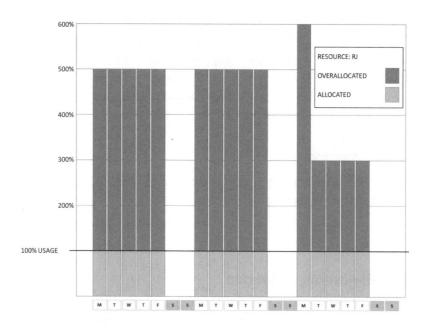

Figure 11.2: Sample resource usage chart

11.5.5 Are there any unrealistic constraints on dates?

Start and end dates for tasks can be constrained in a variety of ways. For example, you can set a task so that it 'must start' or 'cannot start before' a given date.

It is always best to limit the use of these constraints, as using too many can swiftly lead to all sorts of issues with tasks trying to start before their predecessors can finish.

Look through the plan for any constrained dates and check the logic behind the constraint.

11.5.6 'Do you believe it?'

This is a kind of catch-all question that is worth asking. Things may all appear fine but this question may just yield something interesting – a previously unspoken concern, issues within the team or something they did not feel comfortable to express earlier in the conversation.

If you get to this point without any issues, the project is not obviously broken but occasionally this question will reveal a serious problem.

Now we've discussed how to review an existing project, we will move on to how to begin a new project.

11.6 Starting a new project

Organisations have only limited resources and one of the greatest management challenges is using those resources in the best way possible. This means choosing between alternatives, and project managers need to contribute to provide the right level of information to allow such decisions to be made.

A new project will tie up human, financial and technical resources, and so approval can only happen when there is enough information to make an intelligent choice.

When making decisions on which projects to pursue, a project may be rejected or put on hold at the 'concept' stage for many reasons. For example:

- resources necessary for the project are not available;
- the returns are lower than for a similar project concept;
- there are no market channels to exploit the project deliverables;
- the technology risk is too high;
- the project is considered too expensive;
- this project concept is too similar to an existing project;
- the concept falls outside the current business strategy; or
- the project concept does not meet 'customer' needs.

To bring together the information to decide to launch a project, there is a need to carry out some form of structured project kick-off that will detail the scope and objectives of the proposed project. This is known as project initiation.

11.7 Project initiation

11.7.1 Initiation

To initiate a project, organisations need to appoint a project manager before the project is approved. This means the project manager will sometimes take a project concept through to approval – only for it to be rejected. However, the project manager role is vital at this point in the life of the project, ensuring all the different parties are consulted and drawing together the information needed to make the right decision.

CASE STUDY

London Underground

London Underground contractors are constantly refitting the infrastructure but project managers are not included during the project scoping work. Projects are approved by a team dedicated to launching projects and the project manager is only appointed after approval.

This creates problems because the scoping team have less experience of managing one of these projects and so do not understand the reality of infrastructure builds and refits. As a result their budget estimates and timelines are frequently some distance from the real cost of the projects.

The obvious recommendation is that they appoint project managers to take part in the scoping process. This means the person most liable for the success or failure of the project will have a chance to influence it before the plan and budget are approved. In addition, they should be broadening the experience of their scoping team so that they can help spread new and effective practices across the organisation.

11.7.2 Forming the definition team

Once appointed, the project manager needs to assemble a team around them that is capable of carrying out the definition phase. This team is unlikely to be absolutely identical to the team that actually executes the project but must nonetheless have the relevant skills, experience and knowledge necessary.

A project may have been put on hold for a period and different, but still appropriate, people may be available when a decision is taken to approve it.

11.7.3 Objectives of project initiation

The objective of carrying out a well-managed project initiation is to:

- ensure that the project is understood and approved by relevant parties;
- understand the feasibility and level of risk;
- identify an internal champion (sponsor);
- identify a 'customer' for the project – someone who actually wants the project to be carried out. If you haven't got a 'customer' then you shouldn't have a project;
- commit the resources necessary for the initial phases;
- understand the overall resource requirements (human, financial, technical);
- understand how the project fits into the existing portfolio;
- evaluate whether the project should proceed; and
- ensure that the project manager has agreement and backing for the project.

If you inherit a project and you can't identify who the sponsor is (or a 'customer'), then things are serious. Don't mess around with too much diagnosis, just go back to the person who has appointed you to try to understand why the project is going ahead. If you still can't figure out a good reason why the project exists then it probably shouldn't.

There is no substitute for having a senior manager who is championing your work and willing to go to bat for you when you hit problems (and you will). The project champion is hopefully going to break through obstacles in your path and help drive the project to a successful completion. Make sure you keep them informed and keep them on the side of the project – even if things are going badly. Surprising bad news hurts far worse than bad news you've been warned about. This doesn't mean you need to confess every error, concern or problem, but you should keep the sponsor informed of realistic progress in the project and forewarn them of where help may be needed in advance.

11.8 The project charter

The outcome of project initiation is a document that describes the scope of the project in terms of objectives, resourcing, risks and work breakdown. It is called the project charter. This is a structured document that describes the key aspects of the plan including objectives, work plan, resourcing, risks and budget.

At the end of the project initiation work there will be a decision point where the project charter will be reviewed and a decision taken on whether the project should be cleared to proceed, be put on hold or rejected by the organisation.

If the project is accepted, it immediately enters the more detailed planning and execution phase. The project charter then becomes the reference point for the project in terms of deliverables, timescales, etc. A strong and clear project charter agreed by all parties provides the ammunition you need to resist most 'specification creep' you will encounter – the minor changes that people ask for that cumulatively can mean significant changes to the objectives.

11.9 Creating the project charter

The areas you need to cover are very similar but the work required and level of detail will vary enormously depending on the size of the project. For example, digging the Channel Tunnel is inherently more complex and risky than writing a business database. The level of information needed to formally launch the project is therefore very different.

To create the charter, the project manager should:

- ensure that team members who will actually deliver the project are, wherever possible, closely involved in developing the charter;
- obtain input and approval from:
  - internal stakeholders;
  - 'customers' (whether internal or external); and
  - the project champion/sponsor; and
- carefully control changes to the charter once the project is launched.

The best way to start this process is with a kick-off meeting. This will help to create some of the content of the charter and also lets you plan out how you will work with the team to deliver the completed document.

If you have inherited an existing project, you need to go back and review the charter carefully.

If you have diagnosed that the project is in trouble, the only element that you can assume is correct is that the project has been approved. Beyond that, it is safer to assume that the project charter on a troubled project is incorrect until proven otherwise.

The project charter is an excellent way of signalling the true impact of a project and getting early recognition and approval of some of the facts from senior managers and customers alike.

That's a long list of contents and for some projects it will be too much. Some projects will only need a couple of pages. However, others will require hundreds.

If you're the project manager, you need to ensure the project charter delivers the information necessary for all parties and no more. Any more work on the charter is a waste of time until the project is approved.

Whether you are creating the project charter from scratch or reworking an existing one, the charter document should contain the following elements (see Table 11.1).

Table 11.1: Elements of a project charter document

Section	Typical contents
Background/ history	This section is a summary of the situation that has triggered the project. This might be a problem which needs to be resolved or an opportunity that could be exploited by the company.
	It provides an overview of attempts that have been made to date to solve/exploit the situation and describes the impact on the business of not solving/exploiting the situation.
	It should also include highlights from any business case developed to support the project.
Objectives	Include the objectives for the project.
Milestones	List the major milestones through to project completion as clear statements of achievement with the associated evidence.
	If there are any clear decision points where the project logically could be halted, these should also be described along with the criteria that would influence the decision, e.g. results in another project, revised time to completion against deadlines.
Work breakdown	Show the breakdown of major and key work elements below the milestones.
	Describe key resource decisions already made or in question (e.g. using external resources for sensitive work packages).
Timescales	Outline the estimated timescales for completion of key milestones and the overall project – assuming the planned resourcing, specification and quality.
Risks and mitigation	Describe major risks to the project and the contingency or mitigation planned to minimise their probability of occurrence or impact.
Budget	Provide an estimate of the budget through to completion and identify any cost areas that are currently speculative or susceptible to severe change.
Project organisation	Identify the project manager, project team, customers (whether internal or external) and the senior team sponsor.

11.10 The project lifecycle

Figure 11.3 shows how:

- objectives for the project are divided up into measurable states of achievement (milestones);
- milestones are then broken down into the tasks and sub-tasks necessary to complete them;
- the work content is then estimated for each task and the dependencies identified (which task needs to be done first, which is next, which tasks can be finished at the same time, and which tasks need to be completed before the next task(s) start);
- a draft plan is created having assigned resources' true availability to work on the project to tasks they will complete (in other words – identify how long it will take someone to do a task given the other calls on their time); and

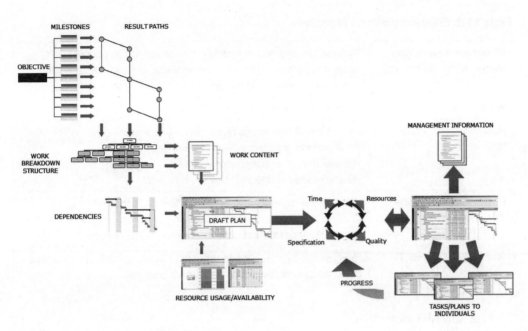

Figure 11.3: Project lifecycle

- the time, specification, quality and resources can then be altered to meet constraints – for example, on the completion date, available resources.

The project is then initiated and:

- plans distributed down to project team members; and
- management information provided to the management team.

We won't be going through all those stages, but the first steps are incredibly important.

11.11 Defining objectives

To create a good and clear objective, we will combine three techniques to build and then check the objective statement is good enough.

11.11.1 Structured objectives

Table 11.2 shows a structure to break down an objective into component parts both to tell the story of what is being targeted for the project and to try to ensure that full information is provided to avoid ambiguity.

Table 11.2: Breaking down an objective

Where are we and **Why** are we doing this project?	You need to describe the context for the project so people understand the background – client needs, competitive situation, performance requirements, etc.
What are we going to do?	What is the project aiming to deliver?
How will we do it and **Who** will do it?	Describe how you are going to deliver the project. What parts of the company will be working on it? Will there be other companies involved? What methods and techniques will be used?
How will we know when it's done?	What are the criteria for when the project is finished? The end point should define any testing or acceptance trials that the project must pass before it is complete.
What will we do next?	How does the project fit into other activities/projects? The next steps could be commercialisation and further phases.

11.11.2 SMART objectives

The most well-known approach to setting objectives is based on the acronym SMART. However, there doesn't appear to be complete agreement over what some of the letters mean. SMART can be broken down into the following characteristics of a well-defined set objectives statement (including alternative meanings).

Specific
Do the project's objectives make it clear what the exact targets are for the project?

Measurable
Is there an unambiguous way that you can 'measure' when the project's objectives have been met? In other words, can you look at the stated objectives and say the project is complete, knowing that no one can or will disagree with you?

Attainable/Achievable
Is it actually possible to achieve the objectives? If it really is impossible, you need to go back to the start and rethink things.

Realistic/Relevant
The 'Attainable' criteria was about whether the objectives were possible. The 'Realistic' term is often used to consider whether the project team is capable of achieving the objective. It may well be possible in theory but impossible for you in practice.

Running the 100 metres in 9.75 seconds is 'attainable' in principle but sadly almost none of us is going to be able to run that fast without the aid of genetic manipulation, an enormous amount of performance-enhancing drugs and a small rocket attached to us. It's attainable but just not realistic for most of us. The same thinking needs to be applied to a project.

Timed

When will the project be completed? People need to know as it may well be linked to other projects for marketing, sales, distribution or whatever comes after your part is finished. You should get agreement on when you are aiming to finish before the project begins.

You use the SMART factors to review the structured objective produced previously to verify that it is complete and that no part has been missed out or inadequately defined. You can't produce a document with a SMART structure. It's a checklist rather than a set of headings.

Kipling's serving men

> I keep six honest serving-men
> (They taught me all I knew);
> Their names are What and Why and When
> And How and Where and Who.
>
> From *The Elephant's Child*, by Rudyard Kipling

You again review the structured objective definition with 'what, why, when, how, where and who' to make sure all of these are well defined within the objective statement.

11.11.3 The race into space – an example objective statement

The following speech was given to a joint session of Congress by President John F. Kennedy on 25 May 1961. It introduced the extraordinary project to get a man on the moon. I've added comments to highlight how this is essentially a very well-constructed objective statement.[1]

> First, I believe that this nation **WHO** should commit itself to achieving the goal, before this decade is out **WHEN**, of landing a man on the moon **WHERE** and returning him safely to the earth **WHAT/WHERE**. No single space project in this period will be more impressive to mankind, or more important for the long-range exploration of space **WHY**; and none will be so difficult or expensive to accomplish.
>
> We propose to accelerate the development of the appropriate lunar space craft. We propose to develop alternate liquid and solid fuel boosters, much larger than any now being developed, until certain which is superior **HOW – TECHNICAL**. We propose additional funds for other engine development and for unmanned explorations **HOW – FINANCIAL** – explorations which are particularly important for one purpose which this nation will never overlook: the survival of the man who first makes this daring flight. But in a very real sense, it will not be one man going to the moon – if we make this judgment affirmatively, it will be an entire nation. For all of us must work to put him there **WHO**.

This was a brilliant speech and a brilliant objective.

You now have a choice of different frameworks to construct a good set of objectives for your project. Using one or more of the models, you can also review an objective to check that you have included all the necessary information.

Next we will look at the important steps in getting to the project objective.

11.12 Milestones

A milestone should not be about doing something, it should be about having arrived somewhere. It's a place in the project that is unambiguous and clear to all in terms of what is meant when it has been achieved.

Milestones, alongside objectives, are an excellent way to identify misunderstandings before the project starts and eliminate nasty surprises later.

Milestones should be:

- phrased around a specific outcome rather than a set of activities. Remember, it is about being somewhere rather than the journey itself; and
- measurable – some part of the milestone should be a statement of the evidence that the milestone has been reached.

A milestone must be a specific, measurable, state of achievement within the project.

Compare and contrast the following two versions of the same intention:

Milestone A:	Take flight BA64 from Heathrow Airport to New York on 22 June next year
Milestone B:	Be in New York City (USA) on 22 June next year and standing at the top of the Empire State Building

Milestone A is a very specific statement and it's measurable. You can tick off that you get that flight and so the milestone is OK – or is it? What happens if the flight is diverted? What happens if you board it but it can't depart because of a problem?

Can you see any ambiguity with Milestone B? If that is ticked off then it can only be that on that day, and before the Empire State Building closed, you are there in New York City!

Consider Table 11.3.

Table 11.3: The milestone is complete when…

State of achievement	and	Quality statement
The draft specification is complete	and	has been signed off by the Director of Design.
The G12 processor batch test is complete	and	the rate passing the Acceptance Test Protocol exceeds 99.999 per cent.
The first 200 customers have been acquired, provided with service	and	the monitoring software confirms that all have transferred at least 1 megabyte of information over the network.

The next logical step is to create more detail under each milestone for the project by developing the work breakdown structure.

11.13 Creating the work breakdown structure

A work breakdown structure divides the project into progressively smaller pieces of work, allowing the project manager to assign the smaller work packages and tasks.

If we think of a project to build a skyscraper, we could have parts of the project to do with foundations, structure, floors, walls and services. The foundations part could involve surveying, digging, inserting piles and pouring foundations. The inserting piles part involves ground preparation, boring and insertion.

Each time we consider one part of the project we can then define the detail at the next level down as shown in Figure 11.4.

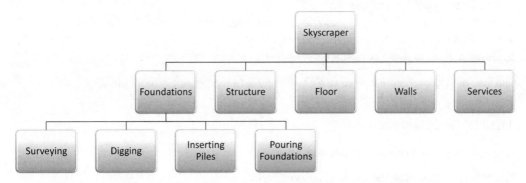

Figure 11.4: Example work breakdown structure for building a skyscraper

The work breakdown structure divides the work into smaller and smaller chunks, and allows you to relate those chunks to one another – knowing what pieces of work contribute to which larger section of the project.

Underneath each work package there will be progressively more detailed tasks/activities. Many pieces of project management software use a numbering system to make the hierarchical relationship between tasks clearer.

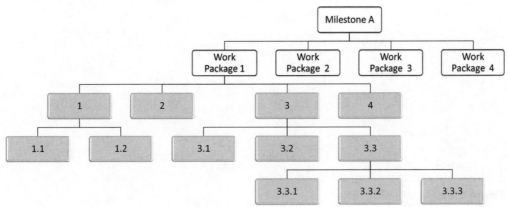

Figure 11.5: Work breakdown structure with numbering

If the objectives and the milestones are correctly formed for a project, it has the best of starts. This chapter is too short to detail some of the other areas in completing the project plan, but will instead focus from now on the activities needed to stay on track.

11.14 Risk management

11.14.1 Identifying and managing risks

There are classically a number of stages to developing contingency plans within a project:

- Identify potential sources of risk.
- Understand the probability of each risk and the effect on the project if it happens.
- Consider the impact of all risks on the overall project.
- Develop ways to avoid or mitigate the risk.

The following sections will look at dealing with risks to the project in more detail.

11.14.2 Risk identification

There are two types of risk that you deal with:

1. certain – will definitely occur at some point; and
2. uncertain – may occur at some point.

For some risks you will know when the risk will occur, while for others there is no way of predicting when it might happen. Figure 11.6 plots the different categories that risks can fall into.

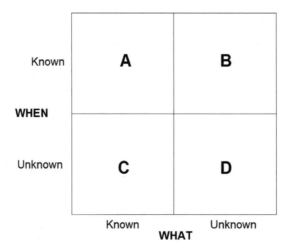

Figure 11.6: Categorising risks

Table 11.4: Categories of risk

	Examples
A	US electricity demand peaks during half-time of the Super Bowl
B	Opening a new bridge Starting up a nuclear reactor
C	Earthquake in San Francisco
D	Could be anything!

You can identify risks in the project at almost any time. You shouldn't just be thinking about risks during weekly meetings with the team – you should be looking for potential risks all of the time. You will identify them during discussions with the team, reading status reports, attending site visits and analysing results. The important thing to do is to make sure the risk is recorded so that it can then be assessed for its impact on the project.

If you don't record the risk, you can't share it with the rest of the team. It doesn't take long to do and your judgement might just be wrong – the risk you think is insignificant might actually be a complete showstopper.

11.14.3 Assessment – evaluating the risk

Some risks are incredibly serious but very unlikely to happen. Some are the reverse, with a very high probability but only a low impact on the project. If you had infinite resources you might chase down every single risk, but you don't and you can't. The skill of a project manager is in juggling limited resources and dealing with risk is no different. You will have to identify which risks you manage and which ones you can ignore.

One way to do this is to carry out an evaluation of each risk as it occurs during the project.

The following characteristics of each risk are then recorded:

- Impact – how severe will it be for the project if the risk happens?
- Probability – what is the likelihood that the risk will happen?

Mapping the project risks may look like Figure 11.7.

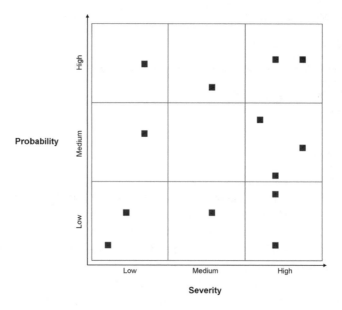

Figure 11.7: Risks – probability vs. severity

So how would you deal with what you see here?

Clearly the first priority must be the risks that are high in both severity and probability – they're likely to affect the project seriously. What's harder is to decide which risks you deal with next.

To illustrate the answer, Figure 11.8 shows the order in which you deal with the risks.

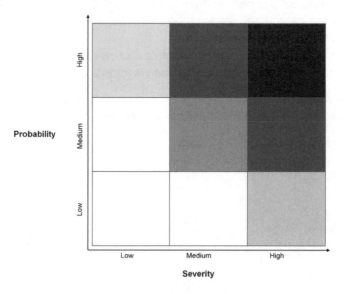

Figure 11.8: Probability vs. severity – risk prioritisation

Note that in Figure 11.8, the shading represents the seriousness and priority of the risk. You manage the darker areas first.

However, in this discussion of risk and probability there is an important element missing – namely time. How quickly should the risk be dealt with?

To factor this third dimension in, we need to create a composite score that combines the rating for risk, probability and time. These factors are then multiplied together to provide a composite score. In the example below, risk number 1 gets a score of 48.

Each risk is added to a risk register (with any reference to external materials, files, photos, reports, etc.). This document is regularly added to during the life of the project as new risks occur.

			A	B	C	=A.B.C	
Number	Problem description	First indicators of problem occur when...	Impact (1 - 5)	Probability (1 - 5)	Time Urgency (1 - 3)	Priority (Result 1 - 75)	Actions
1	Failure to secure mast site	Planning application rejected (at 7 week from start)	4	4	3	48	Begin applications on extra sites to ensure enough sites are accepted to meet the rollout plan.
2							
3							

Figure 11.9: Example risk register

This score can be used to compare different risks and decide which ones should be dealt with and at what priority. The project manager can then set actions for each risk and assign resources to carry them out.

11.15 Issue management

> Everyone has a plan… until they get hit!
> Mike Tyson

Risks and issues are different:

- Issues have already happened.
- Risks are things which may happen in the future and you need to eliminate, mitigate or avoid.

Issues should be prioritised according to some criteria (such as those below), so that decisions can be made on what to do about the issue.

Table 11.5: Prioritising issues

Priority	Response timing	Example issues
1	Immediate response	Project progress halted Immediate delay to the project Technical/quality 'showstopper' encountered Evidence that specification cannot be met under current plan Major shortcut to completion identified Cost/time reduction opportunity Test failures
2	Rapid response	Resourcing problems Changes of availability of equipment
3	Respond when resources allow	Documentation errors

You need to record them so that others involved in the project have a central location where they can check on the issues that exist and how they progress.

The log should include:

● issue number – to help track particular issues easily;
● description – including supporting document references;
● reference;
● date originated;
● priority – 1 to 3;
● status – identified, investigated, resolved; and
● comments – additional information about the resolution or exploitation of the issue.

The issue list should be reviewed formally during the weekly meetings and updated as necessary.

11.16 Scope change management

Managing changes within a project is the process of evaluation and then accepting/rejecting potential changes to the project. Changes within the project may originate from a variety of sources, such as:

● failures in testing;
● customer requests/demands;
● response to competitor actions mid-project;
● issues – problems or opportunities; or
● strategies to reduce risk.

When a potential is highlighted, the project manager needs to record the details in a change log.

This will capture who has raised the change, why they are suggesting it and when this was done.

It is important to capture this to put the change into context. The customer demanding a difficult change is very different from a member of the project team suggesting it.

As well as stating the reason for the proposed change, any supporting documentation should be referenced – e.g. test results, customer specification. A blank change log should look something like this.

Number	Originator	Reason	Date Originated	Impact Assessment	Approval Required From	Approved	Date	Comments

Now you need to start assessing what the impact of change would be in terms of additional cost, delays to the project's end date, increased risk, etc. Evaluating some changes can end up being considerable chunks of work in their own right. Frequently I have seen that the person needed to evaluate a change is also the person who is working flat out on the critical path of the project!

At this point you can decide against doing an impact assessment if you believe it is unnecessary or if you are going to reject the change. This is OK but you need to record this in the change log and put your reasoning in the comments section.

If you choose to carry out an assessment, this work needs to be resourced and planned like the rest of the project.

Summary

Projects are unique and range from the simple to the most complex and impressive piece of civil engineering. Gaining a clear and agreed understanding of the objectives at the start of the project is important to act as a contract between the various parties and prevent changes of scope without prior agreement. Well-defined milestones then support monitoring progress throughout the life of the project.

What's next?

The next chapter introduces tools to support decision making and investigation into issues. These can help keep projects on track but also are very useful as day-to-day management tools.

Note

1.   President John F. Kennedy's 25 May 1961 Speech to a Joint Session of Congress.

12
Problem-solving techniques

To keep on top of the situation as a manager, it can be very useful to have approaches for getting to the heart of a problem. In this chapter you'll find a number of different techniques to help get to the causes of an issue or generate new solutions to a problem.

12.1   Ishikawa diagrams[1]

Ishikawa or fishbone diagrams are different names for the same tool, used to help identify potential causes leading to a problem or the routes to getting to a desired outcome.

To create one of these diagrams, you start with the problem being faced or the change that you want to achieve. The following example is a real situation from a major infrastructure company.

First you create a horizontal arrow (the spine) pointing to the 'effect' being considered. In this case it is issues with project management. Then you work either alone or with the team to brainstorm major causes that could create the effect. These are added to the diagram as diagonal 'bones' that join on to the spine.

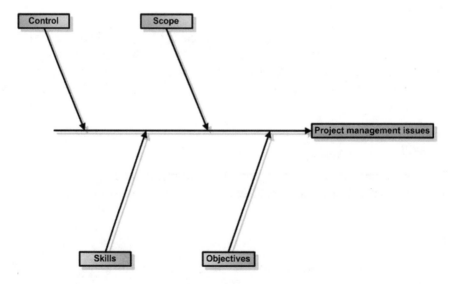

Figure 12.1: Ishikawa diagram – high level

You then add a further level of causes attached to the respective major cause.

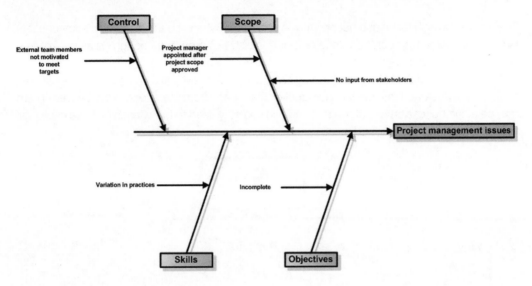

Figure 12.2: Ishikawa diagram – more detail

If causes can be broken down into more detail, these should be attached to the 'bone' to which they relate.

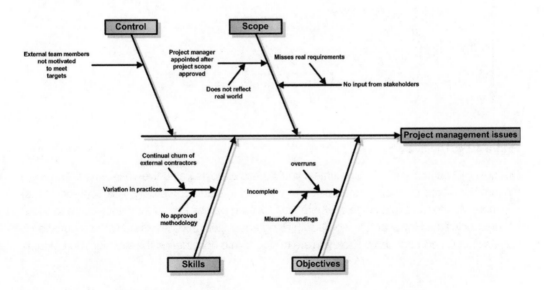

Figure 12.3: Ishikawa diagram – full detail

You may need to reorganise the diagram to move common elements together or possibly split the diagram in two if it becomes too complex.

12.2   The five whys

This is a very simple technique but one that is very useful when you are faced with someone telling you that something can't be done or that is initially not providing enough detail to explain a situation. It is good at getting to the root of an issue fast if used carefully.

The technique is this – just keep asking 'Why'? By asking why five times you will quickly get below the surface and reverse the individual or team back from the effect to the causes. There may be a number of answers at any point and so you may need to follow each of these back until you've asked the question five times.

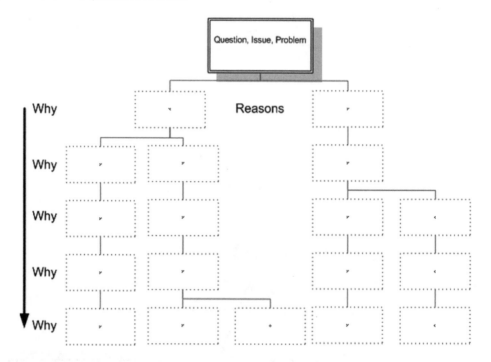

Figure 12.4: The five whys

Obviously, if you just ask 'why' five times, you'll be as annoying as a five-year-old child having a tantrum. However, you can instead ask the 'why' using different wording. Ask someone to tell you more. Ask for an explanation of where their thinking comes from or how they came to a particular conclusion. However it is worded, thinking about going five levels down on a question is very useful to encourage the person you are talking to into considering the situation more deeply.

12.3   Force field analysis

This can be very helpful in understanding a situation and the different forces that support and oppose a potential change.

The process is simple and works well with a flipchart. Draw a line down the centre of the page. Above this line, write the change that is being proposed.

On the left-hand side of the page, the different forces that are supporting the change are listed with an arrow towards the right for each. On the right hand side of the page, you list the forces against the change with an arrow pointing to the central line as shown in Figure 12.5.

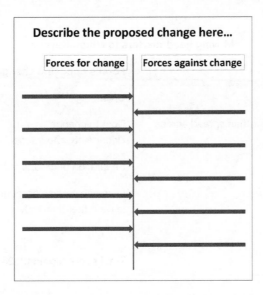

Figure 12.5: Force field analysis

Once the group has exhausted the significant forces for and against the change, you need to score the strength of each particular force.

You can agree a score across the group with 0 being very weak, 5 being average and 10 being very strong.

An alternative is to allow each person in the group a number of votes to distribute as they wish across the whole set of forces (the number of votes for each person should be a multiple of the number of forces identified, e.g. five times). People can then distribute their own votes as they wish to show the most significant forces in their opinion.

Whichever scoring system is used, the total scores are added up for both sides and compared. This might show one or other side being stronger but is not particularly important in itself.

The next stage is to address each force and brainstorm ways to:

- strengthen forces supporting the change; and
- weaken forces opposing the change.

Finally you look at these potential means for changing the forces and:

- decide on which ones you wish to undertake; and
- rescore the assessment considering the actions proposed.

The example below considers a company looking to move its headquarters from London to a regional city.

Moving headquarters to Milton Keynes	
Forces for change	**Forces opposing change**
Cost savings	Unions
Groups co-located rather than spread across London	Cost to change Uncertainty about amenities for children
Better facilities	Separation of groups from central services
Cheaper housing	Loss of expertise (through people choosing to leave rather than move)
Shorter commuting time	
Total score 'for': 35	**Total score 'against': 28**

Figure 12.6: Forces for and opposing change

Considering the ways to strengthen/weaken forces (marked with an asterisk), the completed assessment would look something like this.

Moving headquarters to Milton Keynes	
Forces for change	**Forces opposing change**
Cost savings *Identify and publicise savings internally to help justify the move.	**Unions** *Ensure unions understand the details of the business case requiring the change. *Discuss details of implementation to minimise disruption.
Groups co-located rather than spread across London *Ensure the groups moving are those that need to work together. *Co-locate groups with biggest interaction's together in the new building.	**Cost to change** *Publicise overall figures highlighting total saving rather than the cost to move. **Uncertainty about amenities for children** *Research and provide briefing packs on schools, sports centres, hobbies, etc. available in MK.
Better facilities *Circulate artist's impressions of new workplace. *Buy example office furniture and create 'showroom' area in canteen to illustrate to the staff what they can expect in MK.	**Separation of groups from central services** *Create video conferencing suites and desktop cams for Skype to minimise disruption. *Consider central services visiting MK on rota.
Cheaper housing *Create portfolio of available properties to publicise across the workforce.	**Loss of expertise (through people choosing to leave rather than move** *Identify key individuals to retain and put in place retention strategy.
Shorter commuting time *Calculate reduction in commuting times and publicise.	
Amended score 'for': 45	**Amended score 'against': 23**

Figure 12.7: Strengthening/weakening forces for and opposing change

12.4 Drill-down

This technique is a very straightforward way to get into the detail of a situation.

Figure 12.8 shows a drill-down for a company that manufactures tablet PCs and has a problem with screens cracking on their products.

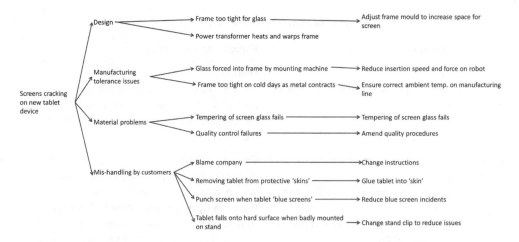

Figure 12.8: Example of a drill-down

EXERCISE

On the left-hand side of a large piece of paper (e.g. several flipchart pages stuck together), write down the issue and then have the group write down potential high-level causes on Post-its.

These can be combined/corrected if necessary and then put vertically next to the problem. From here, each cause can be expanded further using the same approach.

When you have drilled down to an appropriate level of detail about the problems/causes, you can then propose actions/solutions relating to the detailed causes.

The column on the right hand side shows the potential resolutions or improvements that might reduce the instances of screens cracking.

12.5   Swim lane diagrams

When trying to understand and share processes, an interesting alternative to a classic process flow diagram is to use a swim lane diagram. This illustrates the way that steps in the process move from one department to another and can be very useful to ensure all parties understand their role in the overall process. In addition, it can highlight where you need to pay more attention to communication between different groups (e.g. where there are multiple handovers in the process or these are to third parties outside the organisation itself).

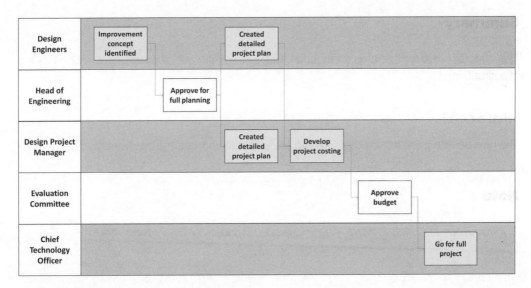

Figure 12.9: Example swim lane diagram

12.6 Interaction diagram

The final technique is similar to the swim lane diagram but shows the specific interactions between different parties. It can be a very useful technique for reviewing a process.

The interactions between the different parties are shown with time flowing down the page to provide ordering of what comes first.

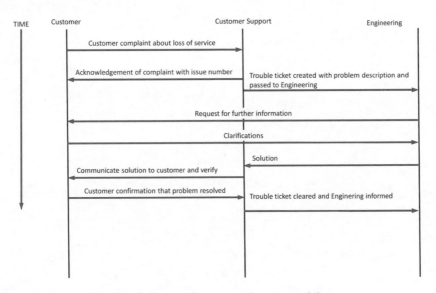

Figure 12.10: Example interaction diagram for a customer complaint

Summary

This chapter has demonstrated a few approaches to gaining and sharing better understanding of a situation.

What's next?

The next section provides a recap of some of the most important themes from the book.

Note

1. *Introduction to Quality Control*, Kaoru Ishikawa, Productivity Press, New York, 1990.

Concluding thoughts

As you've read through the book, you will have picked up on points that are interesting and/or relevant for the unique situation you find yourself in. Hopefully you'll have gained an appreciation of the way that different disciplines in an organisation fit together. You'll know you can't execute a decision if you don't know the direction and if you don't understand the environment around an organisation, you can't work out where to go next.

I wanted to highlight a few points from the book that I think are important in building and maintaining a successful organisation and career. This isn't a definitive list, but the following are fundamental.

Only the right strategy will do

Remember the first point in the book. Of the companies in the US Fortune 100 in 1970 only 57 remained by 1990. Those on the list in 1990 fared worse with only 26 still there in 2010.

Overall, only 16 companies remained on the list from 1970 to 2010 and they were corporate giants like Exxon-Mobil, Coca-Cola and Boeing.

It is getting tougher and tougher for businesses to survive in an increasingly turbulent economic climate. Defining and implementing the right strategy is vital. Changing it as soon as circumstances dictate is just as important.

Learning point

When times are good, even average companies can survive. When times are lean, survival becomes much harder and mistakes are penalised ruthlessly.

Complacency will kill you

Highly successful companies that are making big profits are less likely to recognise the need for, let alone implement, any major changes. The 'If it ain't broke, don't fix it' approach is one reason linked to the bravery needed to confront and address long-term problems. The choice of rocking the boat and reducing current performance to improve the long-term prospects for an organisation is not an easy one. The short-termism of shareholders and managers wishing to build a career in a job for just a few years before moving on will also constrain some organisations from doing the right thing rather than the easy thing.

Success often masks a need to be more competitive. The story of photocopier manufacturer Xerox as well as the demise of Kodak illustrate this, but many other companies have also fallen into this trap.

Learning point

For successful businesses, a significant danger is that there may be no 'lion in the room' pushing them to change when times are good. Even without the obvious need to fix an organisation, it is imperative to keep improving.

If you build it ... they will come

So said Kevin Costner in *Field of Dreams*. However, the problem is that companies imagine that just delivering the great new thing to the market will instantly lead to fantastic sales. Philips sometimes fell foul of this but it was far from alone. Another technically advanced product would appear and the same disappointing sales would ensue far too frequently.

The problem is when companies are technology- rather than marketing-led. Technology can be great but the market is always right. The failure of superior technology like video discs, Betamax and myriad other examples underline this fact. The technology is either in front of market demand or completely misaligned.

Markets are unforgiving places and they react pitilessly to ideas that are poorly thought out or executed. You must understand the market to deliver to it and a scattergun approach to products, launching them in the hope that they find a market, is never going to be the right approach.

As an example, the Segway is a great piece of technology, but when did you last see one in action?

Learning point

Marketing-led companies beat technology-led companies – most of the time. Find out what customers want and give it to them – simple.

Only Apple can do what Apple do

Ansoff's matrix describes the choices an organisation could take when considering options to increase revenue. The most difficult position to get right is entering both a new market and product/service at the same time.

You will hear people justify their ideas by quoting how Sony invented the Walkman market out of nothing or how Apple moved into the mobile phone market – essentially a new product and new market for them. However, the problem is that there are always exceptions like this. For every product that succeeded with such a bold move there are many, many more that perished for trying precisely the same thing.

Learning point

The safe approach is to stick to what you do if it's working. If you want or need to change, then base the move on logic and analysis, rather than a gamble.

Manage your cash

Revenues come in three flavours but only one of them really counts when things are tight.

The revenues booked on a big relationship may flow into the company at some point in the future. Except they might not. The company buying from you may go into administration or bankruptcy and the money will never come. It must have seemed pretty safe dealing with Enron, Kodak, Polaroid, Rangers Football Club and a number of other organisations that looked too big to struggle. However, that 'booked' revenue will never appear for suppliers to some of these organisations.

Billed revenues are those you have invoiced. However, this again means little if the company is going to pay late (meaning you may have to have extra working capital to cover running the business during the time until you are paid) or may never pay if they go under.

The revenues you have banked are clearly the best. It's money sitting in an organisation's bank account. You can use it to run the business and the risks of no or late payment have gone away.

Far too many businesses have gone bust because they have failed to manage their cash. In the current economic climate, you can't even rely on the bank to provide a loan if things get tight. The only answer is to ensure you manage your cash as effectively as possible.

Learning point

Manage cash obsessively! Get every revenue stream to cash in your bank as fast as possible. Change payment terms, encourage early payment or whatever you can to reduce the risk of non-payment and the working capital burden of late payment.

Early issues can be catastrophic

Another reason that companies shouldn't compare themselves to Apple is that their brand appears practically bulletproof. Only Apple's brand could have survived the different problems they have suffered (e.g. battery life on iPods, screen cracking on early Nanos, poor/no signal on the iPhone 4). That's without mentioning the disastrous Apple Newton!

Windows Vista was a bold concept but the level of problems encountered by early users gave it a bad reputation and meant it failed to hit targets. Apple even took to lampooning it in their advertising – increasing the impression that Vista didn't work properly.

Any other company has to get it right first time or Twitter, YouTube, Facebook and word of mouth will harm it in a way that was unheard of 20 years ago. People who didn't like a product used to tell an average of 10 people; now it can be 10 times that number with the ease of access to social media – even on the move. In extremes, we're talking millions of people hearing how bad a company or product is.

Learning point

Launch a product or service as early as you can but only when it, and the organisation that will support it, are ready – never before.

Growing pains

Gordon Gecko suggested in *Wall Street* that greed is good. He'd probably say growth is good too. He'd be wrong at least some of the time.

People imagine that growth is the Holy Grail of business. It certainly has its benefits, but the problem is that companies often fail to realise that growth comes at a price.

A cost problem during the growth phase is that the volumes being sold are constantly rising. In one respect, that seems a good thing, but it can create serious cash flow issues.

In an example in Chapter 4, we saw that a company selling a steady 100 units at a cost of 10 each made an average operating profit of 500. If there was 25 per cent growth period on period, then this average operating profit fell to less than 100. Take into account other costs to the business and the company would be making a loss in the latter case, despite growing very quickly.

You absolutely want to be in high growth markets but you want to combine this with high market share if possible (so you can take better advantage of economies of scale than your competitors). Otherwise, you can end up spreading your management attention and cash across too many products/services.

Learning point

Staying in growing markets requires investment and a company should choose the ones where it can maintain a good market share into maturity or question whether the investment could be better used elsewhere.

Don't be late to the party

In growing markets, the cost of being late can be significant. Every month of delay to launching a product or service means lost customers and revenues. However, this also means another company potentially gaining repeat sales and the benefits to their reputation from the customers that were 'lost' by being late. In markets where customers pay subscriptions, this can be even worse, as being a few months late can result in many more months of revenues that go elsewhere.

The cost to capture a customer when they first start using a product or service is lower than trying to capture them from a competitor. The latter may require discounts or other offers to attract them to become your customer.

Being late therefore results in lower customer numbers, lost revenues, increased marketing costs and lower economies of scale (as your volumes are lower than if you entered the market earlier).

Learning point

Get to the market as early as you possibly can once you are ready – and not a moment earlier. Quality or availability problems will hurt you in the long run so be ready, but once you are prepared, get into the market as hard and fast as possible.

Manage with clarity

The majority of issues in companies seem to happen at the boundaries. Misunderstandings happen at the borders between groups or in the definition of work between individuals. This may be a simple and unimportant hiccup, but the time wasted still adds up. However, the impact might be something very serious:

- A new engine won't fit into an engine bay because nobody said it should.
- Terms of a contract lose money for a company because enough attention wasn't paid to getting it right.
- A tender is won but the project runs at a loss because the team didn't have the right members from the relevant departments.

Learning point

Good companies ensure clarity in decision making and delegation. Objectives set are unambiguous and the organisation has a shared culture of managing with clear objectives and milestones.

The final thought – keep learning

Stephen Covey talks about 'sharpening the saw' in his book, *The Seven Habits of Highly Effective People*. The final thought I'd leave you with is that careers are long, demanding and likely to change direction significantly in the coming turbulent decades. Keep learning, keep reading and keep questioning what you're told. No one idea is right in every situation and you need to build a personal toolkit to help you remain successful in whatever you choose to do.

The ICSA publication series has plenty in it to help develop your skills and they offer professional development for company secretaries and administrators. For those in other industries and sectors, Winmark provides exceptional training across a number of areas and is helping to develop and support leaders across Europe.

As a final thought, if you'd like to discuss the ideas in this book, then drop me a line at richard@richardjones.com. I've learned from working across four continents with tens of companies, hundreds of directors and thousands of delegates, and I'd welcome your feedback.

Recommended reading

The following list of books covers some of the main topics of the book.

Strategy and change

The Art of War – Sun Tzu
Competitive Strategy – Michael Porter
Crossing the Chasm: Marketing and Selling Technology Products to Mainstream Customers –
    Geoffrey A. Moore
Inside the Tornado: Strategies for Developing, Leveraging, and Surviving Hypergrowth Markets
    – Geoffrey A. Moore
Leading Change – John Kotter
The Mind of the Strategist – Kenichi Ohmae
The Strategy Process: Concepts, Contexts, Cases – Henry Mintzberg

Marketing

Competitive Advantage – Michael Porter
Good to Great – Jim Collins
Kotler on Marketing – Philip Kotler
Marketing Insights from A to Z – Philip Kotler

Finance

Management Accounting for Non-Specialists – Peter Attrill and Eddie McLancy
Understanding Company Financial Statements – R.H. Parker

Product innovation and development

Product Leadership: Creating and Launching Superior New Products – Robert Cooper

Organisational design

Designing Your Organization – Amy Kates and Jay Galbraith

Motivation

The Enthusiastic Employee – David Sirota, Louis A. Mischkind and Michael Irwin Meltzer

Leadership

Winning – Jack Welch
Steve Jobs: The Exclusive Biography – Walter Isaacson

Systems thinking

The Fifth Discipline: The Art and Practice of the Learning Organisation – Peter Senge
The Fifth Discipline Fieldbook – Peter Senge

Project management

Project Management Survival – Richard Jones

Bibliography

Books and articles

Abu Latif, Samer. General Manager, Gulf, Microsoft. Speech at Informa Conference, Broadband World Forum 2012, Westin Mina Hotel, Dubai.

Beer, Michael and Nohria, Nitin (2000) 'Cracking the code of change', Harvard Business Essentials, Boston.

Bennis, Warren and Nanus, B. (2003) *Leaders: Strategies for taking* charge, HarperCollins, New York.

Britton, Jennifer (2011) *Effective Group Coaching*, John Wiley & Sons, New Jersey.

Cameron, Esther and Green, Mike (2009) *Making Sense of Change Management: A Complete Guide to the Models, Tools and Techniques of Organizational Change*, Kogan Page, London.

Carroll, Dave (2012) *United Breaks Guitars: The power of one voice in the age of social media*, Hay House, London.

Cartwright, D (1959) *Studies in Social Power*, Research Center for Group Dynamics, Institute for Social Research, University of Michigan.

Catan, Thomas and Trachtenberg, Jeffrey A. (2012) 'Justice Department Threatens Lawsuits, Alleging Collusion Over E-Book Pricing', *Wall Street Journal*.

Chan, Kim W. and Mauborgne, R. (2005) *Blue Ocean Strategy*, Harvard Business School Press, Boston.

Collins, Jim (2001) *Good to Great*, Random House Business, New York.

Collins, James C. and Porras, Jerry I. (2004) *Built to Last: Successful Habits of Visionary Companies*, HarperBusiness, New York.

Cooper, R.G. (2011) *Winning at New Products, Creating Value Through Innovation*, Basic Books, fourth edition, New York.

Covey, Stephen (2004) *The 7 Habits of Highly Effective People*, Free Press, New York.

Cropley, Steve (2011) 'The highs and lows of starting a car company', *Autocar*, Haymarket Cars and Aftermarket.

Deschamps, J-P. and Nayak, P. (1995) *Product Juggernauts*, Harvard Business Press and Arthur D. Little Inc.

Drucker, P. (1996) *Concept of the Corporation*, Transaction Publications, New Jersey.

Drucker, P. (2006) *The Effective Executive – The Definitive Guide to Getting the Right Things Done*, HarperBusiness, New York.

Fielder, Fred (1981) *Leader Attitudes and Group Effectiveness*, Greenwood Publishing Group, Connecticut.

Forsyth, Peter and Gillen, David (2009) *Airport Competition: The European Experience*, Ashgate Publishing Limited, Farnham.

Harvard Business Essentials (2003) *Managing change and transition*, Harvard Business School Press.

Hersey, P. and Blanchard, K (2007) *Management of Organisational Behaviour*, Prentice Hall/ Financial Times, New Jersey.

Herzberg, F., Mausner, B. and Snyderman, B.B. (1959) *The Motivation to Work*, John Wiley & Sons, New Jersey.

Hoffer, Eric (2009) *The True Believer: Thoughts on the Nature of Mass Movements*, Harper Perennial, New York.

Isaacson, Walter (2011) *Steve Jobs*, Little, Brown, New York.

Ishikawa, K. (1990) *Introduction to Quality Control*, Productivity Press, New York.

Janis, Irving (1972) *Victims of Groupthink*, Houghton Mifflin Company, Boston.

Jones, R. (2008) *Project Management Survival*, Kogan Page.

Kotler, Philip (1999) *Kotler on Marketing: How to Create, Win, and Dominate Markets*, Simon and Schuster, New York.

Kübler-Ross, Elisabeth (2008) *On Death and Dying*, 40th Anniversary Edition, Routledge, London.

Lehu, Jean-Marc (2007) *Branded Entertainment: Product Placement & Brand Strategy in the Entertainment Industry*, Kogan Page, London.

Likert, J.G. and Araki, C.T. (1986) 'Managing without a boss: System 5', *Leadership & Organization Development Journal*.

Likert, R. (1981) 'System 4: A resource from improving public administration', *Public Administration Review*.

McDonald, P. (2000) *The Star System: Hollywood's Production of Popular Identities*, Columbia University Press, Columbia.

McGregor, Douglas (2006) *The Human Side of Enterprise*, annotated edition, McGraw-Hill, New York.

McLelland, David (1967) *The Achieving Society*, Simon and Schuster, New York.

Mintzberg, Henry (1983) *Power in and Around Organizations: The theory of management policy*, Prentice Hall.

Mintzberg, Henry (1994) 'The fall and rise of strategic planning: reconceiving the roles for planning, plans, planners', *Harvard Business Review*.

Moore, Geoffrey A. (1999) *Crossing the Chasm: Marketing and Selling High-Tech Products to Mainstream Customers*, HarperBusiness Revised Edition, New York.

Moreton M. (2010) *Jaguar XJ220 – The Inside Story*, Veloce, Dorset.

Mourad, Mohamad, Regional Manager Gulf, Google. Speech at Broadband World Forum 2012, Westin Mina Hotel, Dubai

Newhouse, John (2008) *Boeing Versus Airbus: The Inside Story of the Greatest International Competition in Business*, Vintage Books.

Olson M.S. and Van Bever, D. (2008) *Stall Points: Most Companies Stop Growing – Yours Doesn't Have To*, Yale University Press. Quoted in 'Reinvent your business before it's too late' by Paul Nunes and Tim Breene, *Harvard Business Review* (http://hbr.org/2011/01/reinvent-your-business-before-its-too-late/ar/1).

Peters, Tom, Waterman, Bob and Philips, Julien (1980) 'Structure is not Organization', *Business Horizons*.

Porter, Michael (1980) *Competitive Strategy*, Free Press, New York.

Porter, Michael (1985) *Competitive Advantage*, Free Press, New York.

Qualman, Erik (2009) *Socialnomics: How Social Media Transforms the Way We Live and Do Business*, John Wiley & Sons, New Jersey.

Richie, Pat (2007) *Wisdom for the Busy Sports Leader*, Xulon Press, Maitland.

Rogers, Everett (1983) *Diffusion of Innovations*, Free Press, New York.

Roosevelt, T. (1923) *Social Justice and Popular Rule: Essays, Addresses, and Public Statements*, Ayer Co Pub, New Hampshire.

Russell, Linda and Russell, Jeffrey (2006) *Change Basics*, ASTD Press, Alexandria.

Schendel, Dan and Hofer, Charles (1979) *Strategic management: a new view of business policy and planning*, Little, Brown and Company, New York.

Senge, P., Kleiner, A., Roberts, C., Ross, R. and Smith B. (1994) *The Fifth Discipline Fieldbook*, Doubleday, New York.

Sirota, David, Mischkind, Louis A. and Meltzer, Michael Irwin (2005) *The Enthusiastic Employee*, Prentice Hall, New Jersey.

Slater, Robert (1998) *Jack Welch and the GE Way: Management Insights and Leadership Secrets of the Legendary CEO*, McGraw-Hill Professional, New York.

Society for Personnel Administration (1954) *The Federal Career Service: A Look Ahead*.

Spurlock M. (2004) *Supersize Me*, film directed by and starring Morgan Spurlock.

Treacy, Michael and Wiersma, Fred (1996) *The Discipline of Market Leaders: Choose Your Customers, Narrow Your Focus, Dominate Your Market*, Perseus Books, New York.

Twedt, Dik Warren (1964) 'How important to marketing strategy is the heavy user?', *Journal of Marketing*.

Vroom, Victor H. and Jago, Arthur G. (1988) *The New Leadership: Managing Participation in Organizations*, Prentice Hall, New Jersey.

Welch, Jack (2003) *Jack: Straight from the Gut*, Headline Publishing, London.

Welch J. and Welch S. (2005) *Winning: The Ultimate Business How-To Book*, HarperCollins, New York.

Wheelwright, S.C. and Clark, K.B. (1992) *Revolutionizing Product Development*, Free Press, New York.

Online sources

'16 of the Top 100 Best-Selling Paid Kindle Books in March Are Exclusive to the Kindle Store and Available for Prime Members with a Kindle to Borrow for Free', Amazon press release, 4 April 2012 (http://phx.corporate-ir.net/phoenix.zhtml?c=176060&p=irol-newsArticle&ID=1680062).

2011 Advertising Forecast. Magnaglobal (www.neoadvertising.com/ch/wp-content/uploads/2011/06/2011-MAGNAGLOBAL-Advertising-Forecast-Abbreviated.pdf).

'A billion thanks 25 times over' (www.apple.com/itunes/25-billion-app-countdown).

'A History of Audi – The 1960s' (www.audi.co.uk/content/dam/audi/production/RestOfSite/FleetSales/03_2010/PDF/History/AudiHistory_60s_161009.pdf).

About the Accounting Standards Board (www.frc.org.uk/asb/about).

'Airbus A350 Government Loans to Total $4.6 Billion', Bloomberg, 15 June 2009 (www.bloomberg.com/apps/news?pid=newsarchive&sid=aKB63ZwJ9OZo).

Airbus Global Market Forecast 2011–2030 (www.airbus.com/company/market/forecast).

Airbus Order Book, February 2012, Airbus.com (www.airbus.com/company/market/orders-deliveries).

Amazon press release, 29 January 2011 (http://phx.corporate-ir.net/phoenix.zhtml?c=176060&p=irol-newsArticle&ID=1521090).

Amazon press release, 19 May 2011 (http://phx.corporate-ir.net/phoenix.zhtml?ID=1565581&c=176060&p=irol-newsArticle).

'Amazon Signs Up Authors, Writing Publishers Out of Deal', David Streitfeld, *New York Times*, 16 October 2011 (www.nytimes.com/2011/10/17/technology/amazon-rewrites-the-rules-of-book-publishing.html?pagewanted=all).

Amazon website (www.amazon.com/gp/help/customer/display.html?nodeId=200549320).

Antitrust: Commission imposes € 899 million penalty on Microsoft for non-compliance with March 2004 Decision, 27 February 2008. EU Commission decision reference IP/08/318.

'AOL – Time Warner: Worst Merger Ever?', Michael Hickins, *Information Week*, 28 May 2009 (www.informationweek.com/news/personal-tech/229206374).

'Apple drops "Computer" from name', Mathew Honan, MacCentral, 9 January 2007 (www.macworld.com/article/1054770/applename.html).

'Apple Licenses Amazon.com 1-Click Patent and Trademark', Apple press release, 18 September 2000 (www.apple.com/pr/library/2000/09/18Apple-Licenses-Amazon-com-1-Click-Patent-and-Trademark.html).

'Apple Reports First Quarter Results', Apple.com, 24 January 2012 (www.apple.com/pr/library/2012/01/24Apple-Reports-First-Quarter-Results.html).

'Apple's struggle to defeat Amazon set to be exposed by European eBook inquiry', Juliette Gartside, Guardian.co.uk, 18 December 2011 (www.guardian.co.uk/books/2011/dec/18/ebook-price-wars).

Australians would rather go without food than be without their smartphone, survey shows. INQ Mobile survey (www.news.com.au/technology/smartphones/smart-phones-come-out-on-top/story-fn6vihic-1226050206282).

Author interviews with Tarek Tantawi, former CFO and CEO of Telecom Egypt, Mikael Sandberg, Ventura Team LLP.

'BA to sell Go airline as profits surge', BBC News, 6 November 2000 (http://news.bbc.co.uk/1/hi/business/1009283.stm).

BMW Annual Report 2011.pdf (https://www.press.bmwgroup.com/pressclub/p/gb/pressDetail.html?outputChannelId=8&id=T0125598EN&left_menu_item=node__2201).

'Boeing, Delta Clash on Exports', *Wall Street Journal*, 16 March 2012 (http://online.wsj.com/article/SB10001424052702303863404577285883342797536.html).

Boeing.com, Corporate chronology 1997–2001 (www.boeing.com/history/chronology/chron16.html).

Boeing.com (www.boeing.com/commercial/787family/background.html).

Boston Consulting Group, the Boston Box (www.bcg.com/about_bcg/history/history_1968.aspx).

Boston Consulting Group (BCG) survey of 1,000 respondents, 22 March 2012 (www.dailymail.co.uk/sciencetech/article-2118816/Addicted-com-Americans-alcohol-showers-sex-web.html).

'British law firm "conspired" to hide $50bn debts of Wall St giant' Lucy Farndon, *Daily Mail*, 13 March 2010 (www.dailymail.co.uk/news/article-1257350/Lehman-Brothers-bosses-manipulated-balance-sheet-accounting-tricks-scathing-report-finds.html).

'Business Success Hinges on an Empowered Staff', Shala Hainer, 28 September 2011. (www.womenetics.com/Workplace/business-success-hinges-on-an-empowered-staff).

'Cadbury downsizes Dairy Milk bars and other products', Madii Lown, BBC News, 2 February 2011 (www.bbc.co.uk/newsbeat/12346546).

CNN Money, database of 50 years of Fortune Magazine's list of America's largest corporations (http://money.cnn.com/magazines/fortune/fortune500).

'Compensating the people and communities affected', BP corporate website (www.bp.com/sectiongenericarticle800.do?categoryId=9036584&contentId=7067605).

'Consumers now take more than a quarter of all photos and videos on smartphones', press release, 22 December 2011 (www.npd.com).

Cooperative Group Annual Report 2011 (www.co-operative.coop/corporate/Press/Press-releases/Headline-news/Results-2011).

'Court-Appointed Lehman Examiner Unveils Report' (http://dealbook.nytimes.com/2010/03/11/lehman-directors-did-not-breach-duties-examiner-finds).

Dave Carroll (www.davecarrollmusic.com).

Dell Quarterly Analyst Conference Call (http://hardware.seekingalpha.com/article/18116-dell-too-cheap-to-pass-up).

Earnings Release Q2 FY12 Investor information at Microsoft.com (www.microsoft.com/investor/EarningsAndFinancials/Earnings/PressReleaseAndWebcast/FY12/Q1/default.aspx).

'Easyjet passenger numbers rise To 50m each year', Easyjet press release, 4 February 2011 (http://corporate.easyjet.com/media/latest-news/news-year-2011/04-02-2011-en.aspx).

'EasyJet to buy Go for $525 million', CNN.com, 16 May 2002 (http://edition.cnn.com/2002/BUSINESS/05/16/easyjet.go).

'EBay to buy Skype in $2.6bn deal', 12 September 2005 (http://news.bbc.co.uk/1/hi/business/4237338.stm).

Emissions figures for Aston Martin cars (www.astonmartin.com).

EU Digital Agenda: Major ICT companies join European Commission initiative to reduce electricity consumption. Press release, 28 September 2010. (http://europa.eu/rapid/pressReleasesAction.do?reference=IP/10/1185&format=HTML).

European Patent Office. Case T 1244/07. Publication 1134680. 27 January 2011

European Union Law – Communication from the Commission to the Council and the European Parliament 6 Results of the review of the Community Strategy to reduce CO_2 emissions from passenger cars and light-commercial vehicles (http://europa.eu/legislation_summaries/internal_market/single_market_for_goods/motor_vehicles/interactions_industry_policies/I28200_en.htm).

Eurotunnel corporate information, traffic figure history 2005 to 2011 (www.eurotunnelgroup.com/uk/eurotunnel-group/operations/traffic-figures).

Facebook Newsroom (http://newsroom.fb.com/content/default.aspx?NewsAreaId=22).

'Facebook's Instagram deal: Can one app be worth $1bn?', Tim Weber, BBC News, 10 April 2012 (www.bbc.co.uk/news/business-17666032).

'Facts and Figures – Recent History 1999–2011', UK Charity Commission (www.charity-commission.gov.uk/About_us/About_charities/factfigures.aspx).

'Fatty food tax introduced in Denmark', BBC, 2 October 2011 (www.bbc.co.uk/news/world-europe-15140821).

'Fears Of An Aircraft Order Bubble', *Aviation Week*, 2 April 2012 (www.aviationweek.com/Article.aspx?id=/article-xml/AW_04_02_2012_p30-441893.xml).

Financial Services Authority announcement, 24 August 2004 (www.fsa.gov.uk/library/communication/pr/2004/074.shtml).

'Fisker CEO revamps business plan amid Karma woes', Reuters.com, 4 April 2012 (http://uk.reuters.com/article/2012/04/04/uk-autoshow-newyork-fisker-idUKBRE83305220120404).

Flickr analysis of cameras used to take photos on the site (www.flickr.com/cameras).

Ford corporate website (www.me.ford.com/servlet/ContentServer?cid=1178830507747&pagename=wrapper&c=DFYPage&site=FME).

'GM Announces 2008 Global Sales of 8.35 Million Vehicles', GM press release, 21 January 2009 (http://media.gm.com/media/us/en/gm/news.detail.html/content/Pages/news/us/en/2009/Jan/0121_GlobalSales).

'Go team to fly solo as BA sells airline Benjamin Wootliff', *Daily Telegraph*, 15 June 2001. (www.telegraph.co.uk/finance/2722070/Go-team-to-fly-solo-as-BA-sells-airline.html).

'Heathrow landing fees', 25 January 2011 (www.thisismoney.co.uk/money/news/article-1711438/Heathrow-landing-fees.html).

Help for Heroes (www.helpforheroes.org.uk).

Hershey Company, corporate factbook, July 2011 (www.thehersheycompany.com/assets/pdfs/hersheycompany/global_marketing6-09.pdf).

'How Help for Heroes charity became a £100m fundraising phenomenon', Patrick Barkham, the Guardian, 28 November 2012 (www.guardian.co.uk/uk/2010/nov/12/help-for-heroes-fundraising-phenomenon).

'How Target Figured Out A Teen Girl Was Pregnant Before Her Father Did', Kashmir Hill, Forbes.com, 16 February 2012 (www.forbes.com/sites/kashmirhill/2012/02/16/how-target-figured-out-a-teen-girl-was-pregnant-before-her-father-did).

ICAM Function Modelling Manual, IDEF0, US Air Force Systems Command, June 1981 (www.itl.nist.gov/fipspubs/idef02.doc).

IFRS Foundation (ifrs.org).

'Innocent sells £30m stake to Coca Cola', Jonathan Sibun, the *Telegraph* online, 6 April 2009 (www.telegraph.co.uk/finance/newsbysector/retailandconsumer/5114007/Innocent-sells-30m-stake-to-Coca-Cola.html).

Insolvency Act 1986 (www.legislation.gov.uk/ukpga/1986/45/section/214).

'International Call Traffic Growth Slows as Skype's Volumes Soar', Telegeography.com 10 January 2012 (www.telegeography.com/products/commsupdate/articles/2012/01/10/international-call-traffic-growth-slows-as-skypes-volumes-soar).

'Interview Dyson CEO Max Conze: "Our lifeblood is inventing. That is where we spend all of our money."', Kamal Ahmed, the *Telegraph*, 11 February 2012 (www.telegraph.co.uk/finance/newsbysector/industry/9075642/Interview-Dyson-CEO-Max-Conze-Our-lifeblood-is-inventing.-That-is-where-we-spend-all-of-our-money.html).

Interview with Josh Silverman, CEO, Skype, *Daily Telegraph*, 10 May 2010 (www.telegraph.co.uk/technology/news/7706171/Skype-to-offer-adverts-to-keep-service-free.html).

Interview with Rockstar's Leslie Benzies, *The Sunday Times*, 27 April 2008.

2010 Annual Report, McDonalds (investors-2010-annual-report mcdonalds.pdf).

J D Power Survey 2011, *What Car* (www.whatcar.com/car-news/jd-power-survey-2011/the-results/257096).

'KLM sells Buzz to Ryanair', KLM press release, 31 January 2003 (http://forum.keypublishing.com/showthread.php?t=6574).

'Kodak files for bankruptcy protection', Richard Waters and Tim Bradshaw, *Financial Times*, 19 January 2012 (www.ft.com/cms/s/0/68054e1c-4267-11e1-93ea-00144feab49a.html#axzz1uwqGz99S).

Kodak press release, 9 February 2012 (www.kodak.com/ek/US/en/Kodak_Focuses_Consumer_Business_On_More_Profitable_Growth_Opportunities.htm).

'Kodak: From Brownie and roll film to digital disaster', James Cowling, BBC News, 20 January 2012 (www.bbc.co.uk/news/business-16627167).

'Marketing Myopia', Theodore Levitt, *Harvard Business Review*, 1960, quoted in *Harvard Business Review* (http://hbr.org/product/marketing-myopia-harvard-business-review/an/R0407L-PDF-ENG).

Microsoft CEO Steve Ballmer interview with USA Today's David Lieberman at the sixth USA TODAY CEO Forum, in conjunction with the University of Washington Business School, 29 April 2007.

'Microsoft confirms takeover of Skype', BBC News, 10 May 2011 (www.bbc.co.uk/news/business-13343600).

Nike corporate website (nikeinc.com/pages/about-nike-inc).

Nintendo press briefing, 29 September 2010 (www.huffingtonpost.com/2010/09/30/nintendo-3ds-release-date_n_745654.html).

Nu-Kote Holding, Inc. (www.fundinguniverse.com/company-histories/Nukote-Holding-Inc-company-History.html).

'Online advertising "overtakes TV"', BBC News, 30 September 2009 (http://news.bbc.co.uk/1/hi/business/8280557.stm).

Port of Dover annual traffic statistics (www.doverport.co.uk/?page=AnnualTrafficStatistics).

Proctor and Gamble corporate website information on purpose, value and principles (www.pg.com/en_US/company/purpose_people/pvp.shtml).

Report of the Special Rapporteur on the promotion and protection of the right to freedom of opinion and expression, Frank La Rue, UN Human Rights Council, 17th Session (www.unhcr.org/cgi-bin/texis/vtx/refworld/rwmain?docid=4a044c592).

Research In Motion (RIM) Year-End And Fourth Quarter Results For Fiscal 2012 – RIM investor information (www.rim.com/investors/documents/pdf/pressrelease/2012/Q4_press_release.pdf).

'Revenge is best served cold – on YouTube: How a broken guitar became a smash hit.', Chris Ayres, *The Sunday Times*, 22 July 2009.

'Rosetta's Rise: No 1?', Barbara Figge Fox in US 1 newspaper (www.princetoninfo.com/index.php?option=com_us1more&Itemid=6&key=3-3-10%20rosetta).

Royal British Legion Annual Report 2010 (www.britishlegion.org.uk/media/1642097/annualreport2010.pdf).

Ryanair Annual Report – 1999 (www.ryanair.com/doc/investor/1999/arpt_1999.pdf).

'Ryanair in the dock', 21 February 2011 (www.centreforaviation.com/analysis/ryanair-in-the-dock-46014).

'Ryanair to repay illegal subsidy', BBC News, 28 October 2004 (http://news.bbc.co.uk/1/hi/business/3962797.stm).

'Ryanair's 2011 Traffic Grows 5% To 76m Passengers' (www.ryanair.com/en/news/ryanair-s-2011-traffic-grows-5-percent-to-76m-passengers).

'Saab vs Volvo: a tale of two Swedes', Greg Fountain, *Car Magazine*, 6 February 2012 (www.carmagazine.co.uk/Community/Car-Magazines-Blogs/Greg-Fountain-Blog/Saab-vs-Volvo-a-tale-of-two-Swedes).

'Saab's demise seems inevitable', Jord Madslien, BBC News, 8 September 2011 (www.bbc.co.uk/news/business-14839656).

Samsung Corporate Profile: History, Samsung corporate website (www.samsung.com/uk/aboutsamsung/corporateprofile/history.html).

SAS Annual Report 2011 (www.sasgroup.net/SASGROUP_IR/CMSForeignContent/SAS_%C3%85R2011_eng.pdf).

Scandinavian Airlines System (www.tmiaust.com.au/track_record/case_studies/scandinavian_airlines.htm).

'Slaughter of the Innocent? Or is Coke the real deal?', Richard Northedge, the *Independent*, 12 April 2009 (www.independent.co.uk/news/business/analysis-and-features/slaughter-of-the-innocent-or-is-coke-the-real-deal-1667412.html).

'Social Grade – Definitions', National Readership Survey (www.nrs.co.uk/lifestyle.html).

Social Media Revolution 3 Video – Long Version, Erik Qualman (www.socialnomics.net/2011/07/05/social-media-videos-2011).

Socialnomics statistics (www.socialnomics.net/2012/01/04/39-social-media-statistics-to-start-2012).

'Structure Is Not Organization', Tom Peters, Bob Waterman and Julien Philips (www.tompeters.com/docs/Structure_Is_Not_Organization.pdf).

'Super Bowl Sets Record Viewing Figures of 111M', Glen Levy, Time.com, 8 February 2011 (http://newsfeed.time.com/2011/02/08/super-bowl-sets-record-viewing-figures-of-111m).

Tata Motors information (http://tatanano.inservices.tatamotors.com/tatamotors/home.htm).

Telenav survey of 514 mobile phone users in the US. 3 August 2011 (www.telenav.com/about/pr-summer-travel/report-20110803.html).

Tesco Annual Report 2011 (http://ar2011.tescoplc.com).

'The format wars: of lasers and (creative) destruction', Anders Bylund. (http://arstechnica.com/gadgets/2010/01/is-the-end-of-the-format-wars-upon-us).

Tom Enders, Airbus President and CEO quoted in Airbus press release, 17 January 2011 (www.airbus.com/presscentre/pressreleases/press-release-detail/detail/airbus-celebrates-its-10000th-order-with-virgin-americas-60-a320-deal).

'Top 10 Best and Worst Mergers of All Time', CNBC.com (www.cnbc.com/id/34467713/Top_10_Best_and_Worst_Mergers_of_All_Time).

'Top 10 Primetime Programs with Product Placement Activity', 20 December 2011 (http://blog.nielsen.com/nielsenwire/media_entertainment/nielsens-tops-of-2011-advertising).

Top Gear Survey 2004, BBC, 10 November 2004.

Toyota Global Vision Statement 2011 (www.toyota-global.com/investors/ir_library/annual/pdf/2011/p09_12.pdf).

Toys R Us company website and statements 2009 (www.vuw.ac.nz/~caplabtb/m302w00/toys_R_us.html#history).

'Twenty-Five Years of Groupthink Theory and Research: Lessons from the Evaluation of a Theory, Turner and Pratkanis, Organisational Behaviour and Human Decision Processes', February/March 1998 (http://carmine.se.edu/cvonbergen/Twenty-Five%20Years%20of%20Groupthink%20Theory%20and%20Research_Lessons%20from%20the%20Evaluation%20of%20a%20Theory.pdf).

'Two British Airways directors "sacked" over the Terminal 5 fiasco', Dan Newling, the *Daily Mail*, 16 April 2008 (www.dailymail.co.uk/news/article-559729/Two-British-Airways-directors-sacked-Terminal-5-fiasco--Willie-Walsh-stays.html).

'UK could introduce "fat tax", says David Cameron', Guardian Online, 4 October 2011 (www.guardian.co.uk/politics/2011/oct/04/uk-obesity-tax-david-cameron).

UK Office for National Statistics, quoted in *Daily Telegraph* (www.telegraph.co.uk/finance/economics/9035125/UK-public-debt-passes-1-trillion-for-first-time-reaction.html).

'United Breaks Guitars' video on YouTube (www.youtube.com/watch?v=5YGc4zOqozo).

United States Securities And Exchange Commission Form 8-K Pursuant to Section 13 or 15(d) of the Securities Exchange Act of 1934, 9 June 2008 (http://sec.gov/Archives/edgar/data/320193/000118143108037620/rrd210213.htm).

Volkswagen AG corporate website (www.volkswagenag.com/content/vwcorp/content/en/the_group.html).

'Wal-Mart Asset Utilization' (http://ycharts.com/companies/WMT/asset_utilization).

Wal-Mart investor information, press release, 21 February 2012 (http://investors.walmartstores.com/phoenix.zhtml?c=112761&p=irol-newsArticle&ID=1663026&highlight=).

'Walmart ships free Forza 4 copies after whiffing limited edition' (http://jalopnik.com/5849616/walmart-ships-free-forza-4-copies-after-whiffing-limited-edition).

'When is it OK for a PR to run away?', Maggie Brown, the *Guardian*, 7 April 2008 (www. guardian.co.uk/media/2008/apr/07/marketingandpr).

'When Open Architecture Beats Closed: The Entrepreneurial Use of Architectural Knowledge', Carliss Y. Baldwin (www.hbs.edu/research/pdf/10-063.pdf).

'World Cup 2010: Police arrest women in Dutch orange dresses', The *Daily* Telegraph, 16 June 2010 (www.telegraph.co.uk/sport/football/competitions/world-cup-2010/7830319/World-Cup-2010-Police-arrest-women-in-Dutch-orange-dresses.html).

Index

Bold page numbers indicate figures, *italic* numbers indicate tables.

A

accounts
  balance sheets 142–50, **145, 148**
  cash flow 158–60, *159*
  current assets 146–8, **148**
  current ratio 153–4
  debt to equity ratios 155
  fixed assets 144–6
  gearing *150,* 150–1, *151*
  generally accepted accounting principles (GAAP) 144
  income statements **135,** 135–42, *139,* **140, 141**
  interest cover 155
  key measures and ratios 151–7, **152**
  net assets 151–2, **153**
  net current assets (working capital) 153
  quick ratio 154–5
  return on total assets 156–7
  sales margin 155
  sales to total assets ratio 156
  understanding of 134–5
acid test ratio 154–5
advertising 110–11
Airbus 44–5
airline industry 79–80, 124
Amazon 41–2, 109
amortisation 138
Ansoff's product development matrix 48–9, **49,** *50,* **51**
AOL 31

Apple 37, 41, 177
assessment of organisations
  benchmarks 25–6
  buyers, power of 40–2
  capability-focused approach 21, *21*
  competitive rivalry 40
  duopolies 43–5
  embedding of strategy 21–2
  external forces 39–48, **40**
  failure of, reasons for 18
  McKinsey 7S Framework 19–20, *31*
  new market entrants 45–6
  Porter's Five Forces model 39–48, **40**
  process mapping 23–5
  for strategic planning purposes 17
  substitution, potential for 46
  suppliers, power of 42–3
  SWOT analysis 26–7
  teams for 22–3
  TOWS analysis 27–31
  workshops and interviews 23
assets
  current 146–8, **148**
  fixed 144–6
  net 151–2, **153**
  net current 149
  total current 148
assumption smashing 117
Aston Martin 12
attribute modification 118
Automobile Association 61
automotive manufacturing 12, 45–6, 105–6

B

balance sheets
  current assets 146–8, **148**
  current liabilities 148–9
  example **145**
  fixed assets 144–6
  limitations of 142–3
  long-term liabilities 149
  net current assets 149
  shareholders' equity/funds 149–50
  total current assets 148
  total current liabilities 149
BCG Matrix (Boston Box) 95–100, **96, 97, 98, 99**
Beer, M. 229
benchmarks 25–6
benefit segmentation 83
Bennis, Warren G. 216
Big Hairy Audacious Goals (BHAGs) 218–19
Blackberry 17
Blue Ocean Strategy (Kim and Mauborgne) 118
BMW 135
Boeing 44–5
Boston Box (BCG Matrix) 95–100, **96, 97, 98, 99**
bowling pin strategy 51–2, **52**
buyers, power of 40–2

C

capability-focused approach to assessment 21, *21*
car manufacturing 12, 45–6, 105–6
Carlstedt Elektronik 251
cash 148, 279

cash cycles 153
cash flow 158–60, *159*
change management
  communication 234–5, 241–3
  complacency 235–6, *235–6,*
    277–8
  continuity of change 228
  enemies of change 235–6,
    235–6
  fence sitters in 242
  high level view of 231–3
  hubbers 241–2
  leadership of 234
  metrics and reward structure
    240
  mistakes/problems with 236–8
  models of change 238–40,
    239–40
  need for, recognising 233
  planning change 243
  preparation for change 231–2
  in projects 266–7, **267**
  psychodynamics during
    change **240,** 240–1, **241**
  quick wins 243
  saboteurs in 242
  Satir change model 238, *239*
  structure for 244, *244*
  team formation process 239,
    239–40
  theories O and E 229–31,
    230–1
  top-down approach 236
  types of change 229
  unfreeze-change-refreeze
    analogy 231–3
charter, project 254–5, *256*
churning 123
communication 234–5, 241–3
competence 209–10, **210**
competition, response to 57–8,
  58
competitive rivalry 40
complacency 235–6, *235–6,*
  277–8
contingency plans, development
  of **262,** 262–5, *263,* **264,**
  265
cost leadership *71,* 71–2
cost of sales 137–8

cost reductions 72
Covey, Stephen R. 216
current assets 146–8, **148**
current liabilities 148–9
current ratio 153–4
customers
  intimacy 71
  preferences of 127–8
  retention and loyalty of 120–30,
    122, 125, 126, 129
  understanding 126

D
debt to equity ratios 155
decision making 24, *200,* 200–1,
  201, 209
Dell 160
democratisation of technology
  178–9
demographic factors influencing
  organisation 13, 14
demographic segmentation 82
depreciation 137–8
Deschamps, J.-P. 57
differentiation *71,* 73, *74,* 75
diffusion curve 100–4, **101, 104**
digital cameras 7–8, 11–12, 60
discounted cash flow 163–4, *164*
diseconomies of scale 73
drill-down 273–4, **274**
Drucker, Peter 216
duopolies 43–5

E
early adopters 101
early majority 102
economic factors influencing
  organisations 10, 14
education factors influencing
  organisation 12, 14
emission laws 12
emotions during change 240–1,
  241
environmental factors influencing
  organisation 13, 14
estimation of the market **85,** 85–6
Extended Product Mix 104–10
external factors impacting
  organisations *9,* 9–14

F
fence sitters in change
  management 242
Fielder, Fred 199
films, product placement in 107
finance
  investment assessment *161,*
    161–9, **162,** *164, 165, 166,*
    167, **168**
  see also accounts
fishbone diagrams **268,** 268–9,
  269
Fisker, Henrik 45–6
five whys 270, **270**
fixed assets 144–6
force field analysis **271,** 271–2,
  272, 273
Ford *5*
4Ps (marketing mix) 104–10
free cash flow (FCF) 166–7, **167**
functional hierarchies 190–3, **191**

G
games and games consoles
  112
GE Matrix **53,** 53–6, **55**
gearing *150,* 150–1, *151*
General Electric (GE) 220
generally accepted accounting
  principles (GAAP) 144
Go Telecoms 59
goal setting 218–19
goodwill 144–6
Google *5*
GOST theory 38, *38*
gross domestic product (GDP) 10
gross profit 138
group working 208–9, 239,
  239–40

H
Hawthorne Experiments 208
Heathrow, Terminal 5 129–30
heavy-half theory 83
Help for Heroes 46
Hershey *5*
Herzberg, Frederick 204
Hofer-Schendel Matrix 56–7
Hoffer, Eric 225
hubbers 241–2

hygiene factors and motivators 204, *204*

I
idea generation **179,** 179–80
Immelt, Jeffrey R. 228
income statements
    amortisation 138
    cost of sales 137–8
    depreciation 137–8
    example **139,** 139–42, **140, 141**
    gross profit 138
    interest and tax expenses 139
    limitations of 142–3
    logic in producing **135,** 135–6
    operating profit 138–9
    overheads 138
    revenue 137
    total revenue capacity (TRC) 136
Innocent Drinks 121
innovations, continuous/ discontinuous 103
innovators 101
interaction diagrams 275, **275**
interest cover 155
interest expenses 139
internal rate of return (IRR) 165–6, *166*
inventories 146–7
investigation of organisations *see* assessment of organisations
investment assessment
    discounted cash flow 163–4, *164*
    free cash flow (FCF) 166–7, **167**
    internal rate of return (IRR) 165–6, *166*
    limitations of techniques for 167–9, **168**
    net present value (NPV) 164–5, *165*
    payback *161,* 161–2
    timing **169,** 169–70, **170,** *171*
Ishikawa (fishbone) diagrams **268,** 268–9, **269**
issue management in projects 265–6, *266*

K
Kellogg's 145–6
Kennedy, John F. 219
Kim, W. Chan 118
Kodak 11–12

L
Ladder of Inference **212,** 212–14
laggards 102
late majority 102
launches, product 187–91, *188,* 279–80
leadership
    attributes of 217–18
    Big Hairy Audacious Goals (BHAGs) 218–19
    change management 234
    characteristics of 216–20, 224
    personal 222–5, *223, 224*
    and power 220–2, *221*
    Stockdale Paradox 225
    strength in facing reality 225–6
    styles of management 223–4, *223–4*
legal factors influencing organisation 12, 14
Lehman Brothers 143
Lewin, Kurt 231
liabilities
    current 148–9
    long-term 149
    total current 149
lifecycle, project 256–7, **257**
lifestyle-based segmentation 83
lifetime value of customers 123
Likert, R. 199
long-term liabilities 149
loyalty, customer 120–30, **122, 125, 126, 129**
loyalty cards 127–8

M
market challengers *78–9,* 78–80
market changes and trends
    analysis of 39–48, **40**
    buyers, power of 40–2
    continuous change 60–1
    duopolies 43–5
    growth 280
    new market entrants 45–6

Porter's Five Forces model 39–48, **40, 48**
    and strategy evolution 6–8
    substitution, potential for 46
    suppliers, power of 42–3
market followers *80,* 80–1
market leaders 75–8, *76, 77*
market nichers 81
marketing
    advertising 110–11
    BCG Matrix (Boston Box) 95–100, **96, 97, 98, 99**
    cost leadership 71
    defining 67–8
    differentiation *71*
    elements of the marketing concept 68, *68*
    estimation of the market **85,** 85–6
    focus on segments *71*
    generic strategies 69–75, *70, 71, 74*
    heavy-half theory 83
    levels of requirement 67
    market challengers *78–9,* 78–80
    market followers *80,* 80–1
    for market leaders 75–8, *76, 77*
    market nichers 81
    marketing mix (4Ps) 104–10
    new product development 117–20, *119,* **119, 120**
    perceptual maps **86,** 86–8, **87, 88**
    positioning of products and services **86,** 86–8, **87, 88**
    product diffusion curve 100–4, **101, 104**
    product lifecycle 88–95, *89,* **89, 92, 93,** *94,* **95**
    retention and loyalty of customers 120–30, **122, 125, 126, 129**
    segmentation 81–4, *82,* **84, 85**
    selling, comparison with 67
    strategic alternatives 69
    tactical level 75–81, *76, 77, 78–9*
    v. technology 278
    value disciplines 71–2

value proposition approach
111, 111–12
matrix organisations 193–5, **194,**
196
Mauborgne, Renee 118
McDonald's 28
McGregor, Douglas 204
McKinsey 7S Framework *19,*
19–20, *31*
metrics 240
Microsoft 43
milestones in project management
260, *260*
Mintzberg, Henry 4
mission statements
defining 4–6
examples *5,* 5–6
strategy link 3–4
vision statements compared 4
morale and motivation *205,* 205–6
motivation
assumptions, identifying 206
demotivators, identifying 206–7
five-stage process 206–8
Hawthorne Experiments 208
hygiene factors and motivators
204, *204*
and morale *205,* 205–6
needs theory *201–2,* 201–3
X and Y theory 204, *204*

N
Nayak, P. 57
needs theory *201–2,* 201–3
net assets 151–2, **153**
net current assets 149, 153
net present value (NPV) 164–5,
165
niches 81
Nike *5*
Nohria, N 229

O
objectives, project 249, 257–9,
258
operating profit 138–9
opportunities 27, 29–30
organisational design
balanced/functional matrix 196
functional hierarchies 190–3,

191
matrix organisations 193–5,
194, 196
process vector 195–6
product-based structure 192–3
project-based organisations
193–4
weak/functional matrix 195
overheads 138

P
payback *161,* 161–2
people in marketing mix 109
people management
basics of 198
competence 209–10, **210**
decision-making 200–1
group working 208–9
Ladder of Inference **212,**
212–14
motivation *201–2,* 201–8, *204,*
205–6
perspectives, working with 211
styles of management *199,*
199–201, *200, 201,* 223–4,
223–4
task/relationship-motivated
management 199–200
see also change management;
leadership
perceptual maps **86,** 86–8, **87, 88**
performance measurement
implementation of strategy 39
and strategy 22
personal leadership 222–5, *223,*
224
personal power 221, *222*
personality-based segmentation
82–3
personnel management *see*
people management
perspectives, working with 211
PEST analysis
factors impacting organisations
9, 9–14
telecoms company case study
13–14
Phillips 113
physical evidence in marketing
mix 109–10

place in marketing mix 108
planning
change 243
projects 249–52, **252**
strategic, cycle of 34–9, **35,** *38*
Pole, Andrew 128
political factors influencing
organisations 9–10, 13
Porter, Michael 69–71
Porter's Five Forces model 39–48,
40, 48
portfolio management
assessment of potential
projects 180–5, **181, 182,**
183, 184, 185, 186, 187
idea generation **179,** 179–80
project definition **180**
Stage-Gate processes 185–7,
186, 187
PORTS 61–2, **62**
positional power 221, *221*
positioning of products and
services **86,** 86–8, **87, 88,**
118–20, *119,* **119, 120**
Post Office 61
power and leadership 220–2,
221
presentations software 178
price in marketing mix 106
pricing
elasticity, price 115
importance of 113
planning *115–16,* 115–17, *117*
and strategy 113
willingness to pay 114, **114,**
114–15
problem-solving techniques
drill-down 273–4, **274**
five whys 270, **270**
force field analysis **271,** 271–2,
272, 273
interaction diagrams 275, **275**
Ishikawa (fishbone) diagrams
268, 268–9, **269**
swim lane diagrams 274, **275**
process in marketing mix 108–9
process mapping 23–5, *24*
Proctor and Gamble *5*
product development matrix
48–9, **49,** 51, **51**

product diffusion curve 100–4, **101, 104**

Product Juggernauts (Deschamps and Nayak) 57

product leadership 71

product lifecycle
  decline phase 90
  growth phase 90
  introduction phase 90
  maturity phase 90
  profitability during **93,** 93–5, *94,* **95**
  stages of *89,* **89,** 89–91
  variations on classic 92, **92**

product/market evolution **56,** 56–7, **57**

product placement 107

production, focus on 60

products
  assumption smashing 117
  attribute modification 118
  complexity/simplicity 128, **129**
  democratisation of technology 178–9
  failure of, reasons for *174–7*
  focus on 60
  launches 187–91, *188,* 279–80
  in marketing mix 105
  new product development 117–20, *119,* **119, 120, 172,** 172–9, **173, 174,** *174–7*
  organisational design based on 192–3
  positioning of 118–20, *119,* **119, 120**
  see also portfolio management; project management

profit and loss (P&L) account
  amortisation 138
  cost of sales 137–8
  depreciation 137–8
  example **139,** 139–42, **140, 141**
  gross profit 138
  interest and tax expenses 139
  limitations of 142–3
  logic in producing **135,** 135–6
  operating profit 138–9
  overheads 138
  revenue 137

total revenue capacity (TRC) 136

profitability during product lifecycle **93,** 93–5, *94,* **95**

project-based organisations 193–4

project management
  charter, project 254–5, *256*
  defining **180,** 246–7
  diagnosing current project 247–50, **248**
  importance of 247
  initiation of projects 253–4
  issue management 265–6, *266*
  key dates 250, 252
  lifecycle of the project 256–7, **257**
  milestones 260, *260*
  new projects 252–4
  objectives 249, 257–9, *258*
  plans 249–52, **252**
  resources 251, **252**
  risk management **262,** 262–5, *263,* **264, 265**
  scope change management 266–7, **267**
  teams for 254
  work breakdown structure **261,** 261–2
  see also portfolio management

promotion in marketing mix 106–8

4Ps (marketing mix) 104–10

psychodynamics during change **241**

purpose of organisation, chart for 61–2, **62**

Q

quick ratio 154–5

R

RACI Matrix 62–3, *63*

ratios
  current 153–4
  debt to equity 155
  interest cover 155
  quick 154–5
  return on total assets 156–7
  sales margin 155
  sales to total assets 156

relationship-motivated management 199–200

Research in Motion (RIM(17

resource management, strategy as 3

resources in project management 251, **251**

retention and loyalty of customers 120–30, **122, 125, 126, 129**

return on total assets 156–7

revenue, increasing
  Ansoff's product development matrix 48–9, **49,** *50,* 51, **51**
  bowling pin strategy 51–2, **52**

reward structure 240

rework loops 24

risk management in projects **262,** 262–5, *263,* **264, 265**

S

Saab 98

saboteurs in change management 242

Saint-Gobain 194–5

sales, cost of 137–8

sales margin 155

sales to total assets ratio 156

SAS 124

Satir change model 238, *238*

scope change management in projects 266–7, **267**

segmentation
  benefit 83
  benefits of 81
  demographics 82
  evaluating segments 83–4, **84, 85**
  lifestyle-based 83
  personality-based 82–3
  socio-economic 82, *82*

selling
  focus on 60
  and marketing, comparison of 67

7S Framework *19,* 19–20, *31*

share capital 149–50

short-term debt 148

Sirota, David 205

Skype *5,* 6–7

SMART objectives 258–9

smartphones as cameras 60
social factors influencing
    organisations 11, 14
social media 122
socio-economic segmentation
    82, *82*
staff management *see* people
    management
standards, accounting 144
statement of cash flows 158,
    159
Stockdale Paradox 225
strategy
    Ansoff's product development
        matrix 48–9, **49,** *50,* **51**
    Apple 37
    as blueprint 3
    bowling pin strategy 51–2, **52**
    communication of 21–2, 61–4,
        62, *63*
    competition, response to 57–8,
        58
    data gathering and analysis
        35–6
    decision-makers for 35
    defining 2–4
    drift 34
    embedding of 21–2
    evaluation and selection of
        scenarios 36
    external factors and evolution
        of 6–15
    focus, choice of 60
    GE Matrix **53,** 53–6, **55**
    GOST theory 38, *38*
    Hofer-Schendel Matrix **56,**
        56–7, **57**
    implementation planning 37–9,
        38
    implications of lack of 34
    long-term focus 2–3
    and market changes 6–8
    marketing alternatives 69
    markets, changes in 60–1
    mission statement link 3–4

monitoring 39
and performance measurement
    22
PEST analysis 8–16, *9*
planning cycle 34–9, **35,** *38*
planning pricing *115–16,*
    115–17, *117*
Porter's Five Forces model
    39–48, **48**
PORTS 61–2, **62**
and pricing 113
product/market evolution **56,**
    56–7, **57**
RACI Matrix 62–3, *63*
resource management 3
right, choosing 277
scenario formulation 36
timing of market entry
    58–9
understanding of 22
see also assessment of
    organisations
strengths 27, 29, 30
styles of management *199,*
    199–201, *200, 201,* 223–4,
    223–4
substitution, potential for 46
suppliers, power of 42–3
swim lane diagrams 274, **275**
SWOT analysis 26–7

T
Target 128
target setting 218–19
task-motivated management
    199–200
tax expenses 139
team formation process 239,
    239–40
technology
    democratisation of 178–9
    factors influencing organisation
        11–12, 14
    strategy and changes in 7–8
    v. marketing 278

telecoms company case study
    13–14
television, product placement in
    107
Terminal 5, Heathrow 129–30
Tesco 126
threats 27, 30
total current assets 148
total current liabilities 149
total revenue capacity (TRC) 136
TOWS analysis 27–31
Toyota *5*
trade payables 148
trade receivables 147

U
unfreeze-change-refreeze analogy
    231–3

V
value curve 118–20, **119,** *119,*
    120
value disciplines 71–2
value proposition approach *111,*
    111–12
vision statements, mission
    statements compared 4
Volkswagon *5*
Vroom, V. 200

W
weaknesses 27, 30
Welch, Jack 220
willingness to pay **114,** 114–15
work breakdown structure **261,**
    261–2
working capital 153

X
X and Y theory 204, *204*

Y
Yetton, P. 200